LUCY WIGHTMAN

PRIN CHEY

CESS ENNE

MY LIFE AS BOSTON'S MOST FAMOUS STRIPPER

HAMILCAR
PUBLICATIONS
BOSTON

Copyright © 2025 Lucy Wightman

All rights reserved. No part of this book may be reproduced in any form or by any means, electronic or mechanical, including photocopying, recording, or by any information storage and retrieval system without permission in writing from the publisher.

ISBN: 978-1-949590-87-6

hamilcarpubs.com

Aut viam inveniam aut faciam

For Nanly

Author's Note
This memoir is a true story, as I remember it. It is written from my perspective using journal entries, letters, notes, consultations, research, published media, and memory. Some scenes are condensed or ascribed to different characters to maintain the narrative flow.

CONTENTS

PROLOGUE 1

CHAPTER 1
Lake Forest, Illinois 3

CHAPTER 2
Cat Stevens: Part 1 16

CHAPTER 3
Wild World 28

CHAPTER 4
Pussycat Lounge 42

CHAPTER 5
Combat Zone 56

CHAPTER 6
Naked i 70

CHAPTER 7
Cheyenne 86

CHAPTER 8
Pink Panther 101

CHAPTER 9
Feature Attraction 115

CHAPTER 10
Curzon Street, London 129

CHAPTER 11
Cat Stevens: Part II 144

CHAPTER 12
A'isha.................................157

CHAPTER 13
New Canaan, Connecticut...................171

CHAPTER 14
Fauzia.................................185

CHAPTER 15
Princess Cheyenne.......................195

CHAPTER 16
The Pussy Galore Stag Bar................207

CHAPTER 17
Boulder, Colorado......................219

CHAPTER 18
Andy Kaufman..........................233

CHAPTER 19
Stripper Parade........................248

CHAPTER 20
Motorcycle Cop.........................261

PHILIP'S LETTER 273

ACKNOWLEDGMENTS 277

PROLOGUE

I grabbed the oversized Southern Belle hat with both hands and noticed something peering out at me from inside the locker. It was a forgotten peach, now perfectly ripe. I hooked the hat's chin strap, fluffed my hoop skirt and, having the urge to eat that peach for all to see, headed for the stage, peach in hand.

I settled onto my knees as the song "Great Gig in the Sky," by Pink Floyd, began its vaguely orgasmic wailing. When I presented the peach in the palm of my hand, the audience went crazy. I didn't understand the wild enthusiasm over a piece of fruit. When I rolled it between my breasts, over my abdomen and across my thighs the room stood up.

I was a little hungry. When I bit into the unassuming peach, its juice dripped down my body and I understood the audience appeal.

Peaches became integral to the Southern Belle show, but unfortunately weren't always available. In their absence, I tried plums (mealy nine times out of ten), pre-peeled oranges (too sticky), and bananas (too dry).

There was no replacing the powerful peach.

Dealing with the sticky nectar made me wonder why we didn't have a shower at the Naked i, even for dancers who weren't eating fruit onstage. The club's murky air recirculated into itself, and the churning fog settled into our pores and lungs like resin. No wonder I'd had pleurisy. Customers' well-meaning palms patted our arms, and the stage floors wore a sheath of grime propagated by our bodies and shoes. At the end of the night, the bottoms of my feet were tacky, and the underside of my hair stuck like honey to my neck. I fantasized about riding my bicycle home with clean, wet hair and polished skin. I imagined what it would be like to slide into bed knowing I didn't have to change the sheets the next day.

Who could sleep carrying the weight of the night's filth? A shower was critical.

I approached the manager's table and saw Mel, his legs crossed and one Nike sneaker swaying against his shin.

"Hey, Mel?"

He pulled imaginary taffy from his beard.

"Lucy, hello. You look lovely tonight! And that Southern Belle is spectacular."

"Thanks, Mel. You're looking quite dapper yourself there. How are you?"

"I'm better now. Not that I wasn't feeling great, but you know I like it when you check in with me and come for a chat. Is there something I can do for you?"

"Maybe. What would you think about a shower?"

Mel's eyes shimmered, and he raised his tangled eyebrows.

"Now, that could be tricky, but interesting. We wouldn't want the hardwood floor to get wet."

"Oh, no, gosh, no. I meant a shower for the bathroom upstairs so that I, or possibly, we, well, not you and I, but everyone, can shower after their last show."

Even though Mel wasn't one to ponder, I held my breath. His decisions were quick but firm, no negotiations after the fact.

"You do get a bit messy after eating that peach during your Southern Belle show, so I can certainly understand why you might want a shower. I'll figure something out for you, Lucy. After all, you have received more press than any other dancer besides Gypsy Rose Lee."

"I have?"

"Yes, yes you have. So, my dear, let's get you that shower. But no monkey business in there," he said, waggling his finger and smiling.

Within a month, the royal shower was installed, and I moved on to my next caper—teaching women how to strip.

CHAPTER 1

Lake Forest, Illinois

In my day, girls from Lake Forest, Illinois, became debutantes. I became a stripper in Boston's Combat Zone and was taking it all off before I knew what a debutante was.

WASP parents didn't discuss sex, money, or politics, and certainly not strippers. Informing their offspring about these conversational taboos would have been a waste of time since children learned the social graces by emulating their parents. Children were not seen, heard, or hovered over. We dined alone in kitchens while parents enjoyed cocktails in well-appointed living rooms where dogs and children were forbidden. We complied.

When I was born, in 1959, Lake Forest was 97.6 percent white. Black nannies and other household help made up the rest of the population. Mothers worked part-time at "nice" stores, volunteered, and hosted cocktail parties. Summer camps and prep schools allowed parents their social freedom and protected children from undesirables.

Our mothers' cotillion gowns and grandmothers' long kid gloves lay in wait inside hope chests until we grew up and became women just like them. It was expected that my tuxedoed father would, at the proper time, present me to high society at the debutante ball, and I'd find a suitable husband like him.

I'd marry in the Episcopalian Church, live in Lake Forest, and volunteer at the Junior League. I'd bear blond, pedigreed children, join at least one country club, subscribe to *Town and Country* magazine, and list my domicile in the Social Register, where scandal was grounds for expulsion.

As a child, I learned the fox trot, wore Lilly Pulitzer dresses, and went away to Wyonegonic Summer Camp. I attended the Low-Heywood School for girls before attending public school, where I learned how to sniff glue among other things. I hitchhiked to bluegrass festivals, listened to Pink Floyd, and took LSD five days out of seven. After two alternative boarding schools, I spent twelve weeks at the Emma Willard School before returning to New Canaan High and, at sixteen, opted out of formal education.

I moved into a Vermont commune where I met a divorced, thirty-seven-year-old lawyer and father of four. We saved money from picking apples and making snow at the Killington Ski Resort. Then we traveled cross-country for a year before landing in Boston.

I didn't graduate from high school but did graduate from college. I married several men, none of whom resembled my father, and almost married Cat Stevens, after he morphed into Yusuf Islam. I didn't find work at a "nice" store, but I found the Naked i Cabaret in Boston's Combat Zone, where I became a (literal) poster child for the city's adult entertainment district.

※ ※ ※

The Combat Zone was bordered by Boston's retail hub, Chinatown, the Theater District, and Tufts Medical Center. Peep shows, porn shops, and strip clubs operated legally in the Zone. Chinatown residents toting grocery bags slalomed around hookers, and Filene's Basement shoppers moved along Washington Street, averting their eyes from the seedy scene. Medical students in cerulean scrubs hurried past blinking marquees, and theatergoers walked the periphery, avoiding the area altogether.

The Zone was a manufactured biome, a bucket, its lid designed to contain the spread of smut. It was nothing like the pristine town of Lake Forest.

As a child, nothing about me or my surroundings hinted at my future as a stripper.

My mother, Ellen Fitzgerald Reeves, an only child like me, was tall, with full lips, a turned-up nose, and seeking blue eyes. Although frosty and removed, Mother gave the impression that, with some coaxing, one might come to know her. Her debutante ball was unsuccessful, as none of her potential suitors compared to her father.

My grandfather, "Poomp," was the senior vice president at J. Walter Thompson, an advertising agency in Chicago. In 1945 he coined the

My nanny Roberta used to dance with me on her hip. She had my back.

wartime slogan, "There's a Ford in your future." A lover of words, Poomp kept a 2,300-page dictionary on a bookstand in the living room and lifted me high enough to see the weighty book's tiny drawings.

My mother graduated from Pine Manor Junior College in Chestnut Hill, Massachusetts, then studied secretarial skills at Katharine Gibbs in Boston, where she met my father, Wolcott Howe Johnson, or "Skipper." He was a Harvard graduate from Buffalo, New York, who shared DNA with Edward Crosby (Ned) Johnson III, the eventual owner of Fidelity Investments.

Skipper wore seersucker suits, played squash, hunted pheasant, and sailed. He was athletically trim, with wavy blond hair and blue eyes, and had charm, wit, a contagious laugh, and—most important—an acceptable pedigree.

At some point while they were dating, Mother noticed that her martinis tasted like pennies and her cigarettes like mildew. Her altered palate heralded an untimely pregnancy. There were no books on the subject, and Mother, age twenty-two, couldn't tell her parents or friends. She knew therapeutic abortions involved dire medical circumstances, and adoptions required unexplainable travel. One friend had an illegal abortion and died from the Lysol they pumped into her uterus.

Mother had no choice but to inform my father and, in response, Skipper polished off a handle of vodka, drove his car through somebody's living room, and spent the night in the Lake Forest jail.

It took six months of pregnancy before Mother's parents caught on. Nan, my grandmother, suggested her daughter hole up in a Catholic institution for unwed mothers in northern Wisconsin, and Poomp wanted her to marry immediately, without social fanfare. Skip and Ellen exchanged vows in a meeting room at the First Presbyterian Church of Lake Forest and were escorted to a rented gatehouse guarding an old hobby farm. The newlyweds were forbidden to leave the house, socialize, or use a telephone. Even obstetric care risked scandal.

All four grandparents constructed a cover-up story where Skipper surprised Ellen with a world cruise. Once "returned," my parents could announce the happy occasion of the at-sea nuptials, and later, the stork's delivery. The only requirement for plausibility was a slightly early birth.

I complied. Born nine weeks ahead of schedule, I weighed under two pounds, and Mother said I looked like a rat trying to claw its way out of a bathtub. I barely opened my eyes, slept in twenty-minute increments, and bleated incessantly. When swaddled, I jerked my red, cotton ball-sized fists until whatever constrained me fell to the floor. Feedings and projectile vomiting were synonymous. Three days after I came home from the hospital, Mother took to her bed at my grandparents' house and convinced them to hire a nanny named Roberta.

Roberta wore pale, knee-length dresses with buttoned collars, and freshly laundered aprons. She fed, bathed, and danced with me. When she left for the day, my father wore a yellow raincoat and provided feedings throughout the night. After seven months, Mother finally returned home, but Roberta continued to care for me, allowing Mother time to pursue other interests.

Roberta politely stepped aside when I resisted my mother's irregular caregiving attempts. Dressing, bathing, and feedings were fraught with

Mother's impatient lack of confidence and my uncooperative temperament. As my mobility increased, Mother relaxed, and I toddled full tilt, indulging every whim and impulse with glee.

I considered my entrapment and yearned to escape before I could put a sentence together. Peeking above the second-floor windowsill, I saw the world of things beyond my confines and decided that no day would ever start without me.

One ordinary summer morning, Roberta worked in the kitchen, and Mother sat on the porch fiddling with a needlepoint project. I lined up colored blocks between her feet, bored out of my mind. The phone rang, and Mother reflexively scooped me onto the living room floor. She wound the yellow handset cord in two loops around the arm of a dining room chair and a chirpy phone conversation ensued. She was effectively bound. I knew the look and rhythm of Mother's inattention. It would be a long chat.

Too young to plan but old enough to execute, I heeded the first of many siren calls to adventure and rushed out the door. I advanced beyond the privets and slithered into the dense understory of the vast Illinois prairie.

I moved quickly, turning my body like a weathervane, not wanting to miss a thing. Invigorated, hot, and sticky, I wriggled out of my fussy summer dress and draped it over a bent stalk. Unhindered by clothing, I marched full throttle, my stubby legs working like pistons, churning toward a bright spot ahead. A red pickup truck rumbled toward me, spewing dust. I quickly reversed direction, pulled my dress on, and went home, where Mother stood on the porch. I braced myself.

"There you are. I must have lost track of time talking to Trish."

To my surprise, initial dismay, and ultimate relief, my absence went unnoticed. Roberta, however, noticed everything.

"Long as you don't walk toward strangers or stay out too long, I won't worry. May the good Lord save us both if your mother finds out."

Roberta championed my exploits. She effectively rewound trouble so Mother wouldn't get mad. Without Roberta, Mother's impatience flared, and I got the Ivory-soap treatment. She'd stomp toward me, latch onto my neck, and guide me into the bathroom.

"Lucy Johnson, open your mouth this instant."

I clamped my lips so tight they lost their color. Holding the bar of Ivory soap in one hand, Mother pressed her thumb into my cheek hollows like she was trying to give a dog a pill.

"Open," she hissed through her teeth.

Our eyes met in the mirror.

"Don't you dare look at me."

Mocking her, I squeezed my eyes shut.

"Lucy, now."

As she mashed the cold corner of the soap between my lips, it grated against my teeth. I tried hard not to cry.

"Don't you dare cry," Mother growled.

"It's burning!" I sunk my teeth into the soap, preventing it from sliding further back. When Mother removed it, I had soap shavings between my teeth.

"Go to bed," she said.

"Can't I rinse?"

She let the water run over the bloody soap bar and rubbed out the teeth marks.

"No. Good night."

I went to bed hacking and wiped my mouth all over the pillowcase. Mornings after Ivory soap, Mother was sure to change the sheets before Roberta arrived. The Ivory threat never spoiled my day, though. Eating soap was better than boredom.

Kindergarten promised to relieve some of the monotony of only childhood. My parents said going to school was a chance to make friends, fit in, and learn how to play with others. They hoped I might behave less badly. But being held hostage in an unreasonably hot room and enduring impossibly dull activities with even duller children irritated me. Awash in potential friendships, I made none. It took many years before I learned how to play with others.

At kindergarten, we "napped" on sticky, gray mats that smelled like apple juice and pretended to sleep. Like most things at Lake Forest Country Day School, it was an absurd waste of time. Supposedly, conformity was golden, a sign of future success. I didn't buy it.

Unwilling to be reined in by those in authority, school taught me to take their measure. I hatched a plan to remedy fake napping and collected rocks during recess. I squirreled them away in the back of my cubby, and when it was my turn to deliver the mats, I popped a rock inside each mat cover.

My classmates writhed within minutes. I was the only settled child in the room. The teacher clapped her hands sharply, interrupting my delight.

"Children, children, *children*! Be still!"

The squirming continued, and the teacher paced. She wasn't getting her usual hour off. I waited for my due accolades.

"Lucy Johnson, get up."

I felt pleased. I was behaving.

"Your mat, please."

The sternness in her voice concerned me. She frisked the mat and let it dangle from one hand. Her eyes moved from the mat, to me, to the floor, and back to me.

"For the children who brought rocks up, thank you. It seems that, miraculously, Lucy was the only child spared. She will collect all rocks and put them back where she found them."

My kindergarten report card said, "Lucy is very bright, but spends too much time teasing the boys. Her social skills need work."

"Social skills is just a fancy term for making friends," my father explained. "Watch what everyone does and start talking to girls at recess. Or share your cookies at lunch. It can't hurt to fit in even if you don't like them."

It didn't make sense to work at something I didn't like but I figured my father knew about these things.

Recess was like being given the keys to a car and forced to drive at age six. Girls banded together and controlled playground games and equipment while the boys raced around, conking their heads on the monkey bars before staggering to the nurse's office. I waited in line for hopscotch, but recess always ended before my turn came. When the girls called me weird and a "lonely only," I shrugged and said I liked being weird. I also liked having the last word.

Improving on my father's advice, I pried the gold nuggets off my Tiffany charm bracelet and gave them to my classmates. Nothing changed but the weight of the bracelet and Mother's reproach. It didn't matter. I was *always* doing something wrong. Mother retrieved the charms, and I had Ivory soap for dinner. I went from being called a "lonely only" to an "Indian giver." I tried becoming a class clown, but nothing I said was well thought out and my attempts fell flat. It was fine. I could entertain myself.

In first grade, my grandparents bought us a big house where I tied my sleeping bag to the second-floor banister and hung in it like a cocoon. The fire department retrieved me without incident. At that point, Ivory soap was no longer an effective tool.

"I can't stand this anymore. Honestly, Lucy, there's something wrong with you. I'm calling the doctor and then your grandmother."

I folded my arms. "But I don't feel sick."

"Oh, hello, Dr. Kadison," Mother's voice softened for him. "Yes, it's Ellen Johnson. I'm calling about Lucy. I think it's her brain. The fire department had to rescue her from a sleeping bag suspended above the foyer by a string, and she gave away all the charms from her charm bracelet. Imagine? It was *such* an embarrassment. We can't take her anywhere—no vacations or dinners at the club. I need her fixed. Uh-huh. Yes, oh, really? Keep her awake all night? No, I can't imagine she'll watch *The Tonight Show*. Games, cards? OK. Thank you, Dr. Kadison."

She spun the dial again and called Nan without looking at me.

"Mother. Please don't get hysterical, but there is something wrong with your precious granddaughter. No, she's not perfectly fine and doesn't need to be loved, for God's sake. She is already loved. We're taking her for brain tests."

Ten minutes later, Nan, my grandmother, barreled through the door clutching a boxy, patent leather purse.

"Why, hello, Mother. This is unexpected. Take some tea?"

"No, Ellen, thank you," Nan's voice quivered. "I'm too upset to drink anything. It's senseless, Ellen, damaging, absolute nonsense. Look at her. Lu couldn't be more perfect."

Nan looked at me adoringly with watery eyes. She drew a soft line down my cheek with her gloved fingertip.

"Maybe it's from splitting her head open on the upstairs railing. So typical. Racing to nowhere, not looking where she was going, or, for that matter, thinking what on earth she was doing."

"No child is perfect, Ellen, even *you* weren't perfect."

Nan dabbed her eyes with a tissue. My father walked in, and Mother released a disgusted sigh.

"Fitzie," he said. "Always so good to see you."

Mother began again. "I just spoke with Dr. Kadison. There is obviously something very wrong with her."

My father's eyes widened. "With Fitzie? Fitzie, you certainly look well. I hope it's nothing serious."

"No, Skipper; Jesus, with Lucy. You're as bad as she is. She's scheduled for a brain scan Monday morning."

My father opened the liquor cabinet.

"Don't take it so personally, Ellen. Lucy's just a little more curious and adventurous than most."

"No. Lucy is abnormal. You don't see other children doing these things." Mother glared at him. "It's a little early to start drinking, Skipper."

"I couldn't agree more, Skipper," Nan piped in. "Lu is full of beans. I might need a hot toddy while you're at it. This is the most upset I've ever been."

"Really, Mother? Ever?"

After an EEG and psychological testing, my brain was deemed better than most, with a 140 IQ. Dr. Kadison prescribed Ritalin to make my parents' lives more pleasant. It worked.

Country-club dinners became manageable. I no longer squirmed underneath the table. Instead, I walked to the powder room, where a Black lady sat on a stool reading a magazine. I felt sad she had to listen to people poop all night. When I came in, she pushed a padded chair up to the sink for me to wash my hands and gave me soap shaped like a bird. Then she dotted my palms with purple lotion that smelled like lilacs. Back at the table, Mother rewarded my good behavior with Shirley Temples, vichyssoise on ice, and steak tartare. Sensing an opening, I asked for a pony.

My parents didn't give me a pony but started taking me on trips. I visited Nan and Poomp in Delray Beach, Florida, and my other grandparents at their rustic summer home at Blackstone Lake in Canada.

There, I slept in a room with my cousins, picked wild blueberries, and used kerosene lamps. My grandfather taught me how to spear frogs and cook their bowed legs in lemon and garlic on a wood stove the size of a sofa. There was no electricity, and warm water was off-limits for everyone but my grandmother. The rest of us took "soapies."

Soapies were communal baths held by the lake. Nudity was nothing to be ashamed of for my father's side of the family, but Mother either wore a bathing suit or skipped it altogether. We dropped our towels on the dock, lathered up, and rinsed in the lake water daily.

I was eight years old when I realized that being naked was no big deal—I reasoned I could be shirtless when it was hot, just like the boys. I took off my shirt while eating peach pancakes.

"Lucy Johnson! Put your shirt on this instant!" Mother said, trying to scare me back into my shirt.

The eyes of the extended family turned to me.

"But we're naked every morning," I said.

"Not at the breakfast table, we aren't."

"Some of us are. Look at them."

I pointed to my uncle, father, and boy cousin.

"They're not wearing shirts. Why should *they* get to be more comfortable than we are?"

"Because *they* are men and have hair on their chests. Lucy, stop being a pill."

"It's too hot. I'm leaving my shirt *off*."

My father cleared his throat. "Ellen, I think Lucy has a point."

Mother left the table, and I went shirtless until I was cold.

Like Nan, Poomp, and Roberta, my father endorsed the misfit in me. He gave me forbidden ant farms and sea monkeys. He filled my empty Girl Scout sash with Charlie Brown and Dennis the Menace cutouts. When I swooned over Tiny Tim's gummy smile and falsetto voice, my father hung a larger-than-life poster of his face on my wall. And, after we moved to New Canaan, Connecticut, while I was about to start fifth grade, he took me ice skating on a reservoir that said, "No Skating."

New Canaan was Lake Forest, but with hills and stone walls, and without Nan, Poomp, and Roberta. The new house was a "charming Colonial" with warped windowpanes and crooked floors.

"It's askew because it's early," Mother said. "See these narrow closets next to the fireplace? Back then, they stored babies on shelves. It was much easier."

Neighbors brought tuna noodle casseroles, bags of Fritos, and homemade cookies in tin boxes. The Welcome Wagon lady tied balloons to our mailbox. She presented Mother with a brown wicker basket holding a town map, ruler, potholder, sewing kit, and country-club application.

"I strongly recommend the Mounted Troop and Walter Schalk's School of Dance for your little one," she said. "Once she settles into her new school, of course."

My fifth-grade teacher, Mr. Thompson, had yellow teeth, bad breath, and hair like pine needles. He insisted we hand-deliver our work and wait by his desk while he looked it over. The boys stood across from him and the girls next to him.

I planted my feet where the boys usually stood, but his freckly hand motioned me closer. He corralled me to his side and I stared at the tiny, patterned holes in his shoes. It was the first and last time his cold, wormy fingers parted my thighs. I dug the heel of my loafer into the top of his foot with all my might.

"Fucker," I whispered, grinding harder.

When Mr. Thompson withdrew his hand, I tingled with satisfaction. I wanted to hurt him. Unlike my father, whose drunken antics could be infuriating if not downright dangerous, Mr. Thompson was sober. He meant every disgusting thing he did. My inebriated father became lost in his own house, and I never wanted to hurt him.

Cocktail hours were as regimented as a balanced breakfast in the Johnson household. At 5:30 p.m., my father cheerfully delivered Mother's martini to the kitchen before pouring his own. He settled into the upholstered chair in the library, lit a Kent cigarette, and snapped open the newspaper.

If he only had a few drinks, I could sleep. On stormy nights, he sipped in front of my mother. The moment she turned away, he gulped from the bottle. His fingers started curling toward his palms, and his face became rubbery. I stayed awake in bed waiting for the weighted thuds, muffled gurgling, rough burps, and rounds of booming gags, splatters, and groans.

My father drank until he was nobody. Before becoming nobody, he was an explosive stranger, a lunatic mutation lurching through the house. He left smoldering cigarettes wedged against the sides of upholstered cushions. He prowled, rummaged, and bumped aimlessly along walls while interacting with his hallucinations. Somehow capable of strength and precision despite being drunk, he could swing a fist, or worse, load his duck-hunting rifle and shoot at the walls.

Mother stayed alert to the dangers. When she deemed the risk significant enough, she scooped me out of bed, down the back stairway, and into the front seat of the cold station wagon. We shared a room at Howard Johnson's and had blueberry pancakes for breakfast. I didn't have the

Acting on my eight-year-old objections to gender dress codes.

strength to meet her sadness and looked down while we ate. Once the incident passed, I was instantly happy again.

One Christmas Eve, my father decimated the wrapped presents Mother took months to decorate. He left a trail of red and green sequins, glitter, and crumbled Styrofoam balls. Half-dried vomit stained the tissue paper and streamed down the face of the television. All that Mother made beautiful was ruined. She stayed in her room for eight days and I didn't care about opening presents. I lay on the floor and listened for the turn of a magazine page or a sigh. I took in the scent of Chanel No. 5 from underneath the door.

I committed to improving their lives and deftly replaced half of the vodka with tap water. The preemptive strike backfired. My father went into a sober rage and grounded me for two weeks.

When I asked Mother about drinking, she mounted a fist to her hip and proclaimed that, "Drinking to excess is not something normal adults do, Lucy. It's something that wildly irresponsible adults do, like your father . . ."

My father's appearance aborted the launch.

"Lucy," he said, "what I believe your mother is trying to explain is that being drunk is different than drinking or having cocktails. Sometimes we overeat and get a stomachache, and, on occasion, your father drinks too much and suffers the consequences. Drinking is an important part of society."

"Everyone suffers the consequences, Skipper. Ruining Christmas? Laying comatose on the floor, making your daughter think you're dead? Enough, really. Just knock it off."

Before moving to New Canaan, we spent one year in Summit, New Jersey, where Mother was hospitalized for a kidney stone. My father took care of me and when I woke up for school, I couldn't find him. I called out, again and again, running between all corners of the house. I thought he'd forgotten about me and left for work, but he was unconscious on the sunroom floor, surrounded by vomit.

"Dadee?" I called softly. "Dadee, I have school." Dadee was a nickname derived from my earlier mispronunciation of "Daddy."

I bent down, jiggled his shoulder, and palmed his cold, prickly cheek. After getting no response, I called the police and wondered where my father had gone. The EMTs resurrected him with something miraculous under his nose. My fun, funny father always returned from his vodka abyss.

CHAPTER 2

Cat Stevens: Part 1

My fixation with the British singer-songwriter Cat Stevens started as an unremarkable but time-consuming crush. I listened to the same song forty or fifty times before moving on to the next. I left the shades up and danced, not for rain or recitals, but for the goosebumps. The life-size photograph of Cat Stevens's face inside the *Teaser and the Firecat* album became a shrine on my night table. The more I studied him, the more he consumed me.

My father wasted no time ordering posters for my wall, just as he had for Tiny Tim.

"Honestly, Skipper, we just had the bedroom wallpapered, and now you're going to let her ruin it?"

"Sweetie, I'll use thumbtacks instead of tape."

"Just don't put them up while you're drunk."

From that point on, my mother referred to Cat Stevens as "Poodie," after our tabby cat. They didn't know I was saving myself for him, that I'd rebuffed Jay Sanderson's sloppy kiss at bell-choir practice and avoided boy situations. I attended countless showings of the movie *Harold and Maude* to hear the Cat Stevens soundtrack, and permanently branded his birth name initials, "SDG," on my body with black ink.

Starting seventh grade at a new school lessened my infatuation's intensity, at least for a while.

Low-Heywood was a private, all-girl school whose lackluster slogan was "Knowledge for the Journey." I enjoyed field hockey and Latin classes and hated the scratchy uniforms and ninety-minute study halls. Nobody studied.

During my scenic, 50-minute saunter to and from the most distant restroom on campus, I stopped at the floor-to-ceiling windows where, one day, I spotted an adjacent tray of lemon-yellow paint and, conveniently enough, a roller. I'd never painted on glass and wondered what it felt like. I dipped the roller into the paint, raised my arm, and pulled down like I was closing a shade.

I was kicked out of Low-Heywood that afternoon and started at Saxe Junior High the following morning.

I latched onto the school's marijuana and LSD factions. Both groups wore flannel shirts and frayed, lampshade-sized bellbottoms. Pot smoking was a giddy event ritualized by gurgling bong hits, hash under glass, and Pink Floyd music. Smoking weed was best pursued after school. LSD, however, was more straightforward in its application and made classes more tolerable.

My social preferences continued into ninth grade. The most plentiful type of LSD at New Canaan Public High was "Windowpane." The translucent squares were no larger than a piece of confetti and purchased through a series of nods in the cafeteria. I'd set a tab under my tongue and wait for the familiar, hot buzz. Next came strobing trails, fractals, melting tables, and hallways filled with clear jelly. There were clouds at my feet, crows wearing cowboy boots, robins in tunics, and sparrows in top hats. Even a mundane object became a spectacle.

During occasional LSD droughts, rubber cement was the hallucinogenic substitute of choice. Deep breaths into a plastic sandwich bag were good for brief fractals, significant headaches, and losing IQ points.

The least concerning contraband was our parents' cigarettes, at least until I was expelled for smoking in the bathroom. Being ejected from New Canaan Public High necessitated visits to "alternative" schools. Months after starting at The New School at Lenox, it closed, and I was shipped to Vershire, Vermont. When I gushed to my parents about learning to operate a backhoe and joining the horse program, they plucked me out and deposited me into what was once the Troy Female Seminary, renamed the Emma Willard School, in upstate New York.

Ex-nun and Principal Frances O'Connor espoused honesty and assured us there would be no ramifications to baring it all, but the tiniest fib would result in immediate expulsion. What a relief, I thought, since I'd bungled every lie I told.

Classes were held at round tables, and teachers facilitated vigorous discussions. At long last, learning captivated me, and friendships came quickly. As a seasoned contrarian, I captained the debate team. I learned how to play bridge, and I thrived. My parents were thrilled.

We went to a co-ed dance at the Kent School, where the main attraction was Southern Comfort. The next morning, we were instructed to file

I was finally happy at the oldest all-girls school in the country.

through Frances O'Connor's office one at a time. The room smelled of stale peppermint. I wasn't worried. All I had to do was tell the truth.

"Hello, Louise. You know why you're here. You drank alcohol at the dance last night."

"It's Lucy, and no, I didn't drink."

"Let me smell your breath."

"OK." I leaned over her desk and blew air at her puffy face.

"Again, please."

"I don't drink alcohol."

"Did you brush your teeth this morning?" she asked.

"Yup."

"Did you use mouthwash, Louise? To disguise the foul smell of Southern Comfort?"

"No, Lucy doesn't have mouthwash."

"I hear you didn't dance much. What were you doing?"

"Hanging out with friends."

"What friends were you drinking with?"

"Mrs. O'Connor, Miss O'Connor, I wasn't drinking. I don't drink. If you don't believe me, take me to the hospital for a blood test."

"I want names."

I'd seen girls chugging from Southern Comfort bottles that Mr. Preston, a faculty chaperone, pulled out of his book bag. Sex with teachers was a student aspiration and happened regularly. One could only hope to be chosen for the club.

"I have one name: Mr. Preston. He supplied the bottles."

This was clever and honest enough.

O'Connor sat back and removed her glasses.

"Mr. Preston? I think you are still intoxicated, Louise. That's what I think."

"I think you are wrong, Frances. I did not drink, and I do not and will not drink. I also won't have sex with teachers. The only thing I do is occasionally smoke pot."

"Thank you, Louise. You may go."

Relieved, I walked out, and my shoulders dropped away from my ears.

Within the hour, faculty members had packed my trunk and loaded me into a train before I could say goodbye to my friends. The Emma Willard School kept a full year's tuition and freed up space for another paying student. Not having mastered the stiff-upper-lip routine, I cried on the way home. Instead of feeling aggrieved, I felt guilty. The train slowed into the New Canaan station, and Mother stood on the platform, dabbing her eyes with the backs of her hands. I was cruel to make her feel sad. She shoved tissues into her purse, and we both tried to smile. I'd never seen her tears.

"Lu, I am so sorry. So, so sorry."

Mother framed my face in her long hands and kissed my forehead, lingering through several breaths. For the first time ever, I soaked her in. It felt like the Holy Spirit.

As did the piece of newspaper she left on my bedside table: Cat Stevens was playing on February 28, 1976, at the New Haven Coliseum, and tickets went on sale that Saturday. I'd hitchhike to New Haven and spend the night waiting in line.

Mother didn't try to stop me.

"Dress in layers," she said, nervously buttoning my pea coat. "Don't you ever stop to think that I worry about you, Lu?"

"Sorry. I don't want you to worry. I really don't. I'll be OK, I promise. And I'll come back right after I get the ticket. I just want to be first in line. I still can't believe this!"

Mother emptied coins into my hand. "Good grief, I'm shaking. Call me, please. Tonight."

"I will. I'm sure there's a payphone there."

I wished she weren't shaking.

The ticket window at the New Haven Coliseum was covered in frost. I took my place behind five people wrapped in sleeping bags. Cat Stevens music warbled from a boosted cassette player. An official-looking man in a long wool coat handed us green index cards with place numbers. People started to bargain.

"Hundred bucks, and I'll trade places."

"How about two-fifty for you in spot number three?"

"Hi. I'm Carole, green ticket number seven," said the woman beside me.

"Hi, I'm Lucy, green ticket number six."

"You're young," Carole said.

"I'm sixteen. How old are you?"

"Nineteen. Did you run away?"

"No, but shoot, I need to call my mother."

After my call, I huddled against the cold night, bought a front-row ticket, and hitchhiked home. I was engulfed in everything Cat Stevens until February 28. I knew his gaze better than anybody's and believed we'd find each other. Mother insisted on driving me round-trip to the concert and stopped at a florist shop on the way there.

"You must bring him roses, don't you think? Isn't that what fans your age do?"

"I guess. I feel bad that you'll be hanging around New Haven all alone. I can probably get a ride home if you want."

"I'm already here."

"But what if I meet him?"

"Oh, Lucy, don't be ridiculous. Honestly."

"You never know."

"Lu-Lu, you're so out of touch. Just because you want something doesn't mean you get it. But if you meet Poodie, bring him over tomorrow night for meatloaf."

Ushers stopped me at intervals and herded me toward the front. The people from the ticket line waved, and I saw Carole, green ticket number seven, in the seat next to mine. She poked me.

"What the heck are those for?" she asked.

"My mother said I should bring him flowers."

"Your mom? Really? Your mom is pretty cool. You know he always picks one rose and puts it on his microphone stand."

"How do you know that?"

"This is my fourth Cat Stevens concert," Carole boasted, leaning forward to scan our row. "I'll be right back. I gotta see something."

She skipped along the front row and back again. "Guess what?"

"What?"

"There's not one other person in the front row with flowers. Are you a fainter?"

"I don't know. This is my first concert. But I am crazy about him, so I might. I tattooed SDG, on my hip. Crazy. Messed up."

"SDG? Oh yeah, for Steven Demetre Georgiou, his birth name. A homemade tattoo?"

"With a little sewing needle and some India ink. It's not very pretty."

"Lemme see."

"I can't show you, but it's right here." I straightened my left leg and pressed on the area between my thigh and hip.

The lights dimmed. The emblazoned tiger on the shimmering metallic curtain rippled, and people stood.

"Here we go," said Carole. "Stand up, silly."

A light flared from behind the curtain, and two magicians pushed out four brightly colored boxes and stacked them into a tower. After a gentle spin, they released the doors simultaneously. Steven Demetre Georgiou, Cat Stevens himself, stepped out of the tower wearing gray corduroy pants, green work boots, and a white linen shirt with a waist tie. He mouthed a humble thank you and perched on a red stool. The shock of him gripped me. It was close to unbearable.

"The rose," said Carole.

I couldn't collect myself.

Carole leaned back to examine me. "Hello? The rose?"

I was floating.

"You're crying, a mess."

"I'm not crying," I insisted, while raising one hand to my wet face.

Carole cupped my elbow. "Are you always so daffy? Jeez. Now's the time. Quick. Chop-chop. Get a move on."

She reached down and extracted one of the roses from the paper cone underneath my seat.

"What about thorns? I don't want him to get hurt."

"There are no thorns. They take them off at the florist. Now, here." Carole wrapped my fingers around the rose stem and nudged me forward with her shoulder. "Now go."

When I stepped forward, a man wearing all black came closer. I smiled, and he gave me a thumbs up, so I walked to a metal bar outlining the front of the stage.

The same man yelled into my ear, "Squirm under the bottom rail."

I wobbled under the barricade. The stage floor was at my chest. I tentatively raised the rose above my head. Cat Stevens's legs and green boots moved toward me. He took the rose, grazed the back of his hand on my cheek, and attached the rose to the microphone stand. I was numb.

The coliseum filled with tiny dots of light, and the crowd strained closer. The end was near. I was overcome.

I met Carole Hollander in line for Cat Stevens tickets and we remained friends until her death.

"Are you going backstage?" Carole asked.
"Backstage? Me?"
"Yeah, you know, to meet him."
"Nobody's going to let me backstage."

The music ended, the curtain fell, and the crowd drained from the seats. Men unsnapped black trunks on rollers and circled cables around their elbows and hands. Racks of lights descended from the ceiling, instruments were wrapped and taped, tripod stands collapsed, and the stage floor rose in pieces.

"Now what?" I asked Carole. "We just sit here?"
"Patience," she wagged her finger.

A security man wearing a lanyard and laminated pass swaggered over. "You ladies want to come to meet and greet?"
"That'd be great, thanks," Carole said.

He escorted us around to the side of the stage and through double doors. A handwritten sign that said "Meet & Greet Here" was taped to something resembling a corral.

"What is meet and greet?"

"Just like it sounds. You go in and say a quick hello. Don't act all wacky. Keep it together."

I didn't meet or greet. Instead, I listened for clues and learned Steve was staying at the Pierre Hotel in Manhattan and, most critically, would go to a bar called JP's after his last Madison Square Garden show on March 5. I had four days to prepare for concerts I wouldn't attend.

Once home, I circled the names of tour personnel from the Majikat Earth Tour program and studied a map of Manhattan. I packed a toothbrush, extra underwear, and a full-length, sunflower-colored dress my parents had brought from Mexico. Before leaving, I left my mother a note. I didn't want her to worry.

"Dear Mother, I know you'll be upset, but I want to see Poodie again. He's playing in New York City. I promise I'll call. Lots of love, Lu."

My hair wafted with the scent of Herbal Essence as I floated out of the house, feeling like I knew things. My mission required impenetrable confidence, and I vowed to keep any daffiness in check.

I arrived by train and surveyed the outside of Madison Square Garden for open docking ramps, hoping I didn't miss the sound check. I walked through an open door and followed his voice to the back of an arena. His red stool was a dot from where I stood.

"That part's good, OK? It's good enough then," he said.

I wasn't ready to initiate contact. Once outside, I walked north to the Pierre Hotel, through its doors, and past the white-gloved attendants manning the elevators. I wanted to find the hotel lobby so I could sit and strategize. Maybe Cat Stevens would need to preen at the hotel following the sound check.

A gaggle of heavily made-up, older women wearing animal-print clothing approached the front desk. One woman removed her sunglasses and flopped the top half of her body onto the counter, causing her bangle bracelets to clatter against the marble.

"Hey, man. Excuse me, sir?"

The man rolled his eyes.

"Ladies, we've been over this, yet you persist. Each time a bit tipsier, I might add. It's unattractive and disturbing to our guests. The answer is still no. He is not staying here. Now scat, or I'll call security. Scat for good this time."

Not wanting to be associated with them, I found the lobby, claimed a chair near the most discreet hotel doors, and promptly fell asleep.

"Sleeping Beauty?" The man from the front desk said, tapping my shoulder. "I'm afraid we can't have you snoozing in our lobby like some hobo."

I straightened.

"Oh, gosh, I'm so sorry. Of course, you can't."

"Are you waiting for your parents?"

Before I could answer, a man emerged from a commotion near the front doors.

"She's waiting for us," he said, signaling with raised eyebrows. "Good to find you, darling."

"Right. I've been waiting here a while." I stretched.

The hotel employee hitched his hands behind his back and left.

The man, Micky, was as old as my father. He dragged an upholstered chair next to mine and prattled on about life on the road with the Cat Stevens Majikat Earth Tour. He discussed the roadie hierarchy, merchandisers, riggers, mixers, managers, and groupies. His breath smelled like the rotting-leaf water at the bottom of a vase.

"Are you a groupie, my little bird?"

"A groupie? Me? I don't think so."

I wasn't a little bird, either.

"You don't know those wretched girls who got thrown out, do you?"

"I saw them but no. They were gross."

"Maybe so, but they take care of a man's needs and ask little in return, maybe just a shitty, stick-on backstage pass, not a laminate."

"Good for them," I said.

"You're a bit on the young side. Jailbait. How old are you, love?"

"Old enough to choose between tampons and pads."

"Witty, I see. We get fourteen-year-olds sometimes. No matter what age, it's about fucking a famous cock. Have you eaten?"

"I don't think I'm hungry, but thanks."

"Hospitality suite is on the eighteenth floor. Plenty of food there. What floor are you on?"

"I don't have a room."

"No place to eat and no place to sleep. Tsk-tsk. I'm used to sharing, if you need to sleep." He winked. "Two beds, mate. Right then, gotta run."

As vile as Micky was, he was tolerable and potentially indispensable. I opted for the free food. Who else might be in the feeding room?

※ ※ ※

"Here so soon?" Micky chided. "I don't bite, love, unless asked. You know that Stevie prefers to spend most of his time alone? But not me. I'm a social fellow."

Stevie? "You don't say." I scooped steamed vegetables into a paper bowl.

"I do say. I'm an unusual bloke, so don't miss your chance. I imagine the boys'll be heading to le club. Will you be joining them?"

His words were blurry and slow.

"No, I don't think so."

I didn't want to meet Steve inside a packed nightclub with hordes of beautiful models crawling over him or be a dull, gray fish in the deep, colorful pond. But I had nothing else to do. If Micky became a problem, I figured I could deal with it. We walked to a nondescript building without any signs identifying it as a nightclub. I noticed Micky swirling on his feet while showing his laminated pass to the bouncer.

"Are you OK?" I asked.

"Just the daily buzz," he said.

"From what?"

"Napping, working, Quaaludes, fast food, booze. It's all right. There's always something to counteract the other something. A cosmic chemical balance. C'mon."

A whooping clump of people clutching toy-sized bottles locked us in. They inhaled vapors from poppers.

"Happy poppers. That'll do the trick. Excuse me, mate," Mickey said, stepping up to a young man inhaling vapors. "What'll it take to get a few poppers for my little lady and me?"

"Hey, man, that's a Cat Stevens pass. Cut it out," the man said, producing three bottles and giving them to Mickey. "Free for you, my man."

"That's very kind, thank you. Try some?" Mickey asked me.

"No, and I am not your little lady."

"You're a square?"

"I guess. When it comes to this stuff. I prefer hallucinogens. By the way, you're drooling."

"Lemme take a pop then."

Micky swaggered into a pole with misguided determination, then inhaled some amyl nitrate.

"Yick. Smells like sweaty socks," I said. "Time to go."

I sounded like my mother's refrain to my plastered father.

A disembodied arm holding a doll spoon filled with cocaine shot toward Mickey. He slumped against a wall and accidentally swatted it away. *Great. Here I am, in a nightclub, in Manhattan, shepherding an inebriated roadie lacking motor skills.* It was a long, groggy ten blocks back to the Pierre Hotel.

"Maybe you should go to nursing school, love. You've been an outstanding caretaker. Take that bed. I do get lonely, but you can have it all to yourself, promise."

He lied, but not significantly. When I woke up, Mickey, still dressed, was snoring into my neck. Half his clothed body draped over mine like bags of sand. I lifted one limb at a time, gingerly pushed out from under him, and slipped into my shoes. I felt a weird tenderness toward Mickey as I closed the door.

The next stop was JP's on First Avenue and 77th Street.

I walked past the Pierre's front desk, wondering if I'd be back under more spectacular circumstances. If not, then JP's was the end of my road and I'd be on a train back to New Canaan instead of inside Steve's hotel room.

CHAPTER 3

Wild World

I walked next to Central Park, to 77th Street and JP's. The building looked unassuming, like any other bar in the city. Before I could knock, the door swung open and a giddy man in a black terrycloth robe waved me in. Water dripped from the tips of his corkscrew hair.

"Come on in! I'm JP, and I'm exceptionally clean."

"I'm meeting a friend," I said, "and I'm way early. Are you serving food?"

"We sure are. Care for some cocaine before lunch? Oh no, that's silly. Then you wouldn't want lunch. Order anything on me and join us upstairs when you're done. Just through that door."

I didn't know what cocaine was.

JP's use of the pronoun "us" reassured me. I finished lunch and went upstairs. As it happened, without me there was no "us." In between phone calls, JP talked incessantly. I heard about Trax, a nightclub he was opening, pop-star dramas, record-company executives, and his main concern that day: Stevie Nicks and a pesky drug problem.

"It's one thing to recreate and another thing altogether when a drug becomes your god, but is really your demon," he added.

JP, or James Pullis, was known for maintaining a discreet, relaxed environment for impromptu performances, business dealings, and after-show decompressions.

"It's not so much for the public, but for the trade," he explained.

Unbeknownst to me, JP assumed that, once in his lair, I might relieve his sexual tensions. To that end, he stayed in his bathrobe. I couldn't rebuff him, he was far too valuable. I politely twisted away when he grinded against me. Clearly, there was a lot to learn about sex, including frottage. JP eventually dressed and attended to business downstairs. I fell asleep on his couch.

When I woke up, I flipped the deadbolt, brushed my hair and teeth, and changed into the yellow, embroidered dress my parents brought back from Mexico. I complemented the look with socks and Birkenstock sandals. I was the antithesis of sexy but felt brazen and prematurely triumphant.

I descended the stairs to the sounds of ice shakers, eating utensils, and cheerful chatter. Not wanting to draw attention to myself, I surveyed the cave-like room from the doorway and spied one empty table farthest from the entrance. A propped-up "Reserved" sign was in its center, clearly meant for Steve and his entourage. Not wanting to appear intrusive, which I was, or worse, like a platitudinous fan, which I also was, I inched over to take my post at a safe distance. I made sure my facial expression was neutral, relaxed my shoulders, checked my posture, foot placement, and where my arms hung. I averted my eyes from the door and kept my head still.

Ear-piercing shrieks disrupted the relative calm. Security personnel tugged on the door from the inside while a squall of disallowed groupies tried to force their way in like a football team's offensive line. JP maneuvered quickly around the tables, finally locking the door. I glimpsed a white tunic moving through the darkness. Conversations hushed, and forks rested across plates.

Steve faced the back of the room toward me and slid his hands into his pockets. People stood, eagerly offering accolades and hellos. He looked right at me. I reasoned with myself that, of course, he didn't. The man was hungry and tired of crowds.

I felt like a restaurant hostess standing by the table. My mantle of magical thinking frayed, and I turned away. A thorny list of *why nots* scrolled in my head: *sexually oblivious, don't know how to kiss, never have kissed, sixteen years old, zits, hairy legs, cute, not exotic, and wearing a muumuu.*

After I'd come so far, I couldn't stand thinking of myself as inept, but my plan was clearly ludicrous.

A polite tap on my shoulder signaled for me to move.

"Would you have some dinner? With me?"
That voice.

I whipped around. The air hummed. Shadows brightened around Steve's golden face, the same face from the album cover propped up on my night table at home. It was an effort to keep my eyes pinned on his. Stunned into repose, I wondered what I'd summoned. *This was no album cover.*

"I would love to," I pronounced with astounding confidence.

"Right, then," he said.

He smelled like musk. *This is happening.* He pulled a chair out. "Please, sit with me."

I gave up hitchhiking once I could drive.

Vermont fiddling contests were better than LSD.

Please? "Don't mind if I do." I sounded like my mother.
"I'm glad you're here."
What? Did he think I was someone else? Was I someone else?
He unfolded a napkin and smoothed it onto his thighs.
"Must be proper at the pub," he said. "I'm a bit hungry. You?"
"I could eat."
That was true, but I wasn't sure I could swallow.
"Let's order," he said, motioning for the waiter's attention. "I'll just have a plate of sautéed mushrooms. And my lady will have?"

My lady? This was going better than I imagined.
"Mushrooms sound perfect, thank you. And chopsticks, please, if you have them."

"Two pair if you would," said Steve, smiling and patting the top of my hand. "You eat with chopsticks? Amazin'."

I settled into my body, the chair, the impossible. Steve held multiple conversations around the table, and I stabbed at my plate of mushrooms, making sure we finished at the same time. I didn't assume; I knew we'd leave together.

"Let's go," he said.

He offered his arm, and I accepted. We walked into a rush of chilly air. Velvet ropes barely contained two embankments of frantic women on either side of the door. Men triaged the situation by pressing backward with open arms. Steve closed his elbow against his body and covered my hand with his. He was shivering.

"Where's your coat, young man?" I asked.

He pressed closer. "Don't need one now. Where's the bloody driver?"

The frenzy of female fans was layers deep, a multiform throng dressed in halter tops, camisoles, pea coats, furs, low-slung jeans, and wide belts. I was the only one in a Mexican muumuu.

"Who the fuck's that broad?" "Yeah, who's that hippie chick?"

I smiled directly into their glares, and Steve placed himself between them and me. The driver opened the limousine door and jumped back when a cascade of flowers tumbled out. Steve bent down, taking me with him, and scooped the arrangements out of the gutter and into the car.

"Sir!" the driver shouted. "In the car now, please!"

"We can't just leave 'em. They're livin' things," Steve said.

Our door closed against the intensifying screams. The driver, unable to see out the side windows past the flowers, opened the streetside door and pushed the flowers toward the floor. Locks snapped, and we were sealed in.

"Where to, sir?"

Steve looked at me.

"Sir?" the driver repeated.

"Somethin' 'bout you," Steve said, staring at me.

A woman escaped the corral, then, like displaced termites, another, and another, until dozens of palms pressed in on the windows. The glass separator inside the limo dropped.

"Excuse me, sir?" asked the driver, hanging one arm over the seat. "Where are we going?"

"How about a tour of Manhattan then? The skyline at night, then the Pierre."

"Certainly."

We moved in stops and starts through Manhattan, eased into the Lincoln Tunnel, and cruised along the Hudson River. The reflections followed us like the moon.

We arrived at the Pierre, and Steve darted out to hold my door.

"Young lady?"

"Sir!" the driver scolded him, "Might I remind you that you are in my charge."

A whisper of snow tingled my face.

"You're too kind, really," I said.

"And your manners are fantastic. What to do with all these flowers then?"

The driver raised his eyebrows. "Sir?"

"Your limo is filled with hundreds, maybe thousands of flowers. They must come out," said Steve.

"There's a dumpster at my lot," the driver winked.

"No dumpster. We'll send someone out to fetch 'em."

We matched strides into the lobby toward the front desk, and Steve stopped abruptly. He noticed something by the doors.

"Maybe it'd be best if you ask about the flowers," he said. "I'll wait back here, out of sight."

"Excuse me, could you help us?" I asked, approaching the reception area.

"Miss?" the man behind the counter replied, looking past my shoulder at Steve.

"We need someone to get flowers out of the limo, if that's possible," I said. "There are a lot."

The man tapped his desk blotter with a pen.

"Otherwise, they'll die," Steve piped in.

"Not a problem." The man cleared his throat. "We'll send them to your room after the flowers are settled in vases."

"That would be great," I said. "Our room number is?" I asked, turning toward Steve. *Our* room number.

"I know the suite number," the man said, eyeballing a group entering the lobby. "Very well. Consider it done."

Five bedraggled women lurched toward the desk, the same women I'd seen the day before. When I looked for Steve, he was gone. My stomach dropped to my arches.

"That's the girl from JP's," said one woman. "It could be his daughter," said another.

I wheeled around, still searching.

"Ladies," the man intervened. "In spite of my efforts to dissuade you, I see you've returned."

One of them thrust a wad of cash toward the counter and he rolled his eyes.

"Don't start this again."

"Just his room number, pretty please? We'll throw in a quick blow job with the cash. Every man loves a little head."

"Oh, for goodness' sake," the man flushed. "Shall I call to have you removed? Again? Call the police for trespassing? Or worse?"

"That won't be necessary," said one. "We'll be nearby, if he wants special services. It doesn't look like the little lass is experienced."

"That will be enough, ladies," the man said. "Be on your way now. Shoo."

The women disentangled, regrouping on the sidewalk outside.

"Boo," Steve said, releasing a warm puff of air on the back of my neck. "Don't worry. C'mon, let's take the stairwell then. These types ride up and down the lifts lookin' for me, or whoever."

I expected candles, incense, flowers, and sacred texts placed reverently on an altar inside his room. The door opened, and my thoughts went dark.

"I'd say join me in the shower, but that'll spoil the mystery, eh?" Steve asked, removing his boots.

"I'll take one after you," I said casually, as though scheduling a shower around Cat Stevens's hygienic needs was part of my daily drill.

The bathroom door closed, and I flipped off my Birkenstocks to wander around the living room. I picked up one of his boots, smelled the inside of it, and spied a concert set list, which I promptly shoved inside my sock. I lingered at a low table covered in bamboo print fabric. On top was an orange hardcover book called *The Qur'an*. Inside were columns of unfamiliar script and what I assumed to be English translations, but the room was too dark for me to read. Instead, I plunked down on the king-sized bed where I knew I would soon lose my virginity.

I wondered where my toothbrush was, what to do if I bled on the sheets or, worse, on him, how much it would hurt, and if I could avoid looking like a complete spaz. I knew nothing about having sex but wanted to stay relaxed. Thinking about a checkbook supposedly helped dampen anxiety, but I'd never had a checkbook.

Steve appeared in a white robe. "I hung your robe on the warmin' bar."

I peed quietly so he wouldn't picture me sitting on a toilet and stretched up, scanning the sink for some of his stray hairs to save. Turning the water on, I considered my jigsaw puzzle notion of sex. Sex education class wasn't helpful. All I'd learned was that sperm left the top of a penis and searched for an egg inside of a woman. Putting my lack of experience aside again, I quietly opened the bathroom door and faced the polished copper skin of Steve's naked back. I'd waited for this night, always believing it would happen. In the pause, I knew myself fully. I was unstoppable, audacious, and persistent. There was nothing to shake off. By default, I acted in good faith and was ready to experience what others dreamed about.

"Come close," Steve said, turning toward me.

Taking a seat, I leaned into him and sighed.

"I've never done anything like this," I said.

He leaned over and brushed his lips over mine.

"It's a natural thing," Steve said, putting two fingers on my chin. "Look at me."

We kissed and my brain stopped thinking. Then my teeth cracked against his.

"How embarrassing," I said. "Sorry."

"It's OK; sweet, really. Will you undress for me?"

I stood, dropped my robe, and moved between Steve's legs without looking down. *I hope he doesn't notice my stupid tattoo.* When he stood, I put my head on his chest and my arms around his waist. Then I pushed through my toes, and kissed him like a pro. We simultaneously leaned back to look at each other and grinned before landing on the bed. He bowed his head, grazed the front of my body with his hair, and disappeared between my legs. The air felt cold and empty. I missed him so I reached for his head and brought him back to me.

"You OK?" he asked.

"I am."

He straightened his forearms, and I pressed forward.

"This?" he asked, moving slightly.

"Yes," I answered.

Nothing hurt. I shut my eyes.

"Open your eyes," he said.

I opened them, and the space around me dissolved. I didn't know what was happening.

"Sweetness," was all he said.

Afterwards, he slept. I didn't. Something oozed out from between my legs. I listened to the air move in and out of him until the pink light of dawn tinted his face. After cupping my hands and checking my breath, I started kissing his face. He hummed and rolled me on top of him.

The moment Steve went into the bathroom, I called my mother.

"Hi Mother. You'd better make that meatloaf because I'm at the Pierre Hotel. With him."

"More lies? Honestly, Lucy, I've had it with you. You'll never amount to anything at the rate you're going."

At least she suggested I could amount to something.

"I'm not lying, I swear. I'm here."

"Then stay there, and don't bother coming back."

Click. She hung up. Maybe she couldn't help hating me. Maybe something froze her from the inside out. But it wasn't the time to brood about her.

I walked to the altar and looked at the orange book again. Before I could kneel to investigate further, Steve walked up behind me and pressed against my back. He hung his bearded chin over my shoulder, and I stretched one arm behind me, spreading my fingers into his hair.

"Curious, that book. My brother, David, brought it back from Jerusalem, thinkin' it might suit me. He was right. I've not ever come across a book like it."

"What is it? A prayer book?"

"Really, it's more of a divine map, like instructions from God. I've always had faith, you know, in somethin' higher, but haven't found my place. You must believe in somethin'."

I did believe in fateful coincidences and exceeding the odds but didn't have a clue where my place was. I turned into his chest wanting to stay there forever, call it my place. Preserving the miracle felt like life or death to me, but for Steve, it was just another night. Before I left, we didn't exchange numbers, promises, or plans. He didn't even know my name. I was old enough to know that celebrity crushes were normal but playing them out was not. Crushes wore off, and mine didn't. It wasn't a crush: it was destiny. It wasn't supposed to happen. It did. It would never happen again. It would.

Spellbound, wobbly, and transformed, I knew who I was. I passed the profusion of flower arrangements lining the hotel hallway from the night before. I thought about giving him the rose in New Haven only days before and how he put it on the microphone stand. I wanted to turn around, but instead rode the train back to New Canaan.

Thinking about a return to New Canaan Public High School the next day felt impossible, as did facing my mother's criticisms. It was time for this bird to fledge, to see other things. My vaguely inspired exodus needed specifics. A Vermont commune called the Wander Inn came to mind. I'd heard about it at a fiddling contest that past summer. People supposedly grew vegetables, shared chores, and functioned like a large family.

Even though Mother told me not to come back, I wrote her a note on the back of an envelope, assuring her I was exploring, not running away. Underneath the envelope was a birthday card Mother received from my father announcing... "Next! My departure! Considering your actions, and your words, this should be your most valued and appreciated birthday present."

I later learned Mother forced my father to leave after he ran a truck off a bridge while drunk. It would be decades before I knew that the truck driver was killed.

Self-absorbed adolescence combined with my WASP upbringing insulated me from acknowledging the unspoken traces of their failing marriage. I felt a twinge of sadness that my father left without saying goodbye. I wished I could have felt more for my parents.

The Wander Inn was a large log cabin once used as a stopover for travelers on horseback coming over the Brandon Gap. I rented a room for $50 a month and became the Wander Inn's youngest resident. We cooked vegetarian meals, played charades, and made music with pots, pans, and hollowed-out gourds from the garden. I slept on a futon and got seasonal work picking apples. Another resident named Ed convinced me to take a Silva Mind Control course in Middlebury, where we learned focusing techniques developed by a television and radio repairman named Jose Silva.

Ed gave me a book called *Be Here Now*, by Baba Ram Dass. While driving back and forth to our seasonal job, Ed shared enthusiastic tangents about out-of-body experiences, karma, Esalen, the Bread and Puppet theatre, Wavy Gravy, Medicine Story, and Timothy Leary. He showed me how to season a wok and wax cross-country skis. We ran for exercise and skied the fantastical trails at Blueberry Hill in nearby Goshen. When apple season ended, we worked nights at the Killington Ski Resort, arranging snow cannons and giant tripods on the dark slant of the mammoth mountain.

Mother eventually recovered from my abrupt departure and sent care packages with lighthearted notes. "Aren't you glad I'm not like the creepy Muther in the Runaway Bunny?! You know I'll always love you. Xs and Os" said one note. "I presume you will not be joining the circus. Lots of Love, Your One and Only Muther," said another. The packages contained Reese's Peanut Butter Cups, Bazooka bubble gum, playing cards, flashlights, paper, and stamped envelopes addressed to her. She sent me a pair of substantial hiking boots and wrote, "Mud season will soon be upon you." I kept busy to sidestep missing her. I'd always missed her.

No longer worried about my virginity, I was free to start a relationship, which I did. I didn't tell my mother. Ed was newly divorced, had four children, and was 18 years my senior. When my mother was pregnant with me, Ed was in the Great Books program at St. John's University in Annapolis, Maryland. While he studied law at Catholic University, I foraged for fireflies in the gatehouse yard. But, for all the obvious differences between us, we connected through convenience, friendship, and a desire to grow up and into ourselves. Our shared desire to travel caused us to leave the Wander Inn and travel cross-country in Ed's Country Squire station wagon, just like the one my mother had. Our first stop was New Canaan.

"Lucy, for Pete's sake, he is more than twice your age. Don't you see where this is headed?" Mother implored.

In Manhattan, my father kissed each of my cheeks and said to Ed, "I am watching you, Mr. Webby. One must question your intentions here."

Curiosity paced our travel. We backpacked in dozens of national parks, slept in a tent, and cooked meals on a single-burner propane stove. When we needed money, we picked fruit or worked in restaurants. Nan sent cash to general delivery addresses along the way. We stopped outside Chicago to see her, the woman who completed my mothering.

Ed stood at a distance while Nan kissed and hugged me. She rested her cool, white palm on one of my cheeks.

"Oh, Lu," her eyes watered, "I love you so." She turned to Ed. "And you must be Ed Webbly. So nice to meet you."

"Likewise, Mrs. Reeves. Lucy speaks so highly of you. And that's Webby, not Webbly. No L in there. But, please, call me Ed."

"All right, Ed it is. And Lu, you can settle into the guest room while Mr. Webbly goes to the servants' quarters on the third floor. Now, what do you say we have dinner at the Indian Hill Club tonight?"

"Thanks, Nan. Sounds perfect."

"Ed, dear, have you ever been inside a country club?"

The next memorable stop was outside of Taos, New Mexico, at the Llama Foundation. We attended a torturous, ten-day meditation retreat with Ram Dass inside a giant geodesic dome. Ram Dass was bathed in artificial gold light on stage, flanked by enormous flower arrangements and bundles of smoking Nag Champa incense. Devotees perched on stiff meditation pillows, palms facing upward to absorb energy. The syrupy smiles and repulsive nostril breathing made me want to flee, as did the notion of staying still for seven hours.

"Observe without judgment," Ram Dass ordered, while seated in a lotus position. "Note your thoughts without attaching."

I noted my repetitive, shallow thoughts, my judgments, and the unnatural feel of being surrounded by obsequiously obedient people. *Someone smells. Probably the hairy guy breathing like a docked fish behind me. I can only get into the lotus position in a scalding hot bathtub. This is a waste of ten days, and our cabin has colossal spiders.*

I removed my fidgety energy from the dome of submission and pretended to use the bathroom. I hiked a nearby mountain instead. The only time I returned to the dreaded dome was to hear Ram Dass's intriguing experiences while using LSD.

One afternoon, I found him sitting without the usual fan base around him.

"Knock, knock. Hello, Mr. Dass?"

He unfolded his legs.

"Come in, sit," his eyes twinkled.

"I'm a horrible meditator, but I like your stories, especially about LSD. I've taken acid hundreds of times and never experienced anything close to what you did. It was always a bummer."

Ram Dass smiled and closed his eyes. "Who were you tripping with, and where were you?"

"Just other kids at school, you know, during the boring school day."

"Ah." His eyes clicked open. "No one watching over you? Someone who wasn't tripping?" Both of his eyebrows raised.

"No, no, we all wanted to trip together. It was fine, but never awesome."

"My dear, LSD can be messy. Your brain is still developing. Wait a while and try it again with someone you trust to take care of and watch over you."

The retreat ended, even though I thought it never would, and Ed and I followed the Rockies north through Banff and Jasper before skirting the West Coast. We arrived in San Diego ten months after leaving Vermont and drove back east in seven days. The last life-altering stop was the University of Colorado in Boulder.

I'd seen the campuses of Princeton, Yale, and Harvard because my father, being a Harvard man, attended the Ivy League football games. While the adults tailgated, I poked around to assuage my boredom. This time, I wandered CU's campus feeling interested.

"Are you looking for a classroom?" a man in a suit asked.

"No, I'm just checking everything out. It's beautiful here."

"Did you miss the tour when you were interviewing?"

"Oh, no, I haven't interviewed. I'm just passing through and wanted to see what it was like. I've never seen a real college as an adult before," I said.

The man looked at me over the top rim of his glasses. "Never seen a college before?"

"Only when I was a kid."

"I see. Why don't you follow me to the administrative offices."

"Am I in trouble?"

"Not at all. I'll introduce you to someone who can give you some more information about life at CU."

"That would be great, as long as it's not out of your way," I said.

"I'm headed there anyway."

He handed me off to a man behind a desk inside an office. We exchanged pleasantries, and I told him about my educational failures.

"Get in touch when you're ready," he said, handing me his card.

"Thanks. I will."

And later, I did.

Ed and my arrival in Boston heralded not only the geographical end to our circuitous 22,000-mile trip, but our relational end, as well. We agreed that our eighteen-year age difference was insurmountable when considering a more conventional life. Ed wanted to practice law again, and I didn't know what I wanted.

Ed's parents lived in a modest neighborhood in Wollaston, Massachusetts, a southern suburb of Boston. They allowed me to temporarily stay in their home on the condition I sleep in a makeshift bedding area on the screened-in front porch while Ed slept upstairs in his childhood bedroom. The chilly arrangement motivated me to find a place to live, and within a week, I'd rented a third-floor apartment on Marlborough Street in Boston's Back Bay for $245 a month. My grandmother, Nan, helped financially, and I looked for a job in the Boston *Phoenix*, the city's iconic weekly newspaper.

> Exotic Dancers Needed—ALL SHIFTS & EASY CASH
> Visit the Anne Diamond Theatrical Agency
> for FREE dance evaluation!
> Right in the heart of the Theater District!
> Evaluations held every Wednesday from 9 to 5

I took advantage of the free evaluation the following day.

CHAPTER 4

Pussycat Lounge

After pulling on a pair of corduroy bellbottoms and a peasant shirt, I walked to the subway. Sparks showered out and up from underneath the trolley, and its door released a smattering of people before vacuuming shut behind me. Once I emerged from the steamy tunnel, I followed the edge of Boston Common before finding the Theater District. Anne Diamond's ad didn't list an address, so I went into a joke shop for directions.

A cadre of false teeth clacked and vibrated across the glass countertop where a gray-haired man with twinkly eyes stood.

"Hello there, young lady. The name's Sam. Welcome to the world-famous Jack Horner's Joke Shop. Looking for anything in particular? Masks? Magic?" He looked down at the teeth and started to laugh. "Oh gosh, I'm sorry. I don't know what it is about these teeth, but they always break me up."

"Yeah, they're pretty funny in a group. I'm fond of whoopee cushions and laugh bags myself."

"As you can see, we got plenty of good old-fashioned pranks. Itch powder, leaking pens, disappearing ink, fake dog poop, boxes of exploding cigars, rubber chickens, and jumping beans. The fun goes on and on."

"I'm looking for the heart of the Theater District."

"You're in it."

"Oh. Hmm. Then maybe you can help me find the Anne Diamond Theatrical Agency."

"Wait a minute. Isn't that the lady that works with dancers?"

"Yeah, I think she is."

"You want to do that? You look like one of those runaways from Harvard Square."

"Me? I'm not a runaway. I just moved here and figured if it's just dancing, what a great way to make a living. As long as it's nothing gross."

"You seem awfully young."

"I just turned eighteen."

"Anne's in the next building over, second floor," Sam pointed. "Drop in anytime and say hello."

"I will. For sure. I love pranks. Thanks for your help."

There was an open door spilling dazzling lights into the hallway. It was reasonable to assume that an exotic dancer's agency had a disco ball. Instead, two women and two men operated sewing machines on oversized desks, rotating puddles of eye-catching fabric on their tables as fast as their hands could work. Haphazard groupings of decapitated mannequins posed around them in various stages of undress. One wore a bodice covered in crystals and trimmed by miniature hanging pendants. Another was in a full-length, opaque gown decorated in cosmic swirls made from rhinestones.

A woman with hair like bobbed cotton candy bustled out from behind a riot of colored boas lining the back wall. I assumed she was Anne Diamond. Several unruly feathers rode the draft around her.

"What about heat-fixing the rhinestones? That would save time," said a man trailing behind her.

"Buzzy, you know these girls. They want the tiniest details all perfect and then go on and shove their costumes on the floor after every show. Heat-fixing won't work a peck with all that pulling and crumpling." She looked at me and changed her tone. "Well, hello. I'm sorry. My husband and I were squabbling over rhinestones, weren't we, Buzzy dear?"

Buzzy moved next to her.

"Our arguments are almost always about rhinestones. You know, Austrian Swarovski or Asian are glass. The second best, in my useless opinion, is Preciosa, made by the Czechs. She doesn't listen to me, though." Buzzy's head nodded.

"Now, Buzzy, you go on and hush. You know I'm nothing at all without you. You complete me. Now let's take a polite Southern minute to help this girl."

The sewing machines hushed.

"I'm sorry, I didn't mean to barge in."

"We're a friendly sort. That's why the door's always open."

The woman reached to shake my hand. "My name is Hedy Jo Star, and this is my devoted husband, Buzzy. We make costumes for Cher, Elvis, the circus performers, elephants, Ice Capades, magicians, showgirls, and exotic dancers. Are you any of these things, dear?"

"Oh my gosh, no. I'm here to see Anne Diamond."

Hedy and Buzzy looked at one another and then back at me.

"An exotic dancer, then!" Hedy said, clapping once. "Her office is the next floor up. I was an exotic dancer at one time."

"Exotic is right," Buzzy laughed.

"Oh, Buzzy. Stop. Don't be scaring her. This pretty young thing would do justice to our Southern Belle costume."

"So, an exotic dancer is another word for a stripper? I'm just looking into dancing. I don't mind being naked, but I'll probably chicken out."

"Well, let me tell you, the Southern Belle is a surefire crowd-pleaser. It's all white with a hoop skirt, gloves, corset, and hat, decorated with huge roses. Have you never worn a showy costume, dear?"

"No. And never a hoop skirt. I think my mother wore a hoop for her debut. I saw a picture of it."

"How wonderful! Your mother was in burlesque."

"Burlesque? Hardly. She was a debutante."

"We had plenty of those down South where I grew up, all in their fancy getups and too snobby to talk to us hillbillies, right Buzz? And for what? They were no fun. Anywho, now you know where to come for costumes."

"Thanks." I started toward the door.

They stood in the doorway like proud parents as I entered the stairwell where I could hear Hedy Jo's voice. "The aurora borealis is the best, Buzzy. It reflects all the colors around you."

The top half of Anne Diamond's door was a cloudy textured glass with stick-on letters like a private eye's. I assumed there would be a receptionist and waiting area filled with gum-chewing, prospective dancers bouncing their crossed legs and clamoring for work. I opened the door into a single room. A woman behind a metal desk balanced a telephone handset between her ear and shoulder.

"Uh-huh," she responded to the person on the phone and looked at me.

I left my fingertips on the doorknob.

"Uh-huh. Hold on, Raven honey, please."

"Hi," I said.

Her eyebrows closed in toward each other. "Can you not see that I am on this here telephone?" She shifted back to the phone conversation. "I'm right here, honey. Someone just barged in and doesn't have a clue about manners. Just a minute."

She cupped the mouthpiece.

"Child, close that door, if you would. Turn that-a-way and grab that."

Dozens of bangle bracelets clinked as her finger made circles toward a brown clipboard.

"Yes, the clipboard on the wall. Now fill it out, and I'll be back to you. Raven, I'm back. Mm hmm."

I started filling out the Prospective Exotic Dancer Application: First Name, Last Name, Home Phone, Stage Name, Cup Size, Waist Size, Hips, Height, Weight. Previous Experience, Club Reprimands, and Costumes Owned. Relations Status, Tattoos, Scars, Props, Birthdate. Previous Male Entertainment Work of Any Kind. Check all that apply: Escort. Hooker. B-Girl. Cage Dancer.

I completed the form as best I could and surveyed the room. There was a Magic 8 Ball attached to a piece of black plastic on Anne Diamond's desk. Several pens stuck out of the empty triangular hole where the answers to my questions were supposed to be. A fluorescent light fixture suspended by wire coat hangers hung over a plywood scrap in the dark corner.

The phone cradle clicked.

"I didn't catch your name," she said.

"Lucy Johnson." I handed her the clipboard.

"Obviously, I'm Anne Diamond. Now, Lucy. That sure is a plain name. In fact, you are a plain girl, aren't you?"

"I guess."

"Sit down so I can check this out. My, my, you're a young baby girl. But you're eighteen, anyway. As long as you aren't fibbing."

"I'm not. My birthday's June 18, 1959."

"Mm. You ever stripped before?"

"Strip? Nope. Never. I don't even know what it's about. I . . ."

"Hold your questions." Anne Diamond took a pen from the Magic 8 Ball. "Have you entertained men?"

Taking photographs on Boston Common.

"Entertained men? I don't think so, no. Fairly sure not. I did pose for a swimsuit line once."

Anne Diamond raised her eyebrows. "Do you have the pictures?"

"No, it was ages ago."

"Huh, yeah, ages ago. Do you ever hook, escort, or do private parties, baby? Wait, what's this now? Who is this Walter Schalk? Was that some other agent or something? Like a private party booking agent? Because I don't encourage those at all."

"Walter Schalk was a dance school for little kids in New Canaan. We wore white gloves and danced with boys."

"Canaan, was that in Israel or Egypt or something?"

"No, it's in Connecticut."

Anne blew cigarette smoke toward the ceiling.

"OK, let's start this again. Have you ever entertained anybody, anytime, anywhere? Theater? Any kind of performance?"

"I was in St. Mark's bell choir and Walter Schalk's dance revues. Summer camp musicals, school plays. Things like that."

"Are you nervous on stage? Get stage fright or freeze right up?"

"I don't think so. Once, I was a tree in the nursery school Christmas play and threw up in front of the audience, but that was a stomach bug."

"If we could fast-forward to your life as a grown-up," said Anne. "I'd like to be home for dinner. This is about dancing. In adult clubs. Naked."

"Um, OK. I guess no entertaining since I was a kid. But I've danced, like after school in my room, and I've been going to Dance Free in Cambridge on Wednesday nights."

"Stop, please girl, just stop. That's enough. You need to listen to my questions. Pay attention. Are you here because you want a job as an exotic dancer?"

"Getting paid to dance sounds like a blast. I have to think about the naked part. I mean, not because I'm against it, but I wasn't positive it was nude dancing until today. And I don't want to do anything but dance."

"Let's just get you moving. That would be the best thing. If you look good, maybe we can do something. Go on over to the auditioning area right there in the corner. See it?"

She uncurled one finger and directed me to the piece of plywood.

"If you can walk, you can move. You like Stevie? Stevie Wonder?"

Costume-maker extraordinaire Hedy Jo Star and her husband, Dr. Buzzy.

"Sure. Unless you have some Cat Stevens."

"Some who?"

"Stevie Wonder's good. I like him."

I walked to the center of the plywood, stood stick straight, and smoothed my pants over my thighs.

"Turn that upper light on, if you would. Just press that little button."

Anne fiddled with a turntable on the corner of her desk until Stevie Wonder's song "Superstition" began.

"Now what?" I asked.

The needle bounced and made popping noises.

"Hold on there, let's try and figure this out."

She coaxed the needle with one long fingernail embedded with rhinestones and blew a piece of lint from her fingertip. Then she balanced a penny on top of the stylus. I started to sway, and Anne immediately plucked the needle from the record.

"Hold on here. Where's your outfit?"

"I didn't know I had to have special clothes."

"No outfit? I should've figured. Just move around and take off whatever you got on. The sooner, the better."

My corduroys dropped around my feet and covered the Birkenstocks.

"Usually it's the top first but keep going."

"Oops. Sorry." I tilted to the music while removing my shirt.

The last time I was naked for an evaluation was at my pediatrician's office.

"No bra? No underwear? Now, *this* is a damn hoot!"

"I usually don't wear them."

"That explains why you don't know your measurements. But you look all right. Much better than I imagined. Damn young, though. Turn toward me to see if you even have hair on your privates. Are you really eighteen years old?"

"I swear I am."

"If I get you hired, know that just eighteen is fine. Just under eighteen ain't so fine, understand? These club owners got trouble enough. They don't like children working out of their joints. You'll need a lot of work; hopefully, I'll live long enough. Move a little more."

I tried pivoting and swiveling.

"Loosen up those hips. Men like women with nice easy hips, like this."

Anne stood, snapped her fingers, and moved her padded hips in smooth ovals. I heard her pantyhose rubbing together like zippers and tried the same movement. She laughed herself into a choking fit.

"Oh, my," Anne patted her chest. "You got a fine body, honey, fine, and a sweet, plain little face. Cover your stuff up and come sit. Now you'll need a stage name. All girls have stage names."

"And a stage name is?"

"A fake name you use when you dance. You need one, so think about that. You also need something sexy to strip out of, and heels. Do you wear heels? I'm guessing not. Learn to love them. They make your legs look long and round out your flat behind."

Anne tapped another cigarette out of its pack.

"Smoke?" she offered.

"No, thank you. I don't smoke."

"Of course not. That's good, baby, real good. Now listen up. I'll be calling you to tell you where to start. Do you want the night or day shift? Night pays more."

"Definitely day. Nights would be a little too wild for me."

"Night is when men do crazy shit like give you all their damn money because they've fallen crazy ass in love in thirty seconds."

"Maybe after a while. I hate drunk people."

"I suppose you don't drink either?"

"Nope."

"You must be some kind of hippie health nut. Be sure the bartenders and waitresses know, so when you're sitting with those fools for drinks, you get water, not gin."

"Yuck. I have to, like, sit down with men? And talk to them?"

"It's harmless. No monkey business, and you make money on every drink. It's called mixing. Some girls, all they do is mix."

"Mix?"

"You know, mix it up nice and friendly like. Set down and have a drink or two with the fine patrons of the establishment."

"Can't I order water?"

"Let's think about this. If the man is paying for you to get a little more relaxed by buying you a twelve-dollar cocktail, it goes over better if he thinks it's real."

"I don't really want to sit with them. I just want to dance, is all."

"You'll figure out how to take control, create suspense, build tension. Him thinking it might lead to something someday keeps him coming back."

"It sounds misleading."

Anne pulled herself up and fixed her green eyes on me.

"You listen up. I don't want any trouble. This is how I support myself. I trust my girls to know what men want and how to manage them." She relaxed into her chair and laced her fingers.

"Questions?"

"I do have one question."

"Go on then."

"They won't, like, expect more than, well, you know . . . I mean, what I want to know is, will I have to do anything besides dance and talk?"

"Honey, do I look like a pimp to you? Really? I ain't in no pimping business, never was, and never will be because I believe in women's rights. Yes, I do. If women want to go off and turn tricks, at least let them get all the money paid for their craft rather than give it to some pimp. Hate those mother-fucking, hell-destined crawfish."

"No, right, but the club itself, not you. I mean," I stammered. "I didn't mean to say that you were a pimp. Do the people running the club expect more than just dancing?"

"Clubs don't want no trouble with the Vice."

I remembered seeing a strip club in Louisiana after Ed and I toured a Tabasco factory. There was a small stage and a series of what looked like stalls with black curtains. The dancers had numbers pinned to their leg garters and trotted unceremoniously between two brass poles and collected tips. One dancer sat on the floor in a half sit-up position. Her legs fell open, and five ping-pong balls sprung from her vagina. Men scrambled to retrieve the balls and licked them.

Another dancer set an empty Orange Fanta bottle in the middle of the stage.

"Go on now, number 45!" a man whooped.

Number 45 slid carefully into a full split, grabbed the bottle with her crotch, and wagged it up and down like a deviant elephant trunk.

"Number 17 to the booths," a woman announced over the sound system.

Number 17 sauntered to the stalls and disappeared with a customer.

Thinking nothing of the ramifications, I slid the curtain open just enough to peek in. The man's pants were on the ground, and the woman was on her knees, her head bobbing up and down.

We were swiftly dismissed from the club.

"I have your number here," Anne said. "I'll poke around and call you if and when I find something. It might take me a few days."

"OK. Thanks for all your help."

"You should know that my commission comes out of your pay automatically. That way, you don't have to bring it to me. It saves you a trip."

"Commission . . . for . . . ?"

"For agency representation, of course."

"Representing me? Like a one-time fee kind of thing?"

"Yeah, one time a day," Anne said. "We take 15 percent of your daily pay, not drink money and tips. You don't get many tips in Boston with the 16-inch law still being around."

I needed clarification.

"I thought you said we should keep all of our money."

"You should, and you do. I get paid to help you."

"And what's the 16-inch law?"

"A customer has to stay at least 16 inches from a naked person, or a person who intends to be naked, at all times."

My head was muddled. "I guess that's a relief."

Anne answered her phone. I lingered by the photographs on the wall. The older pictures were monochrome, frameless, and attached with rusted thumbtacks. One woman was in a giant champagne glass overflowing with foam, and another in a bathtub. Names were printed on the images; "Barbara the Barbarian, Let Her Beauty Brutalize You," "Bubbles, Miss Nude America 1973," "Brenda Hollis, The Girl with the Freudian Touch," "Siri, The Dutch Doll," and "Brandy Martin, The Society Stripper."

A color photograph showed a woman in an animal-print one-piece; shiny, black boots to the tops of her legs; and a spiked collar with a long chain. She posed in a full split on top of a wooden cage. Inside was a petite man. It looked painful and weird.

"That there is Nikki Wilde, a throwback to the carnival days. She's a feature entertainer at the Naked i Cabaret, next to the Two O'Clock Lounge. One of a kind," Anne piped in.

"Who's that in her cage?" I asked.

"That's her midget. Now go out and get yourself some sexy outfits. And stilettos. Be ready when I call."

Where to find stripper clothes? Bloomingdale's should have the necessary components, I thought.

"Can I help you, young lady?"

A tidy salesman at Bloomingdale's in Chestnut Hill Mall walked toward me. He stood next to me as I pawed through tables of lingerie.

"Looking for a gift for your sister, perhaps?" he asked.

"No, some things for me."

"Have you tried our juniors department?"

"I need something more grown up."

"Aren't you a little young?"

"I'm eighteen for Pete's sake!"

"What did you have in mind?"

"Something with pieces."

He waited for more information.

"I'm taking a job as a dancer and need a starter outfit."

"How wonderful. Congratulations. What company are you with?" He asked, interlocking his hands in front of his groin. "I do know most all of the dance companies in town quite well."

"No, it's not a dance company. It's exotic dancing, as in stripping."

"I'm afraid I can't help you with that."

He turned cold, walked to another table, and started folding camisoles. I left with thick-heeled black shoes and a lingerie set which seemed to belong to someone else.

I removed the bones from the backpack I used for hiking and buying bulk grains and beans at the Cambridge Food Co-op and stuffed the shoes and lingerie inside of it. Anne called.

"Be at the Pussycat Lounge on Washington Street, 11 a.m. sharp tomorrow, and see Peggy. It's the club across the street from the Naked i. You can't miss it."

The underground train rolled on a straight course toward Boston's Combat Zone, the adult entertainment district near Jack's Joke Shop. I cradled the bag on my lap until the train stopped. People exited the train in herds. Some ate bagels and cream cheese from folds of waxy paper, while others read newspapers. I ascended the wide stairs, flanked by streams of ordinary people doing seemingly ordinary things, and turned left into the sun.

I stepped around a large lump on the sidewalk when a policeman approached and tentatively jabbed his nightstick at the pile. A face appeared.

"Hey, man, get up. Someone's gonna step on you," the cop said.

"Yeah? Beats fallin' outta bed," the face replied.

"I was just killing you with kindness. I meant to say, get the fuck up and out of here. Now. Nobody likes to see or smell this on their way to work. Come on."

There was something attractive about the cop. He spread his feet wide and slid the nightstick through a shiny, black ring on his belt. The man on the ground unfolded himself and balanced on his knees.

"Yes, officer. If I don't move, can you take me to jail for some food?"

His earnest eyes were too large for his face.

"I don't have time to bring you in today," the cop said. "Get moving."

The man scraped together his belongings with prodigious inefficiency and sat back down. The officer glared at him from underneath the visor of his hat.

"OK, OK, I'll go, I'll go. I don't know where, but I'll go. It takes me a while to get this old body moving."

The policeman slid some cash out of his front pocket, looked right and left, and tossed it toward the man.

"Thank God, thank you," the man cried.

The cop made a harsh shushing sound and walked off. I was about to cry.

"Excuse me," my words got caught behind a small bubble of emotion. *What a sap.* I tried again. "Excuse me, sir? Where is the Pussycat Lounge?"

He turned around.

"Why?"

"I don't want to be late and always get lost. Like, always."

"It's across the next street there, see it? And, Miss? Please be careful. It can be a dangerous area."

"I will. I'll be careful. And thank you."

I couldn't find the right words to tell him how nice he was to give the man some money.

Keeping a taut focus on the sidewalk, I caught blurs of human movement and heard loud whispering.

"Pssshhhh . . . Little girl, over here. You're a fine thing," said a man's voice. "How much, baby, how much? You need yourself a daddy."

"Yo, blond white girl, go on home to yer mama," a woman shouted from the same direction.

My back tensed. A woman in painfully tiny shorts leaned against a parked car. The driver gave her some cash, and her arm vanished through the window. Another woman stood in the center of a manhole cover enveloped in rings of steam, circling her lips with her tongue. Curious pigeons hopped on long pink feet, foraging in the street gutters.

The Pussycat squatted on the corners of Beach and Washington streets and "Pussycat Lounge" was hand-scripted in black across the top of the building. Its door was propped open. I recognized the song "Flashlight," by Parliament. A policeman talked to the woman perched on a bar stool by the door. Her ample bottom was four times the size of the seat, but comfortably balanced.

Ha-da-dadee-da da-da hava da da.
Flashlight
Spot Light
Neon Light (neon light)
Street light (street light)
Everybody's got a little light under the sun

The song's synthesized stacked bass made me want to move. I waited for the traffic light and a man wearing fuzzy, rainbow-colored bellbottoms and an enormous, equally ridiculous Dr. Seuss hat walked out of the nearby King of Pizza.

"There's my little girl." I recognized his wheezy voice. "You can join my stable, sure you can. I'll start your quota real low."

"No, thank you."

"I see you lovin' my pants though, right? Free tip for you today: No one ever looks both ways in the Zone."

The cop winked at me as I crossed the street.

"May I help you, please?" the woman on the stool asked.

Her pantsuit was thick polyester, the type that traps sweat.

"Anne Diamond sent me," I settled a comfortable distance away and held my backpack in front of me.

"Oh, right. Anne called me about a new girl, and you must be that new girl." Turning to the cop, she said, "Alright, Danny, nice chatting, as always."

"You too, Peggy."

"Hi, honey. My name's Peggy. And you are . . . ?"

"Lucy, Lucy Johnson."

Peggy rocked herself off the stool and clutched my forearm for balance.

"I'm the manager of this chicken coop. Let's show you around. Follow me."

CHAPTER 5

Combat Zone

Peggy lumbered into the artificial night, and I followed her strained breathing. A woman in her underwear sauntered around a dimly lit stage, cackling every other step.

"What'd I tell ya? A chicken coop, or a henhouse!"

Smoke whirled as Peggy opened a hollow wooden door into the dressing room. The light inside illuminated men in hats hovering over their drinks near the stage.

"Where ya from hon'?"

"New Canaan."

"Wherever that is," said Peggy.

"It's in Connecticut, kind of near New York City."

"I've never been to New York. OK, this here's the girls dressing room. The rules are nobody claims a locker or chair. We don't have enough to go around, so you'll bring your stuff in and out every shift, along with your own lock. No drugs, no booze, no stealing. Simple, right?"

The dressing room was poorly lit by two fluorescent bulbs housed inside nicotine-stained plastic panels dotted with dried-up bugs and disembodied moth wings. Above the small counter was a mirror taped together in sections large enough to reflect a face. The countertop was marred with hundreds of caterpillar-size burns. Curling irons balanced on a collection of abandoned drinking glasses holding bloated cigarette butts leaking brown tendrils. I was glad not to wear makeup.

Peggy gestured toward the lockers. "My girls think they're artists."

One locker was plastered with champagne labels and local radio station bumper stickers. Another had names written in lipstick and eyeliner: "Babycake," "Melanie," "Your Little White Dick," "Phoebe," and "Cinnimin." Twists of material erupted from one and a shiny triangle of fabric hung from its door vent.

"Here's the makeup table and, believe you me, these girls will hockey-check you for the chance to outline their lips or reapply lash glue," said Peggy. "As if it helps. I'll leave you to get ready and put you on the schedule for your audition."

"Audition? OK." I was confused.

"Just to be sure. Oh! I almost forgot. Tell me where you worked before?"

"I mucked stalls, made snow at a ski mountain, and picked apples. I picked oranges in Florida, too. Which I hated. Oranges have thorns."

"Shit, snow, and fruit, huh? You won't believe how easy stripping is."

I wanted her to be right.

While living at the Wander Inn, we rode to an apple orchard every morning in the back of a frosty haying truck. Being paid by the bin, it was essential to get an early start. We harnessed framed canvas buckets to the fronts of our bodies, jimmied our ladders into trees, and clambered up. Each bin was the size of a four-person hot tub, and front-end loaders growled impatiently, crawling the lanes for full containers.

"Oh man," breathed one picker, and "No shit," another. We were groaning sloths in the misty, menthol cold, engineering 45-pound buckets down the ladder rungs for ten straight hours. I was confident stripping would be less monotonous.

I put on my Bloomindale's lingerie and plunked down in a chair to figure out my shoes. Suddenly, the door banged open and hit the wall. A Black woman backed herself into the room while yelling out the door.

"All right, baby, I'll finish you, but I gotta get changed. Jesus, the good Lord." Her voice softened. "Oh, hey, I didn't mean to startle you. You new 'round here?"

"Yeah, it's my first time. I thought I'd check it out."

"That's cool. What's your name, anyways?" She sidestepped around a gaping bag filled with buckles, heels, chains, and belts, and plopped hard onto the other chair with no concern for her tailbone.

"My name is Lucy." I addressed her reflection in the broken mirror. "And you are . . . ?"

She blotted sweat from her face with a fist of toilet paper.

"Nervous? Scared shit? I'm kidding. Don't mind me. I'm Cinnamon, or Cinny for short."

I glanced at her name on the locker.

"Yeah, I know I misspelled my name. I can't spell for shit but I get by. Shit, girl, I'm surprised I can form a goddamn fucking sentence seeing as I got kicked out of elementary school—who needs spelling, anyway? It's not like I write. Just give me those Benjamins, and I'm satisfied. Well, damn nice to meet you, Juicy Lucy." She had a friendly laugh. "Goosey Lucy, wait, I got it now, it's coming to my mind," she smiled, holding the pause with one finger. "It's Loose Lucy."

I shrugged. "I don't know. I guess just Lucy for now."

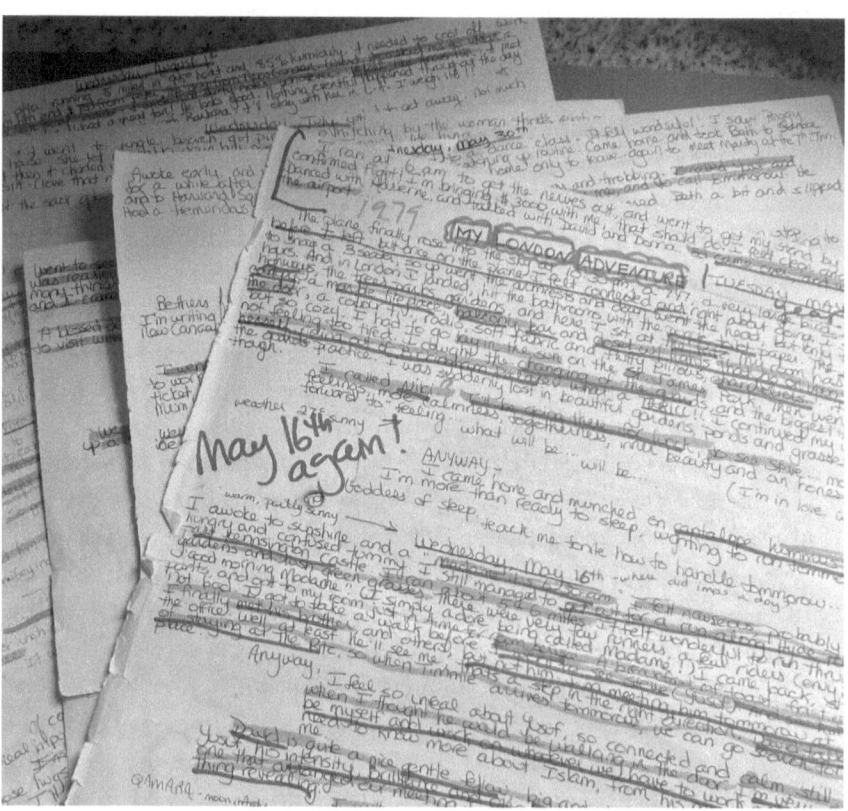

My Diary.

The brightest bulbs in the Zone.

"Who thought up that stage name? Isn't that a person in Peanuts or some shit?" Cinnamon sifted through open rounds of blush makeup the size of Ritz crackers.

"That's my real name, but I don't care if they use it."

I tried to exude confidence through nonchalance, but it felt phony. I desperately wanted to be cool enough to fit in. Cinnamon slid a section of hair through two fingers and smoothed gel on both sides.

"You'll care about your damn name, girl. Where are you from?"

"From Illinois, and Connecticut. What about you?"

"I'm a city girl. You probably got shit like school, good family, all that comfortable shit, but take it from Cinny here with her street smarts, do yourself a favor and use a stage name."

Her attention swung back to the table.

"You must think we are a bunch of pigs. Look at this mess."

"Everyone has their thing," I said, trying to seem unruffled.

"Well, this shit table ain't my thing. I like to find what I want, like, now. You know?" Cinny asked, plucking at squares of eyeshadow and pots of glittered lip gloss. "You know how your sisters took your shit, then used your shit, and then to add to the misery, ruined your shit?" she growled.

"Actually, I'm an only child."

"Lucky, so lucky. I raised my damn sisters. Look at this junkyard in here, man."

Cinny tapped a pink and silver hairspray canister with her long nail. Its top was flipped over and brilliantly transformed into an ashtray.

"This all's my one can of damn wig spray, and some dumb-ass motherfucker turned the cap over for an ashtray. There's a regular old ashtray right here. What the fuck? So, I go and put this here cap back on, like this, see? And all the ashes and shit end up in my hair. And there's a hole melted in the top."

"I don't wear makeup or do my hair, so your stuff is safe with me."

"You're fine. Don't mind me. I like to bark."

Cinny stood up with another fistful of toilet paper and, holding up one breast at a time, swabbed back and forth underneath each one.

"I'm soaking wet. Air conditioning would be nice for us full-figured bitches."

She freed a tiny triangle of material from between her legs and brought it under her nose.

"Yeah, that's me, alright," she said, running her hand between her legs and sniffing it. "I recognize that smell anywhere. You can never be too confident about odors, ain't that right?"

"I guess. This is all new to me."

"Is that why you're staring at me? You look like you just saw a Martian or some shit."

She reached into a plastic grocery bag and extracted another triangle. Its long fabric tail sprouted two elastic strings, the kind that attaches a ball to a toy paddle. She patted the triangle over her pubic hair, lifted one side of her bottom, reached the strings between and up and attached the elastic to the uppermost corners of the triangle.

"Oh wait, when you said you were checking things out, did you mean the club here, or that you've never done this before at all?"

"No, I've never stripped. I have no idea what's going on."

"Oh honey, I hope I didn't scare the bejesus out of you. I think you go on after Melanie, who's up there now." She looked down and back at me. "Them's some ugly shoes, girl. Shit."

A woman with stringy blond hair burst through the door. Cinny rolled her brown eyes.

"What the effing fuck, I hate that place," the woman said, slamming her purse onto the counter. "They are beyond ridiculous."

"I don't wanna ask, but I will," Cinny said. "What place? Go on. Give us all a mouthful, as usual. You and your damn stories. Where were you causin' trouble this time?"

"The Naked i. Just 'cause they heard I might turn a trick or two, I'm hassled. A customer buys me a drink, and there's Ricky, the big fat-ass bouncer, taking up space next to me at the bar while I'm hustling, thinking he's all funny and shit. He's got that fucking smug smirk, the kind you just wanna smack." She paused to look at me as I folded over and struggled to fasten my shoe. "Who the fuck is this? Is she drunk? She ain't gonna puke, is she? Give'r the wastebasket."

"This here is Lucy, and Lucy is brand spanking new and never done this before," explained Cinny. "She's a Combat Zone virgin, ain't that right, Miss Lucy? And this here is Phoebe, who sometimes works here, in between tricks."

"Hi, Lucy. Nice to meet you."

"You too. And I'm not going to barf. I just don't know how to work these shoes."

"Here, I'll help buckle them. But you gonna dance in these? Anyway, yeah, it was, like, harassment all the way. Total discrimination. Bullshit."

Phoebe tightened the shoe straps and both women stared at my feet.

"Them's no dancing shoes, right?" Cinny laughed. "You must know my grandmother. What'd she, give you her church shoes?"

"Oh my God, you can't really dance in those," Phoebe added. "And whoa girl, those are some hairy legs!"

"It's blond," I said.

"I can see that, but we all shave our legs, among other things." Phoebe and Cinny high-fived.

"I hate shaving my legs. They get all itchy. So, I should go out there now? How do I do the music part?"

"You got coins?" asked Cinny.

"Coins?"

Phoebe reached into her purse and produced a small pile of change.

"Here," said Phoebe, "take these and go to the bottom of the stage stairs. Pick your three songs ahead of time."

"Thank you both so much. I'll get the hang of things."

I took four steps to the door and felt the weight of two hands on my shoulders. It was Cinny.

"Turn around a second. You have no makeup on girl. What? You're damn face'll disappear."

"Do I have to wear makeup? I hate makeup."

"She doesn't have to wear makeup," said Phoebe. "Yeah, I guess she doesn't need it like us old, worn-out sea hags."

Phoebe kept ranting as I walked out. "The Naked i thinks they're so fucking great and all, like, college girl revue, my ass. Half the girls in there are turning tricks on their days off; the rest have never been inside a college, never mind attended one, never mind can spell the word. Chicks have IQ's at room temperature. Fucking place is too straight for me and too straight for its own good."

My legs felt weak standing by the jukebox as it rattled the The Commodores' song "Brick House" from its thin speaker.

Ow, she's a brick house
She's mighty-mighty, just lettin' it all hang out
She's a brick house
That lady's stacked and that's a fact
Ain't holding nothing back

Melanie, the woman onstage, wasn't dancing but held nothing back. She eyeballed the men and sat cross-legged on the floor for a quick chat. The volume to the song faded, and Melanie, seized by energy, sprung up, plucked a pubic hair from her crotch, and skipped over to a customer.

"Oop! Time's up. Quick! Here's a little gift from me to you. Everything you wanted and maybe a little bit more from yours truly."

She assumed a deep squat exposing the hefty, dark wings of her crotch. With the pubic hair pressed between her thumb and forefinger she dangled it above the man. He opened his mouth and bobbed his head as though trying to catch a piece of popcorn.

Melanie threw her head back, delighting in her role as a teasing puppeteer and set the hair free. Her intimate souvenir landed in the man's cocktail.

"I am now the proud owner of Melanie's pubic hair, and God knows what else," he announced.

The six men sitting at the stage grumbled their approval. Melanie, still squatting, emphasized her longest finger, wet it with her tongue, and deftly slid it into her vagina up to her knuckle. Simultaneously revolted and intrigued, I couldn't turn away or disrupt the scene by taking my rightful place on the small stage.

"Have some, baby?" she asked, withdrawing her slick finger.

As Melanie lovingly examined her finger, Peggy's maternal voice thundered from the shadows.

"Music, please, and Melanie, exit the stage area, or I'll dock your pay. It's someone else's turn now. This isn't always about you. New girl, start your music."

The men booed in response to Peggy's reprimand, and I initiated my first song, knowing the men would resent me for interrupting such fun. Once the needle scraped into action, I knew it wasn't the bass line of "Disco Inferno" by The Trammps. It sounded like the jangly sound of a little girl's jewelry box. My fingers had unknowingly drifted while engrossed in Melanie's performance and pressed the wrong buttons. Nervously resigned, I stepped onto the stage and was greeted by the tinkling piano and pleading lyrics of "Precious and Few" by Climax. How awful.

I lingered on the top step trying to feel sure enough to walk in my cruel shoes. Meanwhile, Melanie's wet back was slick as a seal. She balled up her clothing in one fist and jimmied down onto the pubic-hair customer's lap before jamming the back of her torso against the bar's edge. The men, absorbed in Melanie's exit, didn't notice me standing there in my saucy coordinated lingerie from Bloomingdale's.

I turned toward the back wall where a large mirror, framed by stapled red curtains, was layered in handprints and body smears. It reflected the circular blurs of men's faces. Melanie continued to strategically grind her weight on top of the man's lap until she abruptly anchored her body on straight arms and said, "No, sir. That shit's for the booth."

I knew enough about male anatomy to fathom the origin of Melanie's objection. The shrinking man searched her face, looked to his crotch, and nodded obediently.

"All right then," Melanie boomed. "Enough said."

She hoisted herself back onto the bar's surface and addressed the other customers.

"You all want to get plump in the pants like this fine gentleman, then just get in line for Melanie cuz, as you saw, thinking of your thick dicks makes Miss Melanie wetter than an otter's pocket."

She positioned her stilettos on either side of the man to push him, and the chair, away from the bar. Reaching down, Melanie made a show of releasing his belt, sliding the zipper, and then, like a magic coin trick, the man's oily little penis appeared between her fingers.

"Look what we have here," she cooed. "Come over to Melanie's secret booth, and we'll empty those tight little mothballs of yours, 'cuz I know you ain't gettin' any at home."

The man gathered his open waistband in one hand and stood. Melanie tucked her wad of clothing under her armpit, coiled an arm around his, and held him steady as they wobbled into the darkness.

"Hey, I left my drink and your souvenir," the man whined.

"Come on, my little honey dripper. Melanie's gonna make you forget all about your souvenir."

The couple disappeared, and the other men turned back toward the stage, readjusting their positions on the short stools. They looked like trolls on tree stumps.

"Man, I am so fucking horny now," said one. "This is like *Playboy* come to life," said another.

I looked away to roll my eyes and then noticed a grim man with an unkempt mustache jiggled his hand furiously inside his pants.

"You have beautiful feet," he said.

Nothing witty or condescending came to mind. I was too niggled by Melanie's whereabouts and how her activities might speak to unsavory expectations at the Pussycat Lounge. I knew how to say no but didn't relish the idea of a confrontation in unfamiliar surroundings. The foot man persisted. I wanted to empty his cocktail onto his lap.

For the duration of the insipid first song, I strode back and forth in an invisible corridor close to the mirror, careful not to touch it. I occasionally tilted my hips toward the men and noticed how, with just a smidgeon of false attention, they leaned toward me. When I retreated or looked away, they slumped. If I fingered the frilled edge of my tie-up camisole, they sat at attention, and when I dropped my finger, they looked away. It was hard not to laugh.

The power I held was so entertaining I forgot about my impending nudity. As the first song faded, I approached the jukebox, hoping to avoid another mawkish song. Peggy met me in the silver glow of the music display.

"Here, let me help you. What other songs do you want? Thing doesn't always behave," she said, tapping the plexiglass. "You can pick your songs beforehand, so you don't have to come down in between. Modern technology and all. What'll it be?"

"Anything but sappy music is fine. Thanks."

Peggy punched in two songs, and I resumed my first stripping extravaganza to "Thank God I'm a Country Boy," followed by "Muskrat Love." I ignored the music, strolled around, taking a turn here and there, waiting to feel something about what I was doing. It was fun controlling the strangers from a stage but the off-stage activities weren't for me.

I decided to leave the Pussycat.

I gathered the camisole around my body and started toward the dressing room when the collective shadow of two men called to me.

"Hey, girlie? Up for some hot, liquid protein? It is lunchtime." They laughed.

Incensed, I closed the dressing room door, put on my regular clothes, and stuffed everything into my backpack. I edged sideways past the two men toward the outline of daylight at the Pussycat's front door. The man who liked my feet intercepted me.

"What's a nice girl like you doing in this shithole, anyway?"

"How do you know I'm nice?" I said, taking my leave.

I didn't belong there. It wasn't nice to disappear without an explanation, but I didn't feel obligated to stumble around in the moist shadows looking for Peggy, as jolly as she was. I infused my limbs with purpose, even though I had none, and pretended I had somewhere to go, even though I didn't. I figured that looking resolute inoculated me against unwanted overtures.

I was in Boston's demarcated red-light district anyway, so I explored what the Zone had to offer, if anything. I headed toward "The Scene," on the corner of an alleyway called LaGrange Street. It peddled "XXX ADULT MOVIES" with "PRIVATE VIEWING BOOTHS" and a "PEEP ARAMA," whatever that was.

I headed down the narrow strip of pavement to the right of The Scene, where the signage continued, "COMPLETELY PRIVATE VIEWING BOOTHS JUST 25 CENTS." That seemed awfully cheap. You couldn't even buy a Butterfinger candy bar for a quarter. The place bore no resemblance to a movie theater and looked inescapable, with no storefront or window.

I looked back toward the Pussycat and studied the assaultive montage of blinking marquees and flashing signs. It was impossible to distinguish one word, phrase, or business from another. "Adult Films," "Open All Night," "Adults Only," "Floor Shows," "Naked," and "Nude." "Peek-A-Rama" was not to be confused with "Peep Arama," "Peep Booths," or "Rap Booths."

Oddly, the businesses were about sex, yet the word "sex" was nowhere to be found. Why didn't they call things what they were? Jerk off rooms, jerk off movies, blow jobs, imaginary sex like you've never had in real life.

I ventured deeper down LaGrange against a pulsing, gritty wind. Disembodied newspaper pages stuck to a drainage grate, tapping the curb like dry leaves. A red-and-white-striped French-fry box tumbled along the ground behind me before finding an intersection of sidewalk and building. A napkin floated and grounded itself before being whisked up high and out of sight. There wasn't a car or a person to be seen, yet the street felt crowded. "Good Time Charlie's" was the only sign I saw.

The one-way alley was ideal for on-demand prostitution. Cars could circle the block multiple times without tying up traffic, men could negotiate through open windows, and horny amblers could skirt the shadows, pay the fee, and drop their pants. There were numerous sunken doorways where pimps could hard-close deals and scrutinize their cash flow.

"Hey, hey you, blond girlie girl!" a woman's voice shouted. "Wait up. It's me, Phoebe."

It was the woman who'd given me change for the jukebox. She wore a fuzzy, baby-pink sweater with a deep V-neck, tight jeans, no socks, and platform stiletto shoes made from clear acrylic. A rhinestone purse bounced at her hip, its strap cutting diagonally between her breasts.

"I am so sorry," I said, reaching into my pocket. "I left so fast I forgot about paying you back. Here."

Phoebe stopped, glanced around, crossed her ankles, and anchored one elbow into the side of her waist to elevate a cigarette.

"That's not why I chased you down, silly. Keep your money. Have you left the Pussycat already? Girl, you didn't even finish your shift."

"Yeah," I answered. "It was gross. Not what I expected. Bad fit."

"I could've told you that the second I saw your white ass. Damn, girl, this whole block isn't right for you. You're lookin' so funny at me. You ain't never seen a ho before, huh?" she asked, her deeply set eyes studying me.

"You look so much prettier in the daylight. You could pass for not belonging here, too."

Phoebe's perfect rounds of cheek rouge shifted as she smiled.

"Hey, thanks. I guess that's why I do so well," she said before tightening her berry lips to drag on the cigarette. "I'm on my break. My pimp's right up there. He's very protective. Then again, I do give him every bit of my cash."

She lazily pointed her cigarette up LaGrange Street.

"See? That's Daddy, there, in the turquoise hat. Come on out, baby," she shouted. "He's even got an emerald embedded in his front tooth. Green for the money, honey. That gold shit's so common."

The Black man who stepped out of a doorway looked seven feet tall. My throat pulsed. He tipped his blue hat toward us and leaned back into the building like a Murphy bed.

"Relax, baby," Phoebe continued in a pressured voice. "He's a good man, my King D. He treats me like a queen. No beatings, quotas, or ass sex. I get top dollar. I'm his only white bitch, and I even train the sister wives. We share this track with other pimps, but they all get along. It's this mutual respect thing. Shit, I'm doing all the talking here. Guess I'm revved up."

"I don't get half of what you just told me."

She tilted her blond head, blowing smoke into the sky.

"You'll get it if you stay long enough. What are you in this for, anyway? Drugs? Runaway? Loans? Gambling? What?"

"I thought it would be a decent job if I could dance without the other stuff. No offense."

"No offense taken, of course. You did know that you had to dance naked, though, right?" Phoebe elongated the word "right."

"Well, yeah."

"So, it's the blow job and stuff? Doing everything but fuck and suck on stage? I get it. We all protect certain things. But don't lose hope, girl, if all you want is to dance. Check out the Naked i. It's about the only club that's strict right now. They won't let me walk past the place, breathe near it, and never mind touch their damn front door. All because I turn tricks. I worked there for two shifts before they got word and tossed my sorry ass out."

"The Naked i? I'll for sure check it out. And by the way, can I ask how you protect yourself? Out here? Assuming it's dangerous."

"Get a pimp!" Phoebe answered. "Just kidding. We can tell you ain't worth groomin' and chattin' up. No pimp wants an unenthusiastic ho."

"Yeah. But, seriously, is it dangerous here?"

"Never had a problem. But I'm smarter than I sound, and I got the calm thing going on, like, I don't get nervous. People think I'm on 'ludes, but I ain't. It's like with King D and his damn dog, Conrad. When a new sister-wife comes around, they're afraid of the dog, even when he's sleeping, but her fear wakes him up. Soon as the ho chills, Conrad's wagging his tail, pushing his clunky, dumb head under her hand. It's just like that, right? People pick up on fear. Shit down here is mostly personal, and since you won't be wrangling and tangling in the street, you'll be good."

"Good to know. I'll check out the Naked i."

"That's the spirit. Just don't tell them Phoebe sent you," she laughed.

"I won't. Thanks for talking."

"Pleasure."

"By the way, where are you from?"

"I grew up in a town called Lexington. My parents still live there. You?"

"Illinois, a town outside of Chicago called Lake Forest. And then we moved to New Canaan, Connecticut."

King D's turquoise hat peeked out from the doorway. Walking towards her, he issued a loud "Psst."

"Coming, Daddy," Phoebe assured him. "Cigarette break's over."

She took one last drag, flicked the filter away, the smoke pausing over her blond head like a thought bubble.

"Sounds like we started off the same way. Be good."

"OK, thanks again."

Combat Zone hookers weren't courtesans by any stretch of the imagination, nor were their hearts of gold visible.

Phoebe unlatched her ankles, and King D opened his arms like a father catching a racing child and smiled.

She looked over her shoulder and yelled, "Good luck at the i. It's at 666 Washington Street. And, hey, shave those legs, girl."

CHAPTER 6

Naked i

The Naked i Cabaret's white edifice and blazing marquee glowed brighter than the rest. "TOTALLY NUDE COLLEGE GIRL STRIP TEASE" was in perfectly spaced red letters across the marquee, bringing to mind coeds with yellow highlighters studying in between naked jaunts. The club's logo was a female eye with legs that repeated jagged half-circles around it like a sprinkler. The eye went dark in between cycles.

A horizontal shadowbox with faded stripper photographs had a sign that said, "Go Go Dancers, Bar Maids and Hostesses Wanted! Apply Within." Four pictures of "The Amazing Nikki Wilde" were in the larger shadowbox. The Amazing Nikki was an unremarkable blond with vibrant red lips wearing a pale-yellow bathing suit. A second entrance around the corner had a small, backlit sign that read, "The Pussy Galore Stag Bar." I opted for the front entrance.

Smoke rushed out as the door closed behind me, and I subsequently tripped over a metal threshold, lurching into a curtain of darkness. The unexpected plexiglass partition forced a left or right turn into the club, so I felt my way around to the bar's end and hoisted myself onto an upholstered stool. I heard a snare drum, and the room's features sharpened as my eyes adjusted.

A narrow walkway projected from a more prominent stage area in the distance. It was surrounded by a U-shaped bar pit, like a castle moat.

Bow-tied bartenders plunged glasses into suds-filled sinks and scooped ice. Diner-style booths lined one wall. I didn't see any curtained booths. Yet.

The snare drum quickened, and the spotlight above me popped on. It was the size of a cannon, suspended above the plexiglass partition by a metal, U-shaped yoke.

"Goddamn, I hate that fucking spotlight," said a woman from one of the booths. "It shows every glob of fat."

A man appeared on stage holding a microphone.

"Thank you, thank you so much. I am pleased to announce now, on the main stage, our lovely Miss, uh, Miss Jasmine, and in the Pussy Galore Stage Bar, Miss Lorna."

He scooped away part of the curtain, where I glimpsed a drum set and keyboard.

"Where is Jasmine's sheet music, for fuck's sake?" the announcer said, unaware of his live microphone.

"It's right here. Jesus fucking Christ, Lenny," said a woman, her voice getting louder as she approached.

"What shit are you playing for her? God, I hate this shit-fucking music. When are we getting a DJ, like the other clubs? Nothing personal, guys," another woman said.

"They're all a bunch of demanding, fucking bitches is all. They're not the bosses of us. Five, six, seven, eight."

A live rendition of "Big Spender" brought Jasmine out in a sprawling gown of greens and blues. The pool of color trailed her. It dripped over the runway like a king-sized duvet on a twin bed. A man wearing a suit and tie leaned into the corner of the bar to get my attention.

"Excuse me, Miss? Can I help you?" he said, speaking over the music.

"Hi, I'm here to maybe see about a job," I said. "Is it OK to sit here?"

"Please, yes, if you're eighteen. I'm Ray, the club manager here at the Naked i. Have you been here before?"

"Nope. It's my first time."

"Excuse me one second. Bruce," Ray barked to one of the bartenders, "arrange your bottles by color, please, and get your limes done. Shine up the coolers with Windex. That goes for everyone. Let's keep it clean and tidy."

Ray had a perfectly round face, mottled cheeks, and eager rodent eyes the same color as his reddish-brown hair.

"Where have you been dancing?" Ray asked.

"Nowhere. I was at the Pussycat for today, but I left. That's it."

Jasmine's gown dropped to the floor with a muffled thud, baring a pear-shaped, pasty-white body. Her big reveal heralded a temporary departure for customers who punctured cocktail napkins with tiny straws to preserve their drinks. They joined a clump of men underneath the illuminated "Pussy Galore Stag Bar" sign. Jasmine persevered.

"We have a higher-class clientele," said Ray, "and waitresses make excellent tips."

"I don't want to waitress; I want to dance."

"Dance? You don't look like a dancer, but sure. If you don't mind waiting, we'll talk," Ray winked. "Be back in a bit."

Patrons migrated back from the Pussy Galore Stag Bar and disassembled their napkins and straws. I noticed how those perched at the bar weren't distracted by the stage lights, bartender banter, or strangers walking behind them. Booth dwellers, on the other hand, wedged themselves into corners with their backs to the wall as if they had to see the club before the club saw them.

Eventually, denizens of the night-shift toted in overstuffed bags, boxes, and trunks, and stopped at a round table. An older, bearded man in a light-gray suit, chocolate-brown fedora, and white Nike sneakers smiled as he checked them in. A woman's crate crashed to the floor as another dancer elbowed past her, causing a momentary stir.

"You motherfucking cunt bag! If my bird is dead, so are you, you amateur piece of crap."

I wasn't sure what relevance a bird would have in a strip club.

Night fell, the live music became more insistent, and men entering the club from the once sunlit streets no longer grappled with temporary blindness. The parade of curiosities held sway.

"Now, ladies and gentlemen," announced a man behind the curtain, "we bring you our first feature show of the evening, the Ravishing Raven, and for your pleasure, at the Pussy Galore Stag Bar, we have Miss Katrina. Please welcome, Raven the Radish, Raven the Ravishing, and Miss Katrina. Why can't you have a normal name?"

"God damn you, Skippy! It's Ravish the Raven," a woman shouted. "You realize you just called me a vegetable, right? How hard can it be?"

"Poor Skippy has to put up with her shit," a woman objected from one of the booths. "It's a stupid-ass name, anyway."

Another woman smacked a small purse onto the table and slid into the opposing seat. "Hey, Dori."

"Hey, Chickie." Dori held a lighter for Chickie's cigarette. "Let the long night begin."

"You doin' a double?" asked Chickie.

"Yeah," Dori said, tapping her cigarette ash on the floor. "I'm already bored as an oyster."

"Hey, who's that Jane Doe?" Chickie pointed my way with her chin.

"Dang if I know."

"You wanna buy us all a drink?" Chickie yelled.

"You're a few peas short of a casserole," Dori laughed.

There was clambering on stage as a shrouded box and coat rack were set to one side. Ravish stomped out in a black corset, eye mask, and boots. She removed her clothes without ceremony and covered one hand with an oven mitt.

I debuted differently than my mother, Ellen Reeves.

"There she goes, baking those dang biscuits again," Dori said.

The dancer unlatched the door to the shrouded box and a live raven hopped out onto the mitt. It fluffed its feathers, yawned, and exposed an arched, pink tongue. Ravish paraded the bird back and forth before it flapped to its coat-rack perch. The corvid regarded its lacquered reflection in the mirrored wall with one twinkly eye while Ravish rolled on the floor, delighting each man with her gyrations.

The next show started with a dwarf rolling a cage large enough for a small tiger onto the stage. It was the same man in the photograph at Anne Diamond's office. The lights turned off and on, revealing Nikki Wilde in her cage. Her diminutive assistant stood by, holding a whip as she bashed the side of her body against the cage. Once free, Nikki snapped into a standing position like a coiled spring and landed her crotch on his nose.

Not a debutante ensemble.

"That seems overly convenient," said a man two seats away from me. "She's no good at plots."

Nikki dragged the argumentative dwarf into the cage and draped herself over it. She moved through a predictable repertoire of cage-top poses before dismounting in a full split. A drumroll ensued, men rustled excitedly, and Nikki pulled her G-string up and between her breasts. This effectively dragged the elastic and corresponding metal hooks through the complexities of her genitalia. Dicey. Once both clips were accounted for, the battle-worn G-string was cast aside.

"Name's Bob." It was the man two seats away from me.

"Hi, Bob." I turned toward him.

"You work here?"

"I'm thinking about it."

"As a waitress?"

Why did everyone think I was a waitress?

"Nope. I want to try out dancing."

"Ah, so this is an investigative, fact-gathering initiative?"

"Pretty much."

Bob moved to the seat next to mine.

"What do you think so far?" he asked.

"After seeing someone drop a pubic hair in a guy's drink, talking with a friendly prostitute, seeing a shy pimp, and now a live raven, and a tuxedoed midget, I'm not sure I can measure up."

"It's a lot to take in, for sure. Weird works well in here."

"Yeah. Do you happen to have the time?" I asked.

Lacking windows, the club simulated continuous night, like an isolation tank.

"It's 7:40," Bob said.

"The time flew. I should get going."

Ray reappeared and greeted Bob.

"I see you've met Bob," said Ray, "our resident. . . ."

"Shh!" Bob said, cutting him off. "I will make my own introductions, thank you, and you know I prefer anonymity."

"Bob comes in for the research."

My head buzzed, and my eyes burned. My curiosity sensors were overloaded.

"I think I'll head home."

"Why not come in tomorrow and try a day shift?"

"As a dancer?"

"Sure. Be here at 10:30 and use the Pussy Galore Stag Bar door. The front doors are locked until 11. By the way, do you read?" Ray asked, walking me to the front doors.

"Do I read? Of course, I read."

"Mysteries?"

"Not since Nancy Drew and the Hardy Boys. Why?"

"That guy, the one sitting next to you? Bob? That's the mystery writer Robert Parker. Comes in from time to time. A lot of famous people come around. I like to think it reflects well on our club."

I left feeling waterlogged and groggy, like I'd been to a foreign country for weeks. Outside, the earth had rolled away from the sun and opened the night trenches. Women had awakened like owls, claimed street-level roosts, and distributed themselves evenly. Preening their feathers, they scanned cars and strip-club exits for prey. I was out of my element, but curious enough to give dancing another try the following day.

As instructed, I entered the club through the Pussy Galore Stag Bar doors in the morning. The room was a subterranean hole, its stage half the size of a boxing ring. It didn't seem designed for stage performances. I scanned for black curtained booths and saw a miniature bar hemmed into the back corner. A man carrying a hardcover ledger and pumping on a cigar walked out from behind the stage.

"Hi, excuse me. Are you the day manager?" I asked.

"I'm better than the manager. I'm the accountant. The manager is somewhere other than here, minding his business. Try the dressing room, sweetheart."

Sweetheart. Yuck. I walked up two broad stairs into the club's main room and pulled on the first door I saw. I was confronted by an orange construction cone in front of a row of urinals and a monstrous yellow bucket on wheels. The next door I tried opened into a long, narrow room where a woman strained toward a mirror, dragging a pencil across one eyelid. Another dancer sucked in her cheeks and brushed powder into the hollows.

"Hi," said one. "I'm Trish."

". . . the dish," said the other. "I'm Emily."

"Hey, I'm Lucy. The accountant said the manager might be in here."

"Accountant?" Trish asked. "You mean the Mafia collections department? Billy, the day manager, will be here soon with the schedule."

"You new?" asked Emily.

"Yeah."

"Better grab a locker before the herd stampedes in," she said. "There aren't enough to go around."

Insufficient locker space was a strip club theme. I donned the lingerie set again as dancers jostled in and clamored toward empty lockers. They discarded their street shoes with decisive kicks and stepped into long, slinky dresses. Those balancing on unharnessed stilettos waited for a chair at the mirror.

"You have to wear a floor-length gown to mix in," Trish said, looking me up and down. "I'll lend you something."

"Knock, knock, ladies."

The stout man was greeted with a barrage of pleas: "Pretty please, don't put me in back of Charlie," "Put me on first," "Can you put me on last?"

"Good morning to all of you, too."

Billy the manager was clearly the inspiration behind Fred Flintstone.

"Ain't there a new girl here somewhere? Or did you lovely ladies eat her for breakfast?"

"Too early to tell if she swings that way, Billy," said Trish.

"Anyway," he coughed, "here's the schedule."

"Hello? I'm new, back here," I waved. "Name's Lucy, for now."

"Thanks, hon'."

Billy scribbled me into the schedule with a pencil stub and pinned it to the back of the door. A woman wafted into the flurry wearing a succession of thin, dove-gray layers of silk and chiffon.

"Ladies," she bowed. "And who do we have in the nether regions of our well-appointed primping area today?"

"I'm just starting."

"Her name is Lucy, for now," Emily said.

"I'm Wilhelmina."

She opened the locker next to mine and scrutinized Trish, on the floor, disentangling silver chains from a thong.

"Maybe there's a more hygienic routine for untangling your decorative dongles. You don't need a degree in microbiology to know living organisms are burrowing in the carpet just waiting for a moist orifice to call home," said Wilhelmina.

"What's with the night girls being around?" someone asked.

"This day's gonna suck wicked bad," divined another. "We don't stand a chance against night girls."

"Competition is part of life, girls," Trish said, relinquishing her seat.

"You all take the day-girl bus, or what?" Emily asked.

It was funny how women were called girls. Billy reentered the dressing room.

"Did these rascals tell you how we do things around here? You know, give you the rules and regs?"

"No, not yet, but they've been super friendly."

"We are a convivial group," Wilhelmina added.

"What the hell does that word mean?" asked Emily.

"Pay her and those big words no mind. I'll do the rules," offered a leggy Black woman from the opposing line of lockers. "Now, lemme see if I can get this right."

"OK, Lorna, let's hear it," Billy said. "This oughta be good."

Lorna took a deep breath. Her smile was wide and bright.

"OK. Dancers must be on time for their sets, which are twenty minutes long. No touching, dating, or promising nothing to nobody. No napping, reading, homework, food, or drugs in the dressing room. Do not get shitfaced. No tips unless it's damn good advice. Stay sixteen inches away from customers while on the stage. Or is it eighteen inches? Fuck, just don't go near them on stage. No boyfriends, pimps, or hoes in the club. When not dancing, keep your ass on the floor. Make your mixing quota. Use the nasty rug behind the curtain for all floor shows. Smile. Um . . . clean up after yourselves, act like ladies, and have some class. Don't play shitty fuckin' music to torture the girl on the backstage."

Elaborations followed: "Don't touch yourself, especially down there." "Tweak your nipples, and you'll get fined." "Tuck your tampon string." "Poop before coming to work. It'll keep your stomach flat and won't stink up the bathroom." "If a girl has pink eye, don't borrow her makeup." "Don't borrow G-strings." "Dump champagne in the bucket, not on the carpet." "Don't take things too seriously." "Don't do anything your mother wouldn't do."

Too late. I already was doing something my mother would never do: making my debut while removing Bloomingdale's lingerie in front of strange men perched at eye level to my knees.

Trish handed me her white, toga-like dress that cinched around the waist and slung over one shoulder.

"Are you sure?" I asked.

"Shit, yeah. You can't walk around in that. And those shoes!"

"So I hear," I replied.

There was no live music for the day shift so I located the jukebox and, per the experienced strippers, noted which dancer I followed onstage. The schedule listed me as "Lucy For Now." I followed "Bunnie," who followed "Udon," who followed "Silver."

Isn't Udon a Japanese noodle?

Rather than overthink myself into a box, I studied the goings on in the dressing room. The mirror rotation was like a NASCAR pit stop, except everyone was naked.

One woman stretched a swath of hair through a curling iron and let it smoke before moving to the next section. Someone else lobbed a foot on top of the makeup counter and inserted a tampon in plain view. Another removed a striped straw from a box and speared her coffee cup.

"What's the straw for, anyway?" someone asked, twisting her hair into a messy bun. "For coffee, tea, red wine, anything that stains my teeth."

"Anyone want my seat?" asked a dancer gathering her make-up.

"I would like it, please," said a taut woman with visible tendons.

She marched forward and planted a three-tiered, metal makeup case on the counter. Using a Kleenex, she cleared a circular patch of ambiguous grease from the mirror, produced tweezers and stretched her breast skin with the other hand before nipping at the erupted black hairs around her nipple.

"Ouch!" A flare of laughter came from Lorna while she adjusted a neon-orange tube dress as tight as sausage casing. "That looks too painful," she said, popping her slick lips at the mirror. "I'm ready to get my beautiful, Black self on stage for these damn fools."

"Ugh, I'm fucking late," a woman in stretch jeans with rhinestones on the back pockets slammed the door and put her nose to the schedule. Squinting, she mumbled, "Bunnie, Bunnie, Bunnie, where is Bunnie?"

"You're after me, sweetheart," said the woman plucking her nipple hairs.

"Oh, good. Thanks, Udon." Bunnie spoke with a lisp and had a wandering eye.

So that was the dancer named for the noodle! Mystery solved. Bunnie waddled to the lockers and, seeing they were all taken, let the bags slide from her shoulders and onto the floor. "Anyone share a locker?"

"You can practically have my locker to yourself," I said. "All I have is what I'm wearing now and my clothes."

"Do you mind if I lock it?"

"No, that's fine."

"You're new?"

"First day." I tried to choose which of Bunnie's eyes to focus on.

"Yeah, I know. These are my fucked up eyes and no, I can't see shit. One minute the eyeball's over here, and then it's way the fuck over there. Tried a patch and a pirate costume, but nothing worked. Anyway, thanks for the locker. I'm Bunnie, that's with an 'ie.' You are?"

"Lucy, for now. I haven't picked a stage name yet."

Something hissed from one of Bunnie's bags, and she emptied its contents onto the floor.

"You motherfucker. My mousse exploded."

Bunnie whisked into the bathroom with her bag. I'd not considered hair or makeup, and I didn't know where to start with either. My face was a featureless disc of skin, in comparison to the other dancers, but it would have to do. I moved to a booth outside the dressing room and watched a dancer named Silver command the stage.

Silver was attractively Lilliputian and round in all the right places, with glossy, black curls to her waist. She galloped before executing a series of leaps and grand jetés that would cripple me. On the fifth song, she dragged a carpet remnant out from behind the curtain and lay down on her side. The lights reflected off trickles of perspiration as she moved through elegant bridges and splits. I was mesmerized until she convulsed into an air-fucking repertoire. The men were rapt. I, not so much.

When it was my turn to part the curtains, I tracked the stage's periphery multiple times and avoided all eye contact. One misplaced heel, and I'd be folded inside a bar trough for my debut. *Was I smiling? Should I smile? Why would I smile when my mood was neutral? What on earth does a seductive smile look like? Is there such a thing? Am I supposed to look at the mirror on the wall? Mirror, mirror on the wall. No, I might lose my balance. Do I take off one item per song? Shorts, underwear, camisole. Shit. Who invented heels and why don't men wear them?*

    I ambled through five generic disco songs on my chunky, loathsome heels and arranged my suburban lingerie in a soft pile by the curtain. After hopping out of my silky shorts, I pinged my gaze from one shadowed head to another, careful not to linger. When I finished, I gathered my clothes but had no idea how to transit from the stage to the dressing room. *Do I put my clothes back on? Or do I bundle the pieces up and race to the door?* I made a run for it and landed in front of Ray.

"Nice to see you," he said, smiling.

I held the fist of clothing in front of my crotch.

"Oops. I didn't think to ask about getting from A to B."

"Most girls bring a towel," Ray said. "Get dressed and come see me in my office. It's the door by the cigarette machine."

Ray's office was a lopsided triangle that barely accommodated a desk and two chairs.

"Was I OK?" I asked.

"I didn't want to make you nervous, so I only peeked. I think we can work something out from the little I saw."

"I can work here?"

"Let's see how you do with a day shift. Billy wrote you into the schedule as 'Lucy for Now.' You can't make this stuff up," Ray laughed. "Billy's a piece of work. OK, let's brainstorm about a stage name. No spices, gems, Disney characters, or cocktails. Town and street names are fine. Oh, and please, not Sabrina or Desiree."

"Could I use my legal name? Louise?"

"Too ordinary. Where are you from?"

"Lake Forest, Illinois, and later, New Canaan, Connecticut. Why?"

Ray raised both eyebrows.

"Lake Forest, I see. Answers usually generate names. How about costumes you always wanted to wear or what you wanted to be when you grow up? No astronauts."

"I'd love an Indian costume, but I have blond hair and blue eyes so that's silly."

Ray dismissed the protest with a wave of his hand.

"What about Cheyenne, you know, from the plains? Now that I say that it is a little plain . . . How about Princess Cheyenne?"

"Yuck. No way."

"Then how does Cheyenne sound?"

The office door opened partway, and a grandfatherly face poked in.

"Whom do we have here?" the man asked.

"I'm Lucy."

"This is Cheyenne, freshly named," Ray said.

"A pleasure. I'm Mel."

He extended his hand, and I instinctively stood.

"Nice to meet you," I said.

"What lovely manners."

"She comes by them honestly. Cheyenne was born in Lake Forest and grew up in New Canaan."

"I see. I look forward to you being here." He tugged the rim of his soft fedora and bowed.

I couldn't imagine why management was so pleasant. They were probably like this to all prospective dancers. If I was a novelty, I didn't know why.

I'd completed my first stripper set, been given my first stripper name, and now needed to procure my first dancer drink. Bopping around without clothes was straightforward enough, but selling drinks was not. Aside from it being unscrupulous, manufacturing insincere dialogue and feigning interest where there was none was not in my repertoire.

I stood by my locker, hoping to change into the toga when Bunnie waltzed in, eyeballing me with her good eye.

"Oh my god, I am so, so sorry. Shoot. I locked you out."

One of Bunnie's irises was half hidden in the far corner of her eye socket.

"It's OK. Maybe give me the combination?"

She straightened and swayed her lower back.

"Yeah, that's a no."

"OK, I'll just grab my stuff then. You're welcome for the locker."

Bunnie squirted powder on her torso, creating a soft white halo on the carpet, and I geared up in my borrowed toga. Once on the floor, I dawdled next to the row of booths like I was considering my options at Disney World. A diminutive man slithered toward me.

"Excuse the intrusion, my lady, but I'd be most honored to buy you a drink."

"Me?"

He had a triangular face like a mantis, and his hair was unprofessionally dyed with auburn henna.

"Yes, my lady. I hope not to displease you."

The vernacular confused me.

"Um, sure. Where do you want to sit?"

"I await your command."

A perky, blond waitress leaned into my shoulder.

"He wants to be your slave," she said.

"My slave?" I asked, looking at her and then at the man standing like a bedpost, his hands folded over his crotch. "Is that true?"

"This could take a while, kids. I'll be back with your drink. Name's Susan, by the way."

"Wait, Susan," I turned away from the slave and whispered, "No alcohol, just water. Or a Shirley Temple."

I turned back to the prospective minion.

"Good grief, I wouldn't know what to do with a slave. A slave? I don't like the word slave. It's offensive. Couldn't we find a better word for this?"

"Servant, my lady? Drudge, serf, vassal?"

"Sure. Whatever. Anything but slave."

I slid into a booth. Oh boy, my first drink. Susan bounded over, stopping to make a silly face behind him.

"Here's my command," Susan said. "Pick a damn seat."

He slid into the seat across from me, looking like he was born at a loss. Susan handed me a light-pink deli ticket.

"A deli ticket?" I asked.

"Oh my gosh, this is your first drink? Turn these in at the end of your shift. You get a dollar on every drink you sell. They really add up."

"My lady?"

"What?" I snipped.

Silence.

"What?" I raised my voice.

He relaxed his posture and asked, "How may I please you today?"

"OK, right. Hmm. How can you please me? I'm thinking. How about telling me your name?"

"Yes, my lady. I am not worthy of my name."

I crossed my arms and looked away.

"I cannot do this," I said halfheartedly to myself. "Fine. Where are you from?"

"I was squeezed from a bar rag, my lady, or so I was told."

My lips tightened as I tried to contain a laugh.

"I'm sorry. But that was very funny. Do you know you're funny?"

"Perhaps your lady has better stock to choose from."

One sip of water and I was irritated to the bone. His servile tone; wet, round eyes; and tiresome, limited script irked me. With some effort, I summoned my curiosity.

"Why are you like this? You know, so interested in lowering yourself?"

"My lady, I am but the dregs of hell."

"Does your family live around here?"

"My lady, I am not worthy of blood relations."

"Where do you live?"

"In the ethers of car exhaust."

"Now that was original."

"Susan? When is he going to stop?"

"He usually stops when you ask for another drink. Poor guy. He doesn't have much money."

"Your lady requires a drink to spend even one more unbearable, wretched second with you," I said. "I'm sorry, but management insists."

"I shall retire from your employ then. Thank you for allowing me to serve you."

"Very well. I dismiss you."

My illiteracy in erotic humiliation failed him. I'd never been asked to criticize, degrade, or discipline someone. A career in dominance seemed unlikely.

Eventually, day strippers stuffed their belongings into bags and counted drink tickets while the night strippers filed in, jockeyed for mirror space, and shed their streetwear. The transitional clothing ran the gamut from jeans, sweats, and flannel to rhinestone-edged leisure suits and fur. One woman arrived in a pair of vertiginous Alberto Fermani stilettos (She called them her "house shoes.") and a powder-pink cashmere sweater tucked into black spandex pants. I assumed that veterans always stayed in full regalia and wouldn't be caught dead without full makeup and heels.

The Naked i's dressing room didn't have changing stalls or curtains. It was more of a locker room feel, an open-floor concept that didn't accommodate modesty. One dancer held her butt cheeks apart so another dancer could accurately apply Nair hair removal cream. Someone trimming their pubic hair elicited considerable group feedback and a woman requested help making sure there was no toilet paper tucked into her crevices. I listened to a vigorous debate on whether tampons, sea sponges, or diaphragms worked best during periods. I also heard the latest on upper-lip hair removers, and Chinese gang hierarchies.

Hungry and soaked in stripper trivia, I left the dressing room, found Ray, handed over my thin ruffle of deli tickets, and pocketed the drink money. A tardy stripper blurred past carrying a padlocked wicker basket. Ray caught the woman's eye and reprimanded her for being late. Then he turned to me. "You might as well stay for this one's show. She's unusual, to say the least."

I wasn't sure how much more unusual I could take in.

CHAPTER 7

Cheyenne

Even though I felt a few peas short of a casserole myself, I reversed course, back into the dressing room. The tardy feature performer, Onyx, held a creature named Simba, a high-maintenance ball python, in the center of a stripper huddle. Like any other good show-and-tell, Simba inspired comments and pressing questions.

"Oooh, he's adorable," "Look at those beady little eyes, just like a criminal." "What about his poop?" and "How much does it weigh?" "What does it eat?"

"It's not an 'it'. Simba is 100-percent male. I had his cloaca probed."

"His what?"

"Clo-ake-a. Birds have them, too. No penises, just holes."

"How do they fuck?"

"They manage."

"Can I pet him?"

"He'll bite if you touch his head, and you'll bleed. Not to mention, he might break a tooth."

No one wanted to touch an ophidian head the size of a small foot, anyway.

"Is he heavy?" "Where does he sleep?" "Wait, do snakes sleep?" "Do you moisturize his scales?"

"Simba weighs around thirty pounds, and he sleeps with me under the covers. I keep my costumes simple for Simba—no beads, rhinestones, feathers, or sequins. Imagine, one of his scales ripped by a sequin?"

Like Ravish the Raven and the Amazing Nikki, Onyx's gimmick overshadowed her.

She was simply the star's handler. One couldn't be anything but mesmerized watching the snake adhere to her body onstage, leisurely encircle her waist, worm between her breasts, and explore her curves. The audience cheered when Simba smoothly negotiated his way into her butt cheeks and geared his head below her pubic hair. Simba stole the show.

Onyx returned Simba to the dressing room, where she zipped him into a padded duffle bag.

"I have to pee so bad," she squeaked, racing to the bathroom and closing the door.

Onyx peed and dancers dispersed. Meanwhile, Simba slithered out of his holding bag without a peep.

"No!" Onyx bleated upon seeing the deflated duffel. "What is wrong with you girls? Didn't you see him leave? Ugh! It's my fault. I hate myself. I'm so stupid! Fuck me!"

Ray, Billy, and Ricky, the night bouncer, quickly located Simba curled up underneath the ice maker in the Pussy Galore Stag Bar and Onyx captured him in a king-sized pillowcase. Reptile crisis averted.

"Nothing personal, but no more animals. I'm done," Ray announced while presenting Simba to his rightful owner. "No more snakes, birds, rodents, cages, midgets, or bands. The days of carnival freak shows are gone, erased, finis. We're sticking to professional, high-class entertainment only."

"What about the big shows?" asked Billy. "Guys love them big shows."

"Everyone here is more than capable of producing shows. The house girls will have to step up. We've got plenty of raw talent and imagination here. Maybe it will inspire the girls to become more invested in shows."

"Not girls, women," I stated.

Having left the club, I walked to the subway and a shadow shifted ahead of me. I tensed but kept walking. A husky woman in yellow spandex pants and an orange button-down shirt tied at the waist leaned against the outside of a XXX movie theater. She glared and flicked her tongue at me like a pangolin.

"Hey, baby. What's up?" It was a man's voice.

"Nothing much," I said, continuing to walk.

My mother's listing in the Social Register.

He grabbed his crotch and grinned.

"You all have a nice night, girl. Peace out now."

"Will do. You too."

It felt important to be friendly in the Combat Zone. I waved to the man and a policeman approached.

"You good?" he asked.

"Yeah, I'm good."

"The Zone doesn't look like your cup of tea."

"It isn't, but it will be. I work at the Naked i now."

It rolled off my tongue like air.

"Oh, OK, right. Then you already know the deal and how nights are a little crazy. Lots of freaks."

"Oh, I'll never work here at night. One drunk is too many drunks for me. I work during the day," I announced.

Aside from avoiding drunks, the day schedule allowed for a pleasant routine. I could still have a life. Every morning I ran along the Charles River, cooked rice with tofu, arrived to work early and nodded to the loners and fetishists who gathered on the sidewalk, waiting for the doors to unlock.

When the club opened, they pressed inside like children vying to be first in line and staked claims on booths. Fetishists wanted table space for their wares, and loners wanted dark corners where nothing could surprise or expose them.

Loners appeared dull and disinterested. Maybe they were intentionally blasé as a means of self-protection. They mumbled into their shirts and rarely made eye contact. Female company was by invitation only and the dancer sat next to, not across from, these circumspect characters. Facing another human being was too daunting. Some had poor hygiene, neglected teeth, dorky clothing, and most lived with their parents. In the club, loners could be invisible, but connected on their own terms. They were in control of the pace and depth of social interactions.

Fetishists, on the other hand, were unapologetic and hygienically inclined. They spoke with candor and excitement about their fixations. When seeking female company, fetishists requested body parts rather than the whole person. "Do any of the ladies here have noticeably high arches?" They did not apologize for ordering up exact shoe sizes, long toes, dirty feet, clean feet, or sweaty feet. "Not everyone understands," they'd say.

Foot and shoe fetishes were at the top of the leaderboard and easiest to indulge in a strip club. Submission, domination, humiliation, and bondage worked best in the privacy of well-equipped dungeons in more private residences, and blood, scat, and urine fetishists weren't tolerated at the club, either. Latex, rubber, hair, stocking, balloon, navel, and pacifier fetishes were acceptable enough, but rare.

Foot fetishists familiar with the club didn't come empty-handed. They brought powder, scent-free lotions, tickling feathers, bottles of witch hazel, paper towels, toenail clippers, nail files and polish, cuticle balms, satin ribbons, stockings, pantyhose, and athletic socks. They wanted to lick, suck, or smell feet or shoes, and dreamed of being penetrated or trampled by them. Ultimately, they wanted to get off in between them.

One especially creative foot man called himself L'Orteil, which, in French, means the toe. He came in every third Thursday carrying a compendium of art supplies and a plastic mailing tube. Out of the tube came a roll of kitchen wax paper and pre-cut, non-fusible, interfacing fabric, which he carefully removed and set aside. He had two palm-sized discs of rubbing wax, the kind used for headstone impressions, a roll of masking tape, and wide rubber bands.

Although counterintuitive, L'Orteil's third Thursday itinerary did not include visits to the King's Chapel or Central Burying Grounds, both significant Boston cemeteries within walking distance. He wasn't after imprints of Samuel Adams's or Paul Revere's headstones. He wanted foot rubbings. One couldn't help but watch as he gingerly secured wax to the bottom of a woman's foot and rubbed until satisfied. L'Orteil then methodically rolled up the day's impressions and dropped them into the tube.

The quotidian flow of daytime customers followed the clock with astounding accuracy. Loners and fetishists left as lunchtime customers arrived, construction workers piled in around 3 p.m., followed by suits at 5:10 and night strippers at 6:45.

Loners and fetishists preferred the unhurried pace of the daytime, as did I. Within weeks, the strip club novelties became less jarring. I felt more at home and less like a fish out of water. I no longer avoided eye contact while on the stage, and wanted each man to feel I was dancing just for him. The quantity of daytime spectators rarely filled the seats, yet my enthusiasm increased alongside the numbers. The audience and male gaze held a strong currency for me.

After three months, I still didn't shave my legs, style my hair, wear makeup, or do floor shows, but I wore stilettos on stage lest I get fired. Excepting only the shoes and hustling drinks, working as a daytime stripper suited me.

The drink hustle was a time-tested charade that pandered to a man's hopes and produced massive profit. After Prohibition ended in the 1930s, drink hustling exploded and, in the 1950s, incited protests bordering on hysteria. Drink solicitors were considered tricksters who wheedled innocent strangers into exhausting their bankrolls. The outrage was warranted when reacting to women who spiked men's drinks to rob them. But most were well-meaning and stuck to basic drink peddling, without cons or false promises. They posed as secretaries, store clerks, or bar patrons, and enticed men to believe they'd found eligible, single women. Most men were aware that carnal entertainment wasn't part of the contract. If he concluded otherwise, it was due to his own weakness and longing.

The first known solicitors roamed the bars of "Storyville," the red-light district of New Orleans, and were called "b-girls." Depending on the source, the "b" in "b-girl" stood for brandy, Bourbon Street, the saying "Busy as a bee, watch out you don't get stung," or just bargirl. B-girls offered companionship in exchange for drinks served in spit cups. The New Orleans spit cup was frosted or metal and cleverly concealed a hollow center.

"I'd like a brandy with a water chaser on the side, please," was the common b-girl request. The "water chaser" was thought to be in the spit cup. She'd take a dainty sip of brandy, pretend to swallow, and end with water. Except there was no water. The b-girl furtively transferred the alcohol from her mouth into the spit cup. Sometimes she deftly emptied champagne bottles into the ice bucket and paved the way for more purchases. She stayed sober as a granite curb while her companion became limbless and cheerfully emptied his wallet. It didn't matter if he drank too much; in fact, it was preferred. The b-girl more easily charmed him into overpriced bottles of rotgut champagne on ice and, of course, water chasers.

B-drinkers were socially savvy, financially solvent, and empowered by the ability to support their families. They knew how to avoid the risks, keep their sexual limits intact, and their vulnerabilities hidden. "Buy me a drink, honey?" coupled with a lingering caress to the upper back was simply a warm greeting and nothing more.

Like contemporary mixers, a successful b-girl was a good judge of character. She made swift assessments from afar, and meticulously bore a hole straight down into the man's vulnerabilities and sexual longings. She broke down sales resistance, and then sustained the transaction until money ran out. With besieged senses and a surging libido, the client submitted to the process like a trained dog. He forgot that having desires is never, ever the same as satisfying them. Inevitably, his hunger was crushed, but he almost always found his way back for more.

Many cities eventually enacted laws against B-drinking. Women could not be employed for the sole purposes of drinking, mingling, or dancing with customers. Men were seen as victims and the laws protected them, not the women.

Mixing at the Naked i didn't stray far from the Louisiana model, but few women mixed without stripping. Pure mixers were older, and strolled in after 11 p.m., prime time to beguile horny men. Mixers viewed themselves as therapists, paid female companions with whom secrets, worries, and triumphs could be safely shared. They could easily sell thirty drinks in three hours, evidence that beauty was less important than proficiency and one's disposition. They stayed as long as they wished and turned in their deli tickets for cash—$1 per ticket—at the bar.

As the Combat Zone accommodated more strip clubs, drink solicitation evolved, often crossing the line into sex for money. "Dirty mixers," although rare at the Naked i, were opportunistic prostitutes determined to turn over every stone in the Combat Zone. They knew how to maneuver their hands under the lip of the bar but didn't escape notice. Once discovered, they were unceremoniously escorted out the front doors.

Inside the Naked i, the tokens of male-female exchanges were eroticism, intimacy, attention, and money. For one drink the customer received a novel, time-limited, friendly encounter. Unlike other areas of the man's life, he controlled how much time and money he spent and with whom. The barstool or booth bore no resemblance to his recliner or stiff office chair, and instead of staring at the same wall or wife, he feasted on a variety of beautiful women in stages of undress. The lowly, single drink could alleviate feelings of worthlessness and inadequacy, dispel loneliness, and relieve boredom. Alcohol, sexual desire, and beauty reinforced its power. Buying the drink made him the frog prince, if only for a moment.

Experienced drink buyers were consumers of fresh conversations with unfamiliar beats. They purchased relational intimacy like any other by-the-hour service and saw mixing as a reasonable exchange of services for goods. They wanted to be seen, heard, and fawned over, to uncover the "true" nature of a women's sexuality, or know how to better please their girlfriends or wives. They wondered openly about their own undoing as fathers, husbands, and partners, the conflicts and confusion. They came in not to have affairs, but to share their angst about having them. Some fell in love and continued to pay for what they would never get for free.

Experienced dancers knew to cultivate stables of devoted, financially sound regulars and schedule them without overlaps. When a dancer said she had a "regular," it meant that she owned him. It was the oral equivalent of a legal notice in the back of a newspaper. We were duly warned.

"One of my regulars is coming in tonight," or, "I'm not working, I came in just to meet with one of my regulars."

An upstanding regular respected the boundaries, abided by the schedule, and ordered as much champagne as his dancer fancied. He didn't smell like a rodeo and his teeth were intact. He gave her jewelry from Tiffany's, or jewelry in a Tiffany's box. He hired a limousine to take her shopping at Neiman Marcus or Bonwit Teller and purchased meals from Maison Robert, the Union Oyster House, or Durgin Park. He sent enormous floral arrangements to the Naked i for all to see. Sometimes regulars and dancers became loyal friends or, rarely, husband and wife.

Regulars didn't care about the alcohol content in a dancer's cocktail. They were discerning consumers of good company and knew what they purchased. For these men, attempting to get dancers shit-faced to sleep with them was ill-informed and tasteless. There were far more good men who removed the discomfort from mixing.

The Naked i's business model relied on platonic drink sales for profit, but training a high-heeled, minimally dressed sales force was a thorny proposition. Fortunately, successful sales came from successful relationships, whether in an appliance store or strip club. Most dancers were gregarious enough to befriend a multitude of customers. The monetization of libido was nothing new, but the array of marketing techniques at the Naked i surpassed anything found in conventional advertising.

A good gimmick accelerated the inveigling. The stripper collective spawned endlessly creative possibilities. Burlesque star Gypsy Rose Lee said, "You gotta get a gimmick if you wanna get applause." Stage gimmicks certainly attracted audience attention, and a few clever dancers used their wiles to corral men into buying them drinks. How could he not be delighted by personal jingles, card tricks, sex advice, or tarot card readings inside a strip club?

The aptly named Karma was never without her tarot cards. Readings were impeccably timed so that halfway through a man's future, she finished her drink. Gulp. If he wanted the full outlook, another drink was in order. Udon offered Iyengar yoga advice based on a man's body typology, and Jazz used her well-trained soprano voice to belt out customized jingles. Jennifer, who once called herself Magic and wisely thought better of it, performed card and coin tricks. Montana presented an assortment of natural treasures like rocks, bird's nests, and sticks. Cupid offered middling (at best) sex advice, and Venus made origami flowers and birds.

Whatever the gambit, breaking through a man's rapture while he was gazing at a naked woman was best done gently. Being startled out of a fantasy increased the likelihood of rejection. But there were always more men.

There were pot-bellied, large-eared, and wormy-fingered men. Men with garlic, beer, and Listerine breath. Bowlegged, pigeon-toed, and flat-footed men. Men who brought books in, and men who didn't read. Men with herpes sores, earwax, nose hairs, and eye crumbs. Mute, loud, coughing, and spitting men. Deaf, blind, and paralyzed men. Blue-collar, white-collar, rich, and poor men. Harmless oafs. Little boys. Men.

The confident and experienced mixer knew all the types. She embodied her worth as an active listener and intelligent conversationalist. Rejection didn't touch her. She knew not to wear perfume, body spray, or glitter lest her primping create a riff at home. She validated the fantastical images men witnessed on stage, and never corrected their reveries. If customers thought whirling stars encircled us, they did. Men didn't always want the truth, and dancers didn't always speak it.

Dancers became skilled hunters and waited for prey near the front doors. The deluge of erotic messages on the street was like foreplay for men en route to the club. Upon entering, they were blinded by the club's artificial night, adequately disoriented and instantly surveilled. After he took a seat and arranged his coat, a dancer approached, lightly touched his arm, and introduced herself in a soft voice. If met by a favorable response, she sat, cooed, and draped distal parts of herself over his hands, arms, and shoulders. She seemed intoxicated by his every word, like a lover would be. She saw, heard, and understood him. Finally, he was laudable. Nowhere else on earth could he find this level of refreshment for a few measly dollars. Like the Velveteen Rabbit, the man was real.

Not every dancer operated with prowess. Some peeked tentatively over customers' shoulders, trotted around the bar like dressage horses, or waited to be approached. The sales quota took care of the rest.

Drink quotas motivated reticent or lazy strippers by charging them for every drink under the quota. Nobody wanted to pay the club. One disorderly dancer tried to get around the quota problem by stealing rolls of deli tickets from a grocery store. Her scheme was exposed once the cash registers closed out, and she was fired.

I excelled on stage and floundered on the club floor. I became an after-the-show opportunist. I lacked the interpersonal proficiencies to sustain plodding dialogues and wandered from stool to booth to bar, to another stool, to the dressing room, and back again like a connect-a-dot drawing. Bopping around buck naked was refreshingly straightforward, but talking to men for money was not. It felt stilted, and shady. To hustle without hustling and ask without asking seemed impossible. I couldn't make the ten-drink quota.

After using up the mixing grace period, I had to pay for my deficiencies every shift. Ray tried to help by loaning me a hideous, lime-green gown from a swag pile of hand-me-downs hanging off flimsy hangers. The clothing had been forfeited by fired, retired, or scatter-brained strippers. It was loungewear gone awry, curtains from a psychic's booth, forgotten prom dresses, or full-length, mother-of-the bride numbers.

"Blonds look best in lime green," said Ray.

He flipped through the hanger hooks like they were pages in a catalog.

"Here, this should work," he said, handing me a waterfall of glowing polyester, and placing an index card on the desk.

"Sign and date here, please," he said. "Think of this as a library. You can borrow for up to three months, but no renewals, and dry-clean it before you return it. Maybe it will bring you good luck."

It didn't.

"And Cheyenne?" Ray continued. "I'd like you to consider working nights. You could develop shows, and mixing would be much easier. They would come to you. I guarantee it."

Ray persisted in trying to onboard me for the night shift, and suggested my aversion was overblown. I politely declined each time. I wondered what I might offer a rapt night crowd standing three feet deep behind the bar stools, whooping, and pumping their fists.

Ray sweetened the deal by purchasing an Indian costume for me. There was nothing Native American about the cobalt blue satin pieces edged in zigzags of white fringe, and adorned with tiny, round mirrors. Native Americans didn't have mirrors or fringe. There was no headdress. No headdress? No feathers, beads, buckskin, quills, or rabbit pelts. Then again, there was nothing Native American about me, either.

The first time I used the costume, Ray stood next to the manager's table, where Mel sat at his post, rocking one Nike sneaker, and peering out from underneath the rim of his hat. They looked like proud parents as I shuffled around to "Half Breed" by Cher.

The ends of filament thread poked at my skin, and the glue underneath the mirrors crackled when I walked. What if the thing didn't come off? To be sure, I reached for the zipper at the back of the skirt, partially released it and repeated the move on the jacket. When my hands returned to the zippers, pieces of fringe had wedged inside the teeth, and I was forced to wriggle the skirt down. I started yanking the jacket over my head, and my hair caught on the edge of a mirror before being ripped out of the follicles.

Aside from its cumbersome fringe, the faux Indian outfit didn't sway me. I wanted something more authentic.

Ray pressed on. "I'll pay you ten dollars more a night." "We'll get a damn DJ." "You can have Nikki's cage." There was no shortage of carrots.

"Nikki's cage? Really? Why? What happened?"

Ray formed an arch in between his forefinger, and thumb, rubbed the front of his scalp line, and sighed.

"She was upset by the sudden changes, and left it behind, told me to burn it."

"You mean the no animals thing?"

"For her, it was the no-midgets thing. Keith, the midget. Nice, nice guy, but I couldn't see what he added to the show besides a freakish, carnival element."

"Huh. Well, I don't know what I'd do with a cage. But thanks for offering."

"Mull it over."

What would anyone do with a cage in a strip club? It was just an open box on wheels. I could see a bed or see-through bathtub, but not a rickety, used wooden cage that once housed a midget.

One morning, before the club opened, Billy, the day manager, and Skippy, the taxi driver and soon-to-be full-time DJ, had maneuvered the cage onto a painter's drop cloth in the Pussy Galore Stag Bar.

"What are you guys doing?" I asked.

"Hey, it's the girl with the golden hair on her legs," said Skippy, bow-legged and always smiling.

"We're about to smash this stupid cage to bits," said Billy, taking up his mallet. "It won't fit in the dumpster like this."

I had an idea.

"Wait, you guys, I might want the cage."

"What? You gotta lion at home?" Billy laughed.

"Or a naughty boyfriend who needs to be whupped?" asked Skippy. "I'll whup him for you."

"Ray told us to get rid of it. You'll have to talk to him," said Billy.

"OK. I'll go find him. Hold your horses. I'll be right back."

I bolted to Ray's office.

"Hi, Ray. I know I never got back to you about the cage, but I think I want it, if it isn't too late. I saw Billy and Skippy back there ready to smash it to bits."

Ray sipped thoughtfully from a paper Dunkin Donuts cup.

"Not for your pet dragon, though. He'll ignite the thing in no time. Seriously, you'll work nights?"

"Don't you want to know what my idea is?"

Ray swiveled toward me and pushed away from his desk.

"Shoot. I'm all ears."

"I'm thinking a Pink Panther show, you know, from the cartoon, with a pink cage, cigarette holder, papier-mâché mask, and Henry Mancini music."

"Pink Panther? I thought you might put a customer in there! But a nod to the classic cartoon character. Hmm. Interesting. Not what I expected but, OK. It would certainly be a stripper first. Iconic, even."

"I didn't even think about the customer idea. That would make it even better, but it wouldn't work with the 16-inch rule. So, could I pay Billy or Skippy to paint the cage for me instead of smashing it?"

"I'm sure you can convince them to paint it for you. Now, when should I put you on the night schedule?"

"What if I hate it? Then what?"

"Hate the costume? Given your exuberance, it's unlikely."

"No, no, working at night. Do I have an out?"

"An out?"

"Like, can I go back to days?"

"No problem at all, Cheyenne. I'll put you on nights next week."

"Can we wait until I have stuff to wear? I'll go see that lady near the joke shop about the Pink Panther."

"Hedy Jo Star? *The* Hedy Jo Star? It doesn't get better than that. How do you know her?"

"I ended up in her shop accidentally, the day I auditioned for Anne."

"Ah. The club is happy to loan you money to get things rolling, and check if she has any used costumes to get you started." Ray beamed.

"I'll go tomorrow before work. Wait, is she that expensive?"

Someone pounded the office door as Ray answered my question. "A few thousand apiece . . ."

"Yo, Mario!" a voice yelled.

"Mario! Get the door, Cheyenne, please."

"Mario, this is Cheyenne, soon to be Princess Cheyenne. And this is . . ."

"How come you call each other Mario?" I asked.

"That's a good question," Mario said. "It's our adorable little way of being family, isn't it Ray? Hey, I remember her from the back room. I think it was her first day. And look at that, the girl's still here. You didn't scare her away," he said, laughing.

"That's woman, not girl," I said.

"Well, my, my. I stand corrected."

"You're the accountant, right?" I asked.

"Accountant. Right," Ray said, blowing air through his lips.

"Okie dokie. Time to settle up. You will excuse us, young lady," Mario said, closing the door.

The following day, I made my way to the costumer's shop.

"Hello, dear," Hedy Jo said. "I remember you. You came to see Anne Diamond that day back in the fall. "Buzzy!" she yelled. "Remember that young thing who came looking for Anne's office?"

"Not really," his voice muttered from behind the curtain of boas.

"She's back to see us. Honestly, Buzz, you could start an argument in an empty house. Now what is the point in being wound up tighter than banjo strings all day?"

Her eyes flickered and she put an arm over my shoulder.

"I'm sure you aren't here to say hello. What can we do for you, dear?"

"I wanted to ask if you'd make me a costume, and also check out your used outfits."

Hedy Jo yelled back to Buzzy. "Princess here would like for us to make her a costume."

"Princess? How did you know that name?" I asked.

"Ray called yesterday and said you're working nights. You have something in mind?"

"Yup. I do. A Pink Panther costume, you know, like the Saturday morning cartoon."

"Fantastic! Yes! A body suit and feathered headpiece? Something that says Pink Panther? Sounds easy enough."

"No feathers, a mask, like a three-dimensional one, made from papier-mâché. I want it to look just like the cartoon."

"Buzzy? Come out here, please," Hedy Jo yelled again. "Can you make something three-dimensional out of papier-mâché?"

Buzzy was of small stature and presence, compared to his wife. He had on brightly stitched dark jeans and a bolo necktie.

"I can try. Gosh, I haven't used that stuff since fifth-grade art class. I could swear we made it with newspapers soaked in potato water. What is it I'm making exactly?"

"A Pink Panther head. Now is the Pink Panther male or female? Or both?" Hedy Jo laughed wildly. "You get it, Buzzy? Or both?"

"I get it all right." (I didn't, but I would.)

"The head of a pink cartoon animal couldn't be sexy even if Lynda Carter was wearing it," Hedy Jo said.

"Who's Lynda Carter?" I asked.

"Oh, child, you need to get out more. Lynda Carter plays Wonder Woman, you know, the female superhero emulated by all the fabulous drag queens."

"Wonder Woman. Hm. That's a cool costume idea. I could maybe burst out of something with sparklers. But Wonder Woman is a cartoon, too, just like the Pink Panther."

"A sexy cartoon. I don't know a soul who's wanted to fuck the Pink Panther. What about a Wonder Woman costume instead of Pink Panther?

Or even better, an Indian costume to match your name? The Southern Belle? A gorgeous gown or two?"

"Maybe later. First, I want the Pink Panther and the head."

"And that's sexy? No, dear. You're selling sexy."

"I just want it to be fun. I don't care so much about it being sexy."

CHAPTER 8

Pink Panther

Despite strip clubs being overtly sexual, sexiness wasn't on my radar. I assumed having fun with a pink cage and silly costume added a layer of interest for customers. It certainly did for me. Maybe my having fun was recompense for avoiding air-grinding floor shows or not looking at all like a *Sports Illustrated* swimsuit model.

"Princess, about your pink thing," Billy, the day manager said, marching after me. "Princess, hello? What are you, deaf? Royalty makes people deaf now. No shit. Cheyenne, hey, hey, hey, wait up, giddy up."

"Sorry, Billy. I'm not used to that name. It sounds ridiculous."

"Gotcha. Listen," he coughed into his fist. "I don't know the exact pink color of the Pink Panther. I watched the cartoon, and I couldn't nail it down."

"It's kind of like a lipstick color, but lighter?"

"That's no help at all. You know how many lipstick colors there are?"

"I don't. That was a bad comparison. When I see Hedy Jo next, I'll get a fabric sample or the paint Buzzy's using for the mask."

"Hedy Jo Star, yeah, she ain't no slouch. Mask? This should be interesting. But yeah, get me that 'cause I ain't going into no paint store asking for Pink Panther paint. I'll sand and prime it in the meantime."

"Thanks, Billy."

"And Ray wants to ask you a favor. He's in the Pussy Galore Stag Bar."

"Yet another ridiculous name," I said.

I told Ray the Pink Panther was in the works and that I'd purchased two used gowns that Hedy Jo was altering for me.

"I have a favor to ask," said Ray. "You are the articulate, bright young lady we need for an upcoming appearance before the liquor licensing board. Of course, you'll be financially compensated. To justify our license to sell alcohol, we show that we're compliant. It's routine."

"But I'm new. I don't know anything about that stuff."

"You know more than you think, Cheyenne. You follow the rules and see how other girls follow them. That's all there is to it. They'll ask a few simple questions, and you give them honest answers. No coaching, no script. Next Thursday, we'll meet at Mahoney, Hawkes, and Goldings at 8:15 in the morning. Yes?" he asked expectantly. "I'm sure you'll dress appropriately."

Ray reached into his breast pocket and handed me a card. "Here's their address. And, if you don't mind, the Joe Oteri Show would like to have you on. It's a small, local talk show."

"Who's Joe Oteri?"

"He's a criminal defense lawyer, a charming Sicilian guy, a swashbuckler if I ever saw one, and boy, does he have stories. He was a divorce lawyer until a client's ex, a Boston cop, shot him outside the courthouse. The man's not afraid to say anything. Morris Goldings, our attorney, will go on the show with you. I gave Danny Schechter, the producer, your number to set things up."

"I've never been on television before."

"You'll be fine. There's one more thing. *Boston* magazine was writing up a blurb about the Naked i and asked to interview you. Also, *Evening Magazine* is producing a segment about the club, and Jack Cole from Channel 7 wants you to come on his show."

While distracted by the dizzying inventory of developments, I was also gripped by the apprehension of telling my parents about my career choice. Maybe I was overreacting. I didn't want to say no but didn't want word of my temporary job reaching my parents before I could tell them. They got their news from New York and surely didn't know about *Boston* magazine. Besides, the article would only be a tiny blurb, and a local television talk show would never air in Connecticut. But I couldn't shake thoughts of it going horribly wrong. I had to tell them. In person. Before the magazine article came out and after the licensing board.

"The Socialite Stripper" was the first article published about me.

I met Ray and Mel at a Greek Revival-style building on Boston's Beacon Hill.

"And you are?" the receptionist asked with a proper British accent.

A suited man walked from behind the enclosed waiting area with one hand tentatively poised to shake mine.

"I'm Lucy, Lucy Johnson."

The man withdrew his hand slightly, and the receptionist looked at him. "I'm sorry, you said Lucy?" he asked.

"From the Naked i?"

Ray burst in carrying a briefcase, and Mel sauntered in behind him.

"This is Cheyenne, the one I told you about."

Ray was breathy, his cheeks plump and red.

"Oh, yes, of course. I am so sorry. I thought you might be a press intern. I'm Morris Goldings. Thanks for coming today. Good morning, Mr. Horowitz. Always a pleasure."

"Nice to meet you, Mr. Goldings," I said.

"Please, Morris is fine. A quick refresher," he noted the time on his watch. "Answer yes or no if possible, and don't volunteer any information."

Morris explained that if the board believed the Naked i allowed direct drink solicitation, its license could be revoked or suspended, with fines.

"Remember that accepting commissions on those drinks is perfectly legal."

"And it's perfectly legal to count cards at a blackjack table," Ray said, winking at Mel.

We arrived at the meeting and sat across from two women and one man.

"Good morning, gentlemen, young lady. Let's start with you. No need to be nervous. We just have a few remarkably simple questions for you. Nothing to be nervous about."

The two women hovered their respective pens above yellow legal pads.

My first television show.

"Now, Miss Johnson, as a performer at the Naked i, are you required to sit and talk with patrons?"

The man looked like a condensed version of Gomer Pyle.

"Yes."

He nodded approvingly.

"Good. How does that happen, you know, play-by-play?"

Morris Goldings nudged me. "Answer every question honestly."

"If a guy wants to talk to a dancer, he has to buy us a drink."

"Then you approach them?"

"Only if they buy a drink."

"What about beforehand? Don't you approach the customer before the drink?"

"Sometimes, yes."

The man smiled and glanced at the two women.

"What do you say when you approach him."

"I say hello."

"How is it that the drink for you arrives?"

"The bartender or waitress brings it."

"I see. Do you ask for drinks?"

"No, never. It's against the rules."

"You never approach anyone, but you sit and talk to the customers?"

"No. I mean, yes. I sit and talk with some of them."

"I imagine it's hard to talk with someone you haven't approached."

I waited for Morris to offer help. He didn't.

"Right," I said. "They approach us."

"Oh, I see. They get up from their seats and approach you wherever you might be. They magically know your whereabouts?"

"No, that's silly. We approach them, you know, walk to where they're sitting once they've asked for us. Then they approach us by asking if we want a drink."

"Why would you approach a customer who hasn't asked for you?"

"If you have a question for him or just want to say hi."

"What kind of question?" he asked, looking hopeful.

"Like, 'Why do you come here?' and things like that. Just if I'm bored."

"Then how do you decide to sit down with someone?"

"Only if they're interesting, or they ask."

"Ask? What do they ask?"

"If they can buy me a drink."

Ray stirred in his seat and the man behind the table continued.

"Talk about you asking them to buy you a drink."

"There's never been a time I've asked anyone for a drink. I don't even drink."

"Never? Not once? What if you're thirsty?"

"I told you that I don't ask men to buy me a drink. Nobody does. The first rule we learn about at the Naked i is to never solicit drinks from the customers. The rule is clear: the customer must ask, and we aren't allowed to. But there's no rule against having a conversation with a customer. I don't know how to say it more clearly than that."

His interrogative questioning annoyed me, like he was trying to trick me into saying what he wanted to hear.

"OK, Tell me about the times you've watched the girls you work with approach customers."

"We don't have girls that work at the Naked i."

I felt Ray's shoulders rise next to me. The man looked toward the woman on his right.

"Hello, and thank you for being here," she said. "To help clarify, is the Naked i a strip club that employs girls willing to dance around naked?"

"The Naked i is a strip club, and the strippers are women, not girls," I said.

A small laugh came from Mel.

"Apologies," the man said, smiling at me.

My mind was going in circles by the time it ended.

"I can't thank you enough, Cheyenne," Ray said, walking me out. "Great job. We appreciate it. I'll make sure to leave an envelope for your next shift. If it comes up again, I hope you won't mind my asking."

"Not at all. It was easy enough even though that guy tried to trick me. And you can put me on the night schedule starting a week from Monday, if you want, and would it be OK if I brought in my own water for drinks? I hate tap water."

"Would Perrier do?"

"It would, yes."

"The Princess has arrived, just in time for spring."

"Ray, it's still winter."

"It feels like spring to me," he said.

I was relieved that the *Joe Oteri Show* was broadcast from a small studio in a residential area of Back Bay, and that the reporter from *Boston* magazine couldn't see me for three weeks. This gave me ample time to visit New Canaan.

My mother, the person most rankled by my existence, sat across from me at her kitchen table on Marshall Ridge Road. I knew that my stripping the light fantastic, no matter how well done, would intensify her past resentments, but I couldn't rewrite the past. Being born early, being born at all, my energy, curiosity, and mutinous ways, protesting naps in kindergarten, challenging the gender inequality of toplessness in Blackstone, getting kicked out of Low-Heywood, New Canaan High, and Emma Willard, panting after Cat Stevens, dropping out of school, leaving home to live in a commune, and traveling the country with a man eighteen years my senior couldn't be erased. I was a quintessential problem child, a black sheep thriving in a shadowy field, to which I was about to call attention. I'm sure she was waiting for me to turn things around.

Only my mother made me anxious. I plunged ahead.

"Mother, there's something I need to tell you," I began, my voice shaking.

"You're pregnant," Mother said, in a clipped tone.

"No, no, no. It's about work," I said, breathing deeply. "I know you're going to be mad, but I work at a strip club. There."

"As a waitress, I presume."

"As a stripper."

"Oh, Lucy. Don't be ridiculous. No one wants to see you naked."

"I may not be a beauty queen, but I am a stripper at the Naked i."

Mother took her sweet time lighting a cigarette, and her voice was liquid ice when she finally spoke.

"And you think this is an appropriate line of work for someone of your upbringing? Although you *are* a high school dropout, so maybe it's fitting."

"I didn't think about it. I saw an ad and went to an audition. I left the first club because it was gross, and found the Naked i. It's wicked interesting."

"Not thinking, as usual. Only you could find degrading, demeaning work exciting. It's disgusting, really."

"It's not like that," I protested. "There's more to it than you think. At least I'm supporting myself."

"Good. You can stop taking advantage of your grandmother. You're missing the point, Lucy," Mother's voice tightened. "You're already an embarrassment. When my friends talk about their children and what they're doing, I want to crawl under a rock. How on earth did you turn out to be so damn selfish? Honestly. You never think about anyone but yourself."

"The reason I'm telling you . . ."

"Instead of lying to me, you mean?"

". . . is because I'm being interviewed for a magazine article. I didn't want you to be surprised."

I wholeheartedly believed I wasn't wrapped up in myself, even though I was.

"Surprised isn't the right word. Too bad your vocabulary isn't as good as mine. No wonder you teased boys in elementary school and insisted on going shirtless in Blackstone. Good grief, those shrinks were a goddamn waste of money."

She shot up from her chair.

"Don't you want to ask me more about it?" I said.

"Not particularly. I prefer to ignore the whole thing, if you don't mind."

I wanted to elaborate on the melting pot of characters, the shows, vibrance, ostentatious displays, unpredictability, and fun.

"You would have made a rotten debutante. Good thing I didn't give you my pearls," Mother continued. "Have you told your wayward father? Or your grandmother?"

I arrived at the real-estate agency where my father worked. I couldn't have predicted his reaction.

"Dadee, I wanted to tell you that I'm working at a strip club called the Naked i in Boston."

"The restaurant on Beacon Hill? Good for you, Loot."

"No, Dadee, you're thinking of the 'Hungry i' on Charles Street, the restaurant. This is the Naked i in the Combat Zone, a strip club. I'm a stripper. A dancer."

"Really?" he said, his eyes lighting up. "A stripper? Isn't that something? Have you thought about the consequences up the road?"

"A little."

Priorities, consequences, and regrets seemed like an older person's problems.

"Maybe someday I'll see you perform. And Loot, be patient when you tell your mother. She won't take kindly to this."

"I told her before I came to see you."

"Have you spoken to your grandmother?" my father asked.

I called Nan from his office.

"Nan? Guess what? You don't have to pay my rent anymore. I'm working as a stripper."

"Oh, Lucy! Have you told your father?" Her voice quivered, and I felt sad.

"Yes, and I told Mother, and you can imagine how that went."

"Well, Lu, I think it's fascinating. Why didn't you fib to her a little?"

"Because a magazine is writing an article about where I work and interviewing me for it."

"I'd love to see the article when it comes out. Oh Lu, what an adventure you're having. I love you so."

"I love you too, Nan."

Telling them was the right decision. People in Lake Forest and New Canaan could talk all they wanted while I distanced myself from Mother's disapproval. I could be as whimsical, provocative, and audacious as I wanted. I could be a blond woman in Native American clothing, or a cartoon character.

Upon my return to Boston, I had several fittings for the Pink Panther, and picked up the altered used gowns. One garish outfit, made from flesh-colored material, included a long train and headpiece, all doused in pink feathers. The other, made from black velvet, was sleek and elegant, with circular cutouts edged with rhinestones. I felt prepared for the night shift.

After the *Boston* magazine interview, I was a guest on Jack Cole's television show. Then a WBZ television crew for *Evening Magazine*, a local TV show, filmed me running along the Charles River, shopping at Erewhon, a natural food store on Newbury Street, putting on makeup I never wore, and dancing on stage. The segment was advertised as "From ingenue to exotic Dancer and the *Boston* magazine article was titled the "The Socialite Stripper." *Boston* magazine barely mentioned the Naked i. It was all about me:

The Socialite Stripper

Why did Ray Comenzo, owner of the Combat Zone's Naked i Cabaret, start serving Perrier? And what could draw WBCN's Danny Schechter, Channel 7's Jack Cole, Evening's Maggie Hines, and off-duty members of the vice squad to the same Washington Street strip joint?

The answer to both questions is Princess Cheyenne, the only exotic dancer in the area who is listed in that index of the upper crust, the Social Register. Certainly her background is toney—father from Harvard, mother from Radcliffe, childhood in New Canaan, prep school at Emma Willard. And her appearance is so angelic that she could be your teenage sister—5 feet three, 110 pounds, straight blonde hair, even a fringe of acne across the forehead—if your baby sister is the type to cover herself with baby oil and ride in the buff on the bar.

"I think my father approves," Cheyenne insists, "but my mother is freaked out." The latest ecdysiast to conquer the hearts and loins of Boston's bump-and-grind enthusiasts started to strip "for the money," but now aspires to higher things: next fall she plans to study with Lee Strasberg and hopes for a career on the stage. Her ideal role, Blanche Dubois in A Streetcar Named Desire.

Isn't a bar in the Zone a perfect place for a sweet young thing to learn to rely, as Blanche did, on the kindness of strangers?

Above the two short columns of text was a photograph of me standing in front of the Naked i, smiling. I read and reread the text, wondering where the reporter's facts came from: Mother didn't go to Radcliffe, I didn't use baby oil (although it wasn't a bad idea), and I had not read *A Streetcar Named Desire*. I didn't know what an ingenue or ecdysiast was, hadn't heard of the Social Register, and my name, Lucy Johnson, was missing. I was excited but found it troubling that a stranger unearthed previously unknown facts and took liberties to define me.

I called Nan, hoping for clarification.

"Nan, the article about me just came out, and I wanted to ask you what the Social Register is."

"Oh, Lu, how wonderful! An article about you. Imagine that. Don't forget to mail it to me will you?"

"I will, first thing tomorrow."

"The Social Register is a listing of all the bluebloods. I can send you one of mine if you'd like. Did the article mention your being in the book?"

"Uh-huh."

"Well, that's tacky. You never tell anyone you're in the book. But it is your birthright."

The navy-blue book with dark orange lettering looked like the White Pages to me, with added details like club and societal memberships, yachts and their owners, marriages, births, deaths, domiciles, academic achievements, and affiliations. I didn't see what the big deal was.

With *Evening Magazine* airing, and my starting to work nights, I checked in with Hedy Jo about the Pink Panther.

"Ooh, look who's here, Buzz, the celebrity stripper," Hedy Jo announced.

The people at the sewing tables stopped peddling their machines and looked at me.

"That was quite a little article," said Hedy Jo. "Sam at the joke shop downstairs taped it up behind the counter and wants your autograph."

"My autograph? That's funny. I don't really get the interest, but, oh well. It's fun anyway."

"Sam says it'll snowball, and I agree with him. It's plain as a pig on a sofa. Your fancy background is big news."

"Maybe in the Combat Zone. And it already is snowballing. I'll be on *Evening Magazine* soon."

"My, oh my, moving into prime time. And to think, we knew her when."

"It's strange. I don't see how I'm a big deal."

"Honestly, neither do I just yet. Once the cows come home, I'm sure I'll see it clear as day."

"Let me know when you see it. Meanwhile, how's the costume coming along?"

"Now give me a Southern second."

Hedy Jo fetched a supersized, transparent plastic hat box and toddled around a wooden fabric-cutting table. She motioned me over, and inside the reinforced box was a perfect replica of the Pink Panther head.

"These here are holes for breathing. Not his breathing, yours," she tittered.

She handed me the box like a dinosaur egg, stepped back, and put her hands to her chest.

"I am about to burst!" she said, waiting for my reaction.

"This is awesome. Just what I imagined. I love, love, love it."

"Buzzy? The Princess loves your head."

Hedy Jo plunged her arm deep into a garment bag and produced what looked like the bathing cap my mother wore swimming, minus the kitschy flowers.

"Since the Pink Panther doesn't have long, blond hair, I made the skull cap big enough to tuck your hair into. Then you position the mask and secure both elastics to the hooks in the back of the cap."

Buzzy popped out from the boa-feather wall, smiling for a change.

"I felt like I was in grade-school art class making that silly head," he said. "Nothing like the smell of wet newspaper in flour, glue, and water. How many layers did I put on, dear?"

"I reckon at least twenty, and you made a mess of my kitchen. He was busier than a moth in a mitten. Each layer had to dry for two days. That's why it took so long. Now, here's the rest, but it needs more tweaks."

Inside the garment bag was a bright pink body suit with a thong, G-string, bra, choker, gauntlets, and a detachable tail. The fabric was laden with interlocking patterns of silver curls, hand-sewn, using tubular beads in varying lengths. Galactic sprays of rhinestones expanded away from the swirls, and the hems were finished with Swarovski crystals. No wonder it took her so long to make things and why her costumes cost a small fortune.

"Wow. This weighs a ton," I said.

"It's the rhinestones and crystals."

"I'm in awe."

"Of course you are, dearie. And the bib detaches."

"The bib?"

"The Pink Panther has an oval of lighter pink on his or her chest. I made a point to watch the cartoon. And this here is your G-string, which you probably know. Given its whereabouts, wipe down the tongue in between every use."

"The tongue?"

Hedy Jo put her large hand on top of mine.

"Aw, it's your first G-string, kind of like your first tampon. While I have you here, go in the back and put the body suit on."

It was skin-tight, causing me to waddle out.

"Now, don't you look sexy."

"I love it," I said, "but it's tight. I hate tight clothes."

"Getting used to a second skin takes time, lovey. Besides, it comes off within minutes. Now step on up here."

Hedy Jo patted a carpeted fitting platform and positioned herself on top of a low stool on wheels. She marked every wrinkle and crease with a pin and asked me to assume several positions while chalking where the material needed tightening.

"I intend to make this panther sexy if it's the last light I see. OK, hop down. I took the liberty of making your negligee a circle and a half of crystalline and rayon. The bottom's weighted making it easier to float."

The fourth song of a 20-minute stripper set was the "negligee song." If well-picked, the music had layers, textures, unexpected drops, and drama. To have the desired impact required musical and kinesthetic senses, and the proper fabric. I'd wanted to try it since I started.

"Come back next week to pick up the finished product, and we'll talk about what's next," Hedy Jo said.

"What do you mean, what's next?"

"As a rising star, you'll be needing more of a wardrobe. If you give it a thimble-full of thought, women dress for other women, because if we dressed for men, we wouldn't wear a stitch of clothing," Hedy Jo said, laughing at her conclusion. "Good luck with your first night."

Fortunately, stripping after dark was less portentous than I imagined. The night accelerated everything. Music, laughter, and voices were amplified, movements were faster, and colors brighter. Dancers wore more makeup, had bigger hair, longer nails, and deeper tans. None danced out of dresses. Only day strippers stripped out of mixing gowns. Night dancers had costumes, themes, and shows. They knew what they were doing. At shift's end, they talked about sharing cabs, going out to "breakfast," and borrowed each other's clothing. I was in a warren of knowing women doing practiced women's things.

The music stopped, and the 2 a.m. house lights exposed the club's dark bones. Bottles clinked, bartenders unsnapped their bowties, and waitresses swabbed tables with wet gray rags. Ricky, the iconic night bouncer and disciplinarian, maneuvered his bloated torso behind the bar. He balanced the metal register drawers on one arm while eyeballing residual customers as they shuffled toward the exits.

Career bouncers like Ricky knew about menacing stares, muscular posturing, and calm. He stuffed his bulk into dark clothing and wore gold chains. Aside from the basics, Ricky parted ways with his colleagues on all other fronts. The bouncers of the universe would have done well to emulate everything that was Ricky, right down to his deepest textures. He was a walking barrel, an army of invisible allies behind him, ready to do his will to maintain peace, preferably in Zen-like fashion. When trouble arose, he approached slowly and without excitement, allowing the parties to avoid a poor outcome. If things escalated, Ricky's chest distended, his arms separated from his sides like a cormorant, and only when pressed would he remove someone by the scruff of the neck like a mewling kitten. Ricky showed up when you needed him.

As fascinating and safe as it was, working until 2 a.m. went against my circadian grain. I slogged through my first nights anonymously. I didn't know it was the calm before the storm, the long, fun storm.

Days before *Evening Magazine* aired, Ray hired a photographer who slid me around on a huge roll of white paper. Within a week, photographs of me replaced those of Nikki Wilde and the old-time burlesque stars. The largest image showed me naked, lying tummy down with my lower legs cocked, feet bare, and ankles crossed. I propped myself up on my elbows and had a mischievous, come-hither look. Happy, relaxed, and not the least bit raunchy, I looked to be greeting the passersby. I didn't see a clueless ingenue, a toney blueblood, failed debutante, or black sheep. The manufactured tart conquering hearts and loins and needing the kindness of strangers wasn't in the poster cabinet. I liked the fun person I saw.

CHAPTER 9

Feature Attraction

I was fired up about trying out the Pink Panther costume and didn't see the man in the cowboy hat. I'd arrived an hour early, sat underneath the spotlight, and watched the action, hoping to settle down.

I set the box with the head on the seat next to mine when someone started rapping his knuckles on the bar. I saw his shadow in my peripheral vision, but refused to turn, knowing he was trying to get my attention. His knocking was out of sync with the music's tempo. I became irritated and shifted in my seat.

When I finally turned, he looked away, and when I looked straight ahead, he stared at me again. The back and forth continued until I couldn't contain my impatience.

"Buddy, what do you want? And, my god, stop knocking!"

The man removed his hat.

"Howdy," he said.

"Wait, I recognize you," I said.

"Nah. Us guys, we all look the same. Never been here in my life."

"Come on. Nobody wears a cowboy hat in Boston."

"You're right," he exhaled. "This needs more work."

Without warning, he tore off his eyebrows and I winced. When he removed the ears and sideburns, I recognized Mel, the club owner.

"Mel? What are you doing here? And why are you wearing a disguise? It's not even close to Halloween, and you don't strike me as someone who gets into that sort of thing. You're more serious."

Although I hadn't known Mel long, his presence demanded respect. Even the most unhinged dancer wouldn't oppose him, and I was getting all over his case.

"I wanted to test it," he replied with a grin, "and see how people would react."

"I guess I haven't seen that side of you until now. It's pretty cool. Kind of like improv."

"You see, Lucy, I enjoy playing blackjack, I enjoy winning at blackjack."

"I don't see what blackjack has to do with costumes."

"I count cards," he explained, "and while it's not illegal, casinos object to the practice."

"You're saying you aren't allowed to gamble in a casino unless you're wearing a disguise? I mean, I've never been to one, but that sounds nuts."

I pictured flashing lights, ringing bells, and hundreds of slot machine levers.

Mel explained that card counting was a strategy he used to estimate the probability of winning the next hand. He kept track of cards already dealt, assigned point values, and eventually knew what cards were left in the decks. This allowed him to calculate the odds of winning and adjust his bets. Because he was so skilled, he was one of the first big-money players banned from Atlantic City. Mel was known as an underworld figure and hired former Las Vegas mayor, and alleged mob lawyer, Oscar Goodman to challenge the bans, but failed. By using disguises, Mel concealed his identity from casino staff as well as surveillance cameras.

"Speaking of disguises, why the Pink Panther?" Mel asked.

"It was just an idea I had, thinking about the cage."

"Show tunes might go well with your new act, as would a floor show."

"I'll try, but floor shows are so tacky. And that rug is disgusting."

"I'm confident you'll make it acceptable."

My harebrained idea for costumes took flight. As the Pink Panther, I lounged on top of the cage, puffed on a fake cigarette, and languidly fiddled with my tail before climbing down. Switching to a negligee and shedding my shoes for the fourth song, I twirled the fabric around me, creating waves, wings, and ripples. I spun fast into twisters and slowed to become clouds. I was mesmerized by the colored motions reflecting off mirrors and cocktail glasses. The best part was knowing I could have this much fun every night.

One of many Hedy Jo Star costumes.

Exhilarated and sweaty, I spilled into the dressing room carrying my performance pieces. Chickie, the dancer I first saw sitting with Dori the afternoon I left the Pussycat, had sidestepped her way in front of the mirror, blocking everyone's view. Despite the protests, she wasn't budging.

"I gotta trim, babes, gotta trim," Chickie said. "Can't trim while standing."

"No one wants your leftover pubes on their ass," someone said.

Chickie was the farthest thing from a baby bird one could imagine. She had large, coltish joints, a hunched posture, and slight underbite.

"You guys, I did it," she pronounced. "It was a little scary, but do you think it's too orange?"

She pulled her tube dress up high enough to reveal a yellow puff perched in the center of her triangular area. The other dancers rolled their eyes.

"Just move and then tell us about it. We gotta get ready," said a dancer.

"I doused it with some shit from a brown bottle, and damn, it looks good, right?" Chickie asked, thrusting her pelvis toward the mirror. "And I promise to be better at cleaning up my hairs."

Chickie frequently trimmed her pubic area using a disposable razor against dry skin. The plastic chairs created static electricity, causing the shaved hairs to leap onto positively charged surfaces like fabric.

"Sorry. It's all I got to show off," she added quietly. "I got no tits and I ain't especially gorgeous."

There was something sad about her reasoning.

In 1978, before vajazzles (genital decorations like crystals and/or glitter), anal bleaching, and Brazilian bikini waxes, a grown woman with a hair-free mons resembled a colossal six-year-old. Back then, having pubic hair was an asset, providing it was trimmed, ornamental, and neat. Women shaped their hair into lightning bolts, hearts, arrows, martini glasses, checkerboards, and initials.

Montana kept it all. She didn't care if it protruded out the sides of her G-string. Kind and soft-spoken, no one criticized her full nest and dark underarm wisps. Montana collected small stones and brought in swaths of cut wildflowers that she thoughtfully arranged for the makeup table and top of the toilet tank. Instead of eating subs or pizza, she gulped nuts from mason jars and chomped on raw zucchini. She hung herbs to dry from the locker vents and occasionally smudged the area with burning sage.

After Chickie's highlighting experiment, we noticed her newly colored tuft glowing purple in the black lights. Men didn't notice the glow, but stopped asking if she was "a real blond." Matching pubic to head hair became a collective quest and was discussed at length in the dressing room.

"Men are so stupid," said Dori. "It doesn't always match any old way."

The nucleus of the Naked i was its dressing room. More complex and informative things happened there than in any other part of the club. Far from a shrine to sensuality and glamour, the dressing room was a refuge, debate hall, and vocational classroom. The curriculum was never the same and included practical and theoretical gems.

Dancers molded plastic shoes with blow dryers, applied lipstick to their nipples, employed sea sponges for menstruation, and created skin art using tanning beds.

Unregulated tanning salons debuted in 1978. Dancers had expendable cash and plugged themselves into rigorous tanning schedules weeks in advance. The coffin-like beds and chicken wire cages presented artistic and aesthetic opportunities. Triangular patches made breasts look bigger, half-bronzed rear ends appeared rounder, and sharp frontal Vs made the torso look taller.

Martha, a tanning expert, had skin like a polished walnut and espoused the benefits of contrasting skin because, "Ya can't tell a tan without lines, so why bother?" She talked about how to avoid pesky crease lines from lying prone on an unforgiving surface. Flesh flattened into folds made fine, white lines underneath the butt cheeks.

"Nothing says fake tan more than crease lines. Grab one cheek at a time, pull it out and let it stick to the glass before you get sweaty. Or use a standing booth. I bend over and stick my ass as close to the lights as possible."

Martha taped a diamond pattern to her body for the Tudor-window-style grid across her torso. Linda applied candle wax and Elmer's Glue to her rear end to create a rose, resulting in her paying extra charges to the tanning parlor for cleaning the bed. Udon painted black fingernail polish onto transfer paper to create white swirls on either side of her hips, and Chickie became a regular at the hardware store, purchasing sticky sign letters to spell out different words, like "hot" and "yes."

Having one's period was a practical problem for strippers. The simplest solutions were either snipping or tucking the tampon string, but there were other options. Montana, the dancer who showed customers her array of treasures from the natural world and set up altars in her locker, explained using sea sponges instead of tampons.

"They're little brown sponges that you stuff up there until it's full. Then you pluck it out, rinse it, and put it back in. You can get them at the health food store."

"I prefer a diaphragm. It's like a dam," Gisele, a new dancer, said.

"I'm cramping up just thinking about it. Then there's the mess," Jazz, an especially friendly dancer, said.

"You take it out in the shower. And if it fits, no cramps," Giselle said.

"No shower here. Then what?" asked Jazz. "You're stuck with a puddle."

"Really?" Giselle rolled her eyes. "It's called a toilet."

"Sponges are wicked comfortable," Montana said, "and all you need is a sink."

"Tampons are fine by me. Just change them more often," Jazz said.

"Fine until one sneaks out during a floor show and glows purple like the head of a torpedo," said Giselle. Anything bleached or white turned an eerie purple in black light.

"How can I get a diaphragm, Giselle?" I asked.

"Just go to your gynecologist. In fact, I have one that's brand new, never used," said Giselle. "I'll bring it in for you."

Brittany, the tallest dancer I'd seen, strolled in with a warm, smirky expression.

"I can hear you hens cackling from La Grange Street. It sounds like the Second Coming."

Her voice was deep and silky.

"Just talking about periods," said Jazz.

"Since I know everything about nothing," Brittany laughed, "I'll tell you."

"No, Britt, you really can't," said Jazz, "You had a penis."

I assumed Jazz's comment was a private joke.

"By the way," Jazz continued, "this is Princess Cheyenne. You may have noticed the photographs of her out front. She's caused quite a stir. Between *Boston* magazine and *Evening Magazine*, who knows what's next?"

The media's power and momentum were exponential. After *Evening Magazine* aired, men I didn't know started asking for "The Princess." One such man arrived with a cooler. I couldn't imagine why a customer needed a cooler in a strip club. The red and white box balanced on a barstool where the unremarkable, compact man stood like a sentinel, guarding the cargo. Upon seeing me, he grinned like a boy on a playground and popped a TicTac into his mouth.

"Hi, you must be the guy who wanted to meet me."

"Oh my god, it's you, the *Evening Magazine* girl. Aw yeah, please sit. Psyched! Name's Guddler. And I know you're The Princess."

An unmistakable fish odor emanated from his clothing, and the customer seated next to Guddler fanned his hand in front of his nose.

"Hey," said the customer, "you're that debutante gal I read about in *Boston* magazine."

"She was just on *Evening Magazine*," Guddler emphasized, pulling his shoulders back. "If you'll excuse me, I asked for her company before you did."

"I'm patient," the man said.

Bruce, the bartender, brought over a bottle of Perrier for me and a can of beer for Guddler.

"That article wasn't exaggerating about the Perrier water," Guddler said, moving his cooler to another seat.

"You aren't carrying someone's organs, are you?" I asked.

"Crustaceans," he whispered.

"Haitians?" asked Bruce, mishearing Guddler's one-word explanation.

"No, no, there are lobsters inside, still alive."

Bruce's eyes enlarged behind his glasses, and he laughed softly. "I gotta say that, of all the firsts, this rates in the top twenty!"

"Aren't you gonna ask why I am walking around with live lobsters?"

"Sure. Why are you walking around the Combat Zone with live lobsters?"

"Lobsters for the famous one here. And they're fresh, on ice. I caught them four hours ago, scuba diving. They're still moving around a little." Guddler swiveled to me. "You have a lobster pot, right?"

"Uh, no, I don't. I'm sorry. It's so sweet of you."

"You brought her lobsters that she has to cook . . ." Bruce slid his hands down his apron. ". . . and crack open? What if she cuts herself? Come on buddy. Where's your chivalry?"

Guddler's chubby little hands dropped to his thighs.

"You are so right, my man. Please put my beer on ice, and I'll be back in an hour or so. And, Princess, I'm wicked sorry. I'll fix this."

He lugged the cooler toward the door, and suddenly there was a thump, followed by spilling slush and two loud voices.

"You should watch where you're going, man! Jesus!" and "Holy fuck, what are those things?"

"My lobsters," he cried, "the lobsters for The Princess. Oh, man, I blew it. I screw everything up."

I didn't expect Guddler to return, but he did, with the meat of five cooked lobsters, lemon wedges, cocktail sauce, a lobster fork, a plastic plate, and seven Wet-Naps.

"I'm wicked sorry again for not thinking to cook them. Ugh!" Guddler said, thumping the heel of his thumb against his temple. "You probably like them hot, with melted butter. I didn't even think of that."

"I like them every way. Any way you want to bring them is fine and beyond generous."

"I'll bring more, don't you worry. Consider me your personal lobster man from this point on."

Guddler didn't pull traps onto a boat. He collected them using scuba equipment. Every month, without fail, my very own lobster man arrived with the same cooler. Since he couldn't afford dancer's drinks. I lingered when he came in and had to convince him I wanted to talk, not for his lobster meat, but for the person he was.

Ray was right. Mixing was easier at night, especially on weeknights, when most regulars came in. They often bought bottles of champagne, which yielded higher commissions, but were more challenging for teetotalers like me. I learned how to pour champagne into the ice bucket or invited other dancers over to help drain the bottles. One dazzled while the other guzzled or poured. I still couldn't trick myself into liking the drink hustle but tolerated it to finance more outfits and guarantee ongoing fun.

As soon as I had enough money, I trotted into Hedy Jo's for more. Within months I'd ordered a Wonder Woman, Las Vegas-style Indian, and a red dress for a total of $12,000, not including the Pink Panther.

"For someone new to the business, you sure are diving in," Hedy Jo said. "Remember that you're the new chicken in the house, my dear, and any time there's a new chicken, that new chicken better sneak into an empty roost in the middle of the night. Otherwise, them chickens will gang up on it and kill it. Imagine? Those sinful chickens."

"Are you saying that chickens don't recognize strangers?" I asked.

"I reckon not."

"And dancers are chickens?"

"I reckon so."

I don't know who enjoyed the shows more, me or the audience. I loved the challenge of brainstorming themes and putting acts together. Although unwritten, the stripper rule of exclusivity forbade performance plagiarism, assuring there was only one bunny, one Wonder Woman, one kitten, or one schoolgirl on the roster.

Strippers loved playing dress up. Rudimentary themes were repetitive and required little imagination. The outfit was thought to be enough. Schoolgirls wore crotch-length plaid skirts and patent leather spiked heels. Some carried metal lunch boxes and rulers to complement their scholarly ensembles. The cheerleader was also in the academic realm. She could have worn sneakers, but none did. Beyond the ribboned pigtails and pompoms, perkiness, splits, and cartwheels were mandatory. One overly enthusiastic dancer incorporated a plastic megaphone and cheered, "Give me an N . . . Give me an A . . . Give me a K. . . ." More than once, I heard a customer say, "Give me a break."

Maids wore the requisite aprons, bonnets, and stockings while flitting about with feather dusters. One generous domestic filled a Windex spray bottle with vodka and administered streaming shots to the audience before she was found out. Nurses, secretaries, and flight attendants were plebeian and short-lived, as were little girls with lollipops and bobby socks.

Feline costumes required drawn-on whiskers, ears, tails, and animal-print fabric to strip out of. Insects got some play in the form of bumblebees and ladybugs but didn't easily lend themselves to sexy interpretations.

Mythical themes abounded. Naturally, devils wore red capes and tiny satin horns and carried glittering tridents. Angels in white attached halos with wire hangers and sprouted generic, flimsy wings. There were magicians, clowns, mermaids and nuns, Cinderellas and Cleopatras, cops and robbers. Anything the mind could play with was fair game.

Then there were the Lolas. Mel appointed the Lolas based on beauty and compliance. If one stripper named Lola left, Mel found another. The

Lolas didn't need themes, shows, or fancy costumes. Their polished skin, impossibly trim waistlines, and cantaloupe breasts were enough. The first Lola I remember had a short finger-wave hairstyle like a flapper and slouched posture, probably from trying to hide her breasts as a young teen. While walking, she scuffed the stage and then, without musical provocation, thrashed about as though seized by an internal storm. At the end of her set, she placed an imaginary dot on her glossy lower lip with one finger, and the crowd went bonkers. I couldn't possibly have balanced my success on one imaginary dot.

All the designated Lolas had acquiescent personalities and beat-deafness. None walked or moved rhythmically, and percussion was ignored. The deficit was most noticeable during the negligee song, when arms chopped the air like hedge trimmers, causing the fabric to clump and twist around their torsos. Like a photographer's eye, a numerical brain, or perfect pitch, the relationship between music and movement either was or was not. Best, then, for Lola to abandon the billowy prop and just walk. Their mysterious beauty efficiently carried them.

Plenty of non-Lolas couldn't dance, either. They could be seen wrangling with their thongs or trying to untwist their bra straps. Lacking body or spatial awareness wasn't a stripper's death sentence if she could perfect her walk and adjust her carriage. A confident presentation and runway model stride could conquer the room. If that wasn't doable, some strippers looked cute when figuring out what to do next.

Although rare, a few dancers were terminally klutzy. I recall one woman making a series of deep knee bends before standing and waiting for someone to clap.

Some fancied themselves modern dancers and took uncomfortably long strides, devouring the space around them like naked banshees.

In its most basic sense, the work required beauty or performance aptitude, but not necessarily both. Both beat-deaf and musically inclined dancers used vintage stripper moves, like bumping, grinding, and the occasional shimmy. More common were the neo-stripper gestures, like butt slapping, facial caresses, hair tugging, finger sucking, tongue waggling, lip licking, hip thrusting, finger pointing, gluteus shimmying, or breast smashing. The worst neo-stripper move was pointing at one's crotch. Come on. Men already knew it was there.

Whenever I lapsed into a cliché move, I felt like a caricature. It felt comical to blow kisses, bite on my lower lip, or paw myself, and I wouldn't put my fingers anywhere near my mouth. When men knew what to expect, they stopped looking.

To perfect or control what men saw, dancers eyeballed their movements in front of every reflective surface, onstage and off, and talking to reflections was standard. I'd break down laughing if I attempted hip circles in front of a mirror or struck some alluring poses. What would I be checking exactly? Even if I knew, my astigmatism precluded visual accuracy. On stage, dancers lost the audience when they watched themselves in the wall mirrors along the runway. When I glimpsed myself, I felt like I was falling into the bar pit.

After several comments about my butt, I looked at it in a mirror, and one time became many.

"What is that dimple on your ass?" many customers asked, to which I replied, "You're being kind. It's more like a dent."

The most original query was, "Did your father take you pheasant hunting and shoot you in the ass?"

The crater on my right cheek came from an unfortunate run-in with a horse at the Vershire School in Vermont. I was in the "horse program," and my steed, Aquarius, disliked having her right rear hoof picked. Picking is done facing away from the rear of the horse. Aquarius coiled her hind leg against her belly, unleashed its strength, and caused the hoof and shoe to pound into my ass so hard I was in the air before slamming into a stall door 10 feet away. It left a noticeable dent in my right butt cheek. Thus, my rear end had a respectable shape and decent symmetry but suffered her forever mark. There was nothing I could do about it, so I stopped looking.

Close body scrutiny sold me on the importance of staying healthy and fit, so I gave up cabs and traveled the sixteen blocks to and from work by bicycle. Boston's conglomeration of one-way streets protected me from being followed to and from, and the fresh air was the next best thing to a shower.

I kept running, with the Boston Marathon in mind. I ran intervals at the MIT track once or twice a week and, on days off from work, ran long, slow distances along the Charles River. I considered body conditioning part of the job.

One morning, while peddling home from the MIT track, a car clipped my bike's front tire, and I fell sideways onto the pavement. I wasn't in pain, but my shoulder joint felt loose and wobbly. A doctor said I'd torn the rotator cuff and suggested surgery or weight training to strengthen the muscles around the tear.

Universe Gym was just past the Museum of Science on the Boston-Somerville line. I climbed the stairs, past a boxing ring on the first floor, and followed the grunts and sounds of heavy objects to the second floor. It was one massive room with mirrors, low-standing racks of dumbbells, and various benches and slanted chairs. The air smelled like rubber, and chunky weights lay scattered next to a handful of men in impossibly tiny sleeveless shirts. One man dropped a pair of dumbbells beside a bench and swayed toward me.

"May I help you, Miss?" the man boomed, walking behind the counter.

"Yeah, hi. I wondered how much it is to use the weights, or join."

He had a goofy smile and hooded eyes. A vibrating thump caused me to whip around. An orange-tanned mass of veins, muscle, and ligament stretched out on a bench, and two equally enormous men pulled large, iron plates from a bar. When they stood, their arms were so swollen they couldn't rest by their sides.

"You're awfully jumpy," the man behind the counter said. "Now, who are you looking for?"

"I want to start lifting weights because I hurt my shoulder, and the doctor said it would be good."

"We ain't got no lady's locker room or bathroom," said the man.

"I guess that's fine."

"If you have to go or change, I gotta clear out the locker room, which the members don't take kindly to."

"Should I go somewhere else? Do you know where I could go?"

"Maybe that Elaine Powers place, a little fitness chain for girls."

"Women," I said.

"OK, darling, women."

"Do they have weights there?"

"Puh, no. Maybe ankle weights. It's the same no matter where you go if you're after weightlifting. Maybe you could time your workouts with that broad, um, what's that broad's name that comes here?"

An anonymous voice answered, "Ina."

"Yeah, Ina."

"OK, when does she come in?"

"Who the hell knows? When she wants." All the men chuckled. "Name's Ralphie."

"I'm Lucy."

Ralphie leaned into his meaty forearms on the counter. "Do you swing the other way?" he lowered his voice.

"No. Why?"

"A lot of bulked-up broads are lezzos. If you're lookin' to get hitched, this isn't the place. You don't want to get wrapped up with these clowns. And what if you can't have kids? There's stuff out there that says muscles make women sterile." He laughed. "Notice I said women, not broads? Pretty good, eh?"

"I'm not looking to meet anyone," I said, "I just want to tone up a little, geez Louise. Do you put men wanting to join through the same crap?"

"Of course not. I'll give you a trial membership for a month, see how it works out, ya know? And, if you're a pain in my ass," he pointed to the entrance, "you're outta here."

"That's great. What should I bring?"

"Look, kiddo," Ralph stood and walked to my side of the counter, "I ain't holding your hand. Wear gym clothes. Bring water, a towel, and gloves."

A blender started up in a separate room behind the counter. "For fuck's sake, Georgy, I'm talkin' here. Like I was sayin', we'll give it a shot."

I noticed a messy stack of *Muscle Builder*, Joe Weider's bodybuilding magazine, on the end of the counter, and a shelf with large vats of protein powders.

"Ok, I'll be in tomorrow. What are your hours?"

"Early and late. Open at 5 a.m. and close at 10 p.m.," Ralphie said.

A man with massive thighs and a stained white towel hanging from his neck waddled toward me before I reached the door.

"Hey, I know this chick!" he said, shuffling faster. "Hold up there. Where the fuck do I know you from?"

"I don't know. I'm not from around here."

"I'll figure it out."

After my bike accident, Mel invited me to lunch at Jacob Wirth's, a German restaurant and iconic Boston venue.

"I'm raising your nightly pay to $65."

"What? $65? Thank you so much. Wow."

"Keep it to yourself."

"I will. Thank you so much, Mel."

"Keep it up, and you'll get more."

"Oh, no problem. Hedy Jo has three costumes in the works."

"Shows are important, but I'm talking about the publicity. Consider yourself the Naked i's first permanent feature attraction."

The red letters on the marquee, "TOTALLY NUDE COLLEGE GIRL REVUE," were replaced by "FEATURE ATTRACTION PRINCESS CHEYENNE."

My deck was stacked, and I knew it.

CHAPTER 10

Curzon Street, London

Despite having been picked for the team and made captain, I didn't always play by the rules. After a year of practice, I could walk in toothpick heels, but not gracefully. My rebellion against makeup covered up my lack of knowledge. When I shopped at department stores like Filene's or Jordan Marsh, I saw women consulting with makeup aficionados and couldn't fathom what they were talking about. I licked my lipstick off within minutes, and mascara ended up on my nose. Getting and maintaining fake nails was a day-long excursion that seemed bound for failure and hair coloring required a schedule I was unwilling to maintain.

I didn't own a purse, blow dryer, or curling iron (forty years later, I still don't). I considered shaving my legs but didn't. Instead, thanks to Hedy Jo Star, I discovered thigh-high boots, the closest I'd ever get to embracing heels.

At the final fitting for Wonder Woman, she suggested that gold boots would complete the show. Thigh-highs had stiletto heels, but with support, like ankle braces.

"What's that bruise?" Hedy Jo asked, pins jutting from one side of her mouth.

"Bruise? Where?"

"On the front of your hip."

I twisted to each side but saw no bruise. Hedy Jo pressed her finger to my leg and sighed.

Native American jewelry was at the top of my Christmas list.

"Right here," she leaned closer. "The upside-down letters."
"Oh, the tattoo I did."
"I know that, child, but what do the initials stand for?"
"It's for Cat Stevens' real name, Steven Demetre Georgiou. Customers and dancers ask about it all the time."
"You could get it removed," said Hedy Jo.
"Maybe," I said, touching the spot with a fingertip. "Not yet, I don't think."
"Eventually, you'll get sick and tired of answering the same questions repeatedly."
"I already am. Especially the question, 'What happened to your ass?' and 'What's a nice girl doing in a place like this?' I hate that question and hate being called a girl."
"Why'd you get the tattoo any old way?"
"He was, or is, an obsession. I lost my virginity to him. Crazy."

Curzon Street, London | 131

From debutante to exotic dancer.

Tonight at 7:30:
Find out why 19-year-old Lucy left her wealthy home in suburban Connecticut for the life of an exotic dancer in Boston's combat zone. ALSO: Linda Harris continues our "great escape" to Hawaii

evening magazine 4

From ingenue to exotic dancer.

Tonight at 7:30:
Find out why 19-year-old Lucy left her wealthy home in suburban Connecticut to become "Princess Cheyenne," an exotic dancer in Boston's combat zone. Then, Evening shows you an unusual group that brings music to deal people. ALSO: Linda Harris continues our "great escape" to Hawaii

evening magazine 4

Our winners (or losers). Princess Cheyenne: Think you've seen everything? How about a Combat Zone stripper who is listed in that index of status and propriety, the Social Register? Well, that's exactly what Princess Cheyenne is, making her noblesse who obliges. Cheyenne, whose real name and initial are Lucy J., struts her high-class stuff at the Naked I. She prepped for this career at the posh Emma Willard School (although only for a month and a half). Her mother attended tony Pine Manor, and her father is a Harvard man and successful realtor in Connecticut. Both, Lucy says, are looking forward to her retirement.

NO SHY ANNE: Princess Cheyenne, feature stripper at the "Naked i Cabaret" in the Combat Zone, is in the Social Register. (Under her real name which is for Eye to know and you to guess.)
Her veddy, veddy socially prominent family lives in Connecticut, doesn't come to her opening nights. Such prudes!
(Also prudish is the management at the Naked i, which adamantly refused to give Cheyenne's picture to the Covered Eye. Is The Page too risque for those sensitive souls?)

The media's snowball effect.

"Not many people get that far with a pop star now, do they?"

"Yeah, I guess. He's a Muslim now. He changed his name to Yusuf Islam and gave up music."

"Sounds like you outgrew him."

I hadn't. I'd reasoned that our initial meeting was preparation for a life together. It had been almost three years since meeting him at JP's in New York and my obsession had not abated.

Hedy Joe's wearable iteration of Wonder Woman included gauntlets, a lasso, a cape, a crown, a corset, and blue shorts marked by white stars. I wanted to add a layer of interest to the ensemble and found that layer in a character I made up named Mildred Schwartz, a stubborn librarian with failing eyesight. When the library let her go, she accepted a position cleaning at the Naked i, or so my story went.

I found Mildred's dull green dress, pillbox hat with netting, cat eyeglasses, argyle knee socks, and clumpy shoes at the Salvation Army. Before the show, I crept behind customers' backs dressed as Mildred and wedged between them to swab the counter with a rag. It was hard to keep a straight face as the customers reflexively lifted their beer bottles and cocktails when they saw her coming. She finished cleaning the bar and her poor vision mistakenly landed her on stage. The audience booed. It was hard to believe they didn't catch on.

A bewildered Mildred cleaned her glasses with her dress sleeve and sometimes a bartender handed her Windex. While resetting her eyeglasses, the pointed rim inevitably snagged on the pillbox netting, leaving the glasses dangling in front of her face. She bumbled along the runway until every light in the club went out, and the audience was plunged into darkness. The Salvation Army ensemble was off in a snap, and I climbed into my gold thigh-highs. The DJ lit sparklers behind the curtain, and Mildred reappeared to the audience as Wonder Woman. Dazzling the crowds with the iconic red, blue, and gold costume was satisfying, but the action was in the prequel.

After the show I bagged up Mildred's clothing and Wonder Woman's patriotic garb. Giselle smacked her rigid box purse onto the makeup table like a declaratory flag as I passed by.

"I see you've become a homeless, unemployed librarian, Princess," she said.

"Yeah. Might as well experiment and have some fun."

"Now that you're *the* feature attraction," her voice slowed, and her hands made air quotes, "you need to start doing floor shows. Obviously. Do you have some religious objection or are you disfigured down there?"

"Neither. It's just a little trashy. Plus, I wouldn't know what on earth to do."

"You do know you're in a strip club, right? Anyway, I have your dam, you know, for your periods. Remember? No blood on the stage. Or running down your legs. That would be unsightly."

"Oh, right. Great."

Giselle had arrived from Florida, first as Brandy, then Tiffany, and finally, as Giselle. When dancers and customers mistakenly called her Gazelle, they were reprimanded.

"It's not GA-zell; it's JI-zell. Everyone knows the famous ballet, Giselle, where jilted brides force men to dance until they die."

Everyone but me.

Giselle's stage presence showed nothing of her caustic personality. She was one of only a few dancers who wore short hair well. The clipped style and ginger color complemented her creamy skin, long neck, freckles, and regal posture. Her joints had little resistance, as though she'd loosened the screws, yet her gestures were precise and purposeful. She always placed her feet in one of the four ballet positions, on or off stage, and held her arms in a classical port de bras.

She claimed to be new to stripping, but had unflappable confidence. She wasted no time kissing Mel's ass by indulging his obsession with Broadway show tunes and beat me to the punch. When dancing to the song, "One," from *A Chorus Line*, she punctuated the melody by flinging one straight, muscular leg upward like it was nothing and unsettled the ceiling tiles. Flakes from the degrading panel looked like snow in the spotlight. Mel looked on, grinning. She finessed "Let Me Entertain You" from *Gypsy*, "All That Jazz" from *Chicago*, and most impressively, "42nd Street" with its bursts of frenetic tap dancing.

No matter how halting a score, she moved from one pose to the next with legs turned out and arms gently curved like feathers. She raised the negligée into a cyclone while spotting perfectly on every turn, her silhouette edged in ghostly blue. Customers watched. Bartenders and waitresses paused. We were all hypnotized.

She effortlessly dropped into full splits and pioneered the carpet-free floor routine saying, "It's gotta be cleaner than that nasty rug." The textile remnant used to shield knees, elbows, and whatever else from hardwood burns was used by countless women with divergent cleanliness standards. Mel happily approved the change, and those willing to bare everything on a bare floor did. The carpet went into the dumpster.

Most dancers eventually performed floor shows to please Mel and to stay competitive. Ideally, a floor show was executed with some elegance. Whether squatting, crab-walking, or crawling, it mattered not how the legs got spread, just that they did, which, by itself could never be elegant. The room always quieted as the dancer's body sunk, and men held their breath, waiting for gynecological intimacy. Once underway, the comments and requests started. My favorite was, "Show me your vagina."

Anyone in a strip club asking to "see" a vagina is misinformed. Under spread-leg conditions, specific anatomy is visible, but not the birth canal. The vagina is inside a woman's body and can only be seen with a speculum.

I put away the plastic box containing the vaginal dam in my locker, and Brittany came striding in. She stood away from the table to assess her white minidress. She looked better than Linda Evans and was close to six-feet tall, with a coiffed platinum bob and shocking tan.

"Have you all been on vacation?" asked Giselle.

"Nope. We purchased a personal tanning bed, which is why we look so fabulous," said Brittany, "and you look so frail and anemic."

"I prefer milky to angry red, peeling, and blistering. And I'll look fucking fabulous when I'm your age," said Giselle.

"I'll give you the name of my plastic surgeon so you can be prepared when the time comes. Staying out of the sun can't save the likes of you," Brittany said.

A feline-looking woman burst through the door.

"Where's my husband?" the woman asked.

"Here and available, as always," said Brittany, kissing the woman on both cheeks. "Cherelle, this is Princess Cheyenne, of unknown royalty."

Cherelle shook her hair while fluffing it with the backs of her hands. She was the color of creamed coffee, compact and beautiful, the outer corners of her eyelids tapered into a neat point.

"Oh my god, wait! Someone just told me about some article and how you're a rich kid, but working here. Is that you?" she asked, cocking one hip and studying me.

"Yeah, but I'm not rich. I'm pretty much disowned at this point."

"So, Brittany, if you're the husband, and Cherelle's the wife, doesn't that mean you have a dick?" Giselle said, changing the subject.

"I'm shocked. That's a narrow view for someone who seems to be so sophisticated," Brittany said. "But, yes, once upon a time, I had a dick the size of my arm. Then I rubbed the genie's bottle, made a wish, and a voodoo doctor turned me into a woman. Before that, I was a lesbian named Bob trapped in a man's body."

Giselle didn't even laugh.

"Yeah, OK. And Cherelle's your wife? Or whatever?"

Giselle postured away from the table, extending her arms and fingers in a useless pose. She always needed to be right.

"Cherelle is the love of my life. The reason I became myself," Brittany growled. "But, seriously, they turned the tip into a clitoris and my ball sack into a labium. I'm a rarity, a medical miracle."

Dori painted triangles on the outer corners of her eyes with liquid eyeliner. They looked like tiny, black wings.

"Hey, how do they all do that shit anyway?" asked Dori, pausing her handiwork. "I mean, it sounds gross at first, but now that I know you and shit, it's interesting."

"I thought you'd never ask. Give me one second."

Brittany returned from her locker with a flashlight, turned a chair away from the mirror, and sat down.

"Oh my god, honey," said Cherelle, her hands resting on Brittany's shoulders. "What makes you think anyone is interested? Please don't do this."

"I know that everyone is fascinated," she laughed. "Besides, I live for this. Ladies, come over for the tour. It's not going to bite. Who wants the flashlight? Dori, get your pale self over here and stop messing with your makeup. There's no one here to see it anyway."

"Fine. Gimme the dang flashlight," Dori said, opening her palm. "I ain't afraid of no plastic vagina."

"It's called vaginoplasty, and there's no plastic. The surgery wasn't pretty, but the results were," Brittany said.

Dori snapped the flashlight on, and a few dancers gathered beside her.

"I hope I don't have gas," said Brittany with a laugh.

"Me too. It looks like a regular old cooch," said Dori, passing the flashlight. Is there a vagina in there?"

"They turn the shaft of the penis inside out," Brittany spoke quickly, "and pop the tip through a tiny hole in the skin for the clitoris, and the rest becomes a canal called the neo-vagina."

"Do you get your period?" Chickie asked.

"Really? Let's think about that," said Giselle. "You need a uterus and ovaries to menstruate."

"To what?"

"Oh my God. To bleed." Giselle rolled her eyes.

"No period. I bled from the surgery. I had to rinse with a lubricant and use a catheter every day. After the packing was removed, I dilated the inside with an expander. I still do. Otherwise, it would collapse."

"Where does your pee come out?"

"The same place it always did, only with a shorter trip."

"You can't come, right?"

"Of course I can. Your clitoris has a shaft that fills up with blood like a dick. Everything's attached to nerves and muscles. My orgasms are positively wild," Brittany said, reaching for Cherelle's hand. "Right, honey?"

"What did you think when you first woke up?"

"I cried like a baby. I've never been so relieved."

"Do your kids call you Mom or Dad?"

"They call me Dad."

"Why did you go through all of that?"

"To become who I've been my whole life. People told me I was crazy and to give up. Surgery didn't make me a woman; I already was a woman. Giving up on your dreams is never an option, ladies. Never. Go for what you want, all the way. There's no time like the present."

Brittany was right. There was no time like the present.

After working six days a week for over a year, it was time for a vacation. Yusuf Islam lived in London. That fit the bill.

I applied for a passport, got some American Express traveler's checks, and purchased a round-trip ticket to London. Knowing nothing about London hotels, I went to the Boston Public Library, where the most straightforward thing was to search available material and choose something familiar, like the Ritz. I also searched the library's card catalogs for basic information on a religion I knew nothing about, Islam, and learned about the importance of modest attire.

During my first year at the Naked i, everything about Cat Stevens's life had changed. It seemed that fame and fortune didn't lead him to a higher purpose and none of the religions or practices he'd studied resonated deeply enough. He'd sought answers to complex questions after a life-threatening case of tuberculosis in 1968. The quest intensified in 1976 when a riptide off Malibu, California, pulled him far from shore. Believing death was imminent, he promised to devote his life to God if he survived. Soon after, his brother David gave him the Qur'an I'd seen in his room at the Pierre Hotel. Once he answered the Islamic call to prayer, he didn't look back. Cat Stevens changed his name to Yusuf Islam, wore a thobe, prayed five times a day, and studied Islamic texts.

I repeated the name "Yusuf" over and over.

On Sunday, May 13, 1979, I showered twice, packed, repacked, checked and rechecked my passport, cleaned the refrigerator, and remembered the homeless man who slept in the dumpster behind the building.

The frail man survived the winter by burrowing into the warmth of decomposing food. Our waste both protected and sustained him. Although his situation made me sad, I marveled at his common sense. I regularly packed up leftover food and slid it into the dumpster. If he was inside, he popped his face over the green rim and smiled. I wondered how he managed his life with such civility. Before leaving for the airport, I emptied my fridge and taped a note to the food bag.

"Dear Sir, I am going away for a few weeks and won't be able to leave food for you. But I will be back. Please don't give up. I am glad that it is getting warmer for you."

I slid the bag onto the container's ramp, and he emerged from his nest.

"Here's some food. I'll be away for a little bit. I'm sorry."

He grumbled unintelligibly and pulled himself up, his hands shaking while he considered the note. I'd not heard him speak.

"Where you off to?"

The clarity of his speech surprised me.

"London, England."

"For a British boyfriend?"

"I don't know about that."

"You be good."

I arrived at Heathrow International at dawn the following day, hailed a taxi, and checked into the Ritz Hotel.

"Good morning, Madame," a uniformed man said, bowing.

He pulled a luggage cart toward me and handed me a key attached to a white marble square engraved with the room number.

"Oh, thank you. How on earth am I supposed to carry this gigantic thing in my pocket?" My voice cracked.

"Pardon me, Madame?"

"Oh gosh, nothing, sorry, just talking to myself. Thank you. A little tired."

He showed me to the room, snapped open a mahogany luggage rack with one hand, and flipped the suitcase onto its straps.

"Madame," he bowed.

"Right, one second, please. Let me get something."

I hadn't yet changed my currency and handed him a $50 bill.

"I'm so sorry. I haven't changed my money over."

"Madame, this is most generous. Might I suggest asking the front desk to exchange your foreign currency? They'd be more than happy to accommodate, and I'll happily accept less."

"No, please. I've never traveled overseas before. I mostly have traveler's checks anyway."

"Oh, my. Thank you ever so much. Once you settle, sign your checks, and visit the front desk. They will happily exchange them for pounds. And, if your agenda allows, afternoon tea is not to be missed."

"I'll try it. Can I ask why you all wear white gloves on your shoulders?"

"One must always be prepared to greet Her Royal Majesty or other royal family members. This is only done while wearing gloves. Oh, and please don't hesitate to ask for a map or directions."

"OK. That reminds me. I'll need a map. And you don't happen to know where Curzon Street is, do you?"

27 Curzon Street was the management address on the back of one of Cat Stevens's last albums.

"It is a seven-block walk from here, Madame. The front desk will prepare a route for you."

In the spirit of being overly prepared, I wasted no time retrieving the map and asking the front desk to look up the telephone number to Yusuf's office. I called before I had time to think.

"Good day, this is Nicki."

"Good morning, Nicki. I just arrived from the United States to see Yusuf and wanted to know what time he would be available."

"Oh, yes, he is due to be in tomorrow, just after lunch time. If this suits you."

That was easy.

There was nothing in my way. I skipped dinner and fell asleep underneath crisp, heavy sheets surrounded by unfamiliar sounds on the street below my balcony.

The next morning, I awoke to clacking hooves below me. When I went to the window, I saw the backs of horses filling the street with only a few riders directing the herd. They were the Windsor Greys and Cleveland Bays, the front engines to the royal carriages, exercising in the empty London streets.

Feeling sleep-addled, I decided to take a run. I jogged past Buckingham Palace, through Kensington Gardens and continued onto Curzon Street, where I located number 27. I felt a hitch in my determination. Yusuf, a newly converted Muslim, was about to meet me, a newly converted stripper who'd hurtled across the Atlantic Ocean believing in far too much. Finding this man for a second time was statistically impossible. I kept running until I arrived back to the hotel.

I nibbled on cold, room-service toast with honey and considered God, faith, and destiny. God was far beyond my understanding; my beliefs changed every time the sun rose, but fate held appeal. No matter. It was time to get dressed, abandon my doubts, and walk to Curzon Street.

I used the knocker, and a British male voice called out.

"I'll be there in one moment."

It must be him. I leaned in with one ear, and the heavy door whooshed open before I could shift my posture. I windmilled my arms.

"Oh my," a lanky man said, cracking the door.

It wasn't Yusuf.

"Is this 27 Curzon Street?"

"Indeed, it is. May I help you with something?"

He left his fingers on the door's edge.

"I'm supposed to meet Yusuf here at one o'clock."

The man leaned back to get a better look at me. "And you are, Miss . . . ?"

I wanted to mount my hands onto my hips but didn't dare look defensive.

"Johnson, Miss Johnson," I said, emphasizing the word 'Miss.' "My first name is Lucy."

I hated sounding breathy.

"I'm David. A pleasure."

He let go of the door and swooshed me inside.

"Right then, Miss Johnson, the American. You are here from what part of the United States exactly?"

"I come from Boston."

I felt my insides clench, guarding against the possibility of being screened out, told to go away and never return. The man tapped to his lip.

"Hmm. My brother hadn't mentioned an American, but, funny that. I do believe he was looking."

"Looking?"

After a dreadful pause, David stepped backward to let me take a few more steps.

"Nothing. My apologies. Our assistant, Nicki, happened to mention someone was coming by, but had no name or return number from the call. Please, follow me. Right this way."

I followed Yusuf's brother up the stairs. David walked sideways, crossing one leg over the other, keeping eye contact. I peered into the few small rooms we passed, wondering where Yusuf was. We entered a cozy room with a small couch, its walls studded with gold and platinum records and framed artwork of Yusuf's making.

"I am so terribly sorry. I assumed you were a meddling stranger. Yusuf would be most displeased if I'd turned you away. I'm sure you can appreciate how protective we are, though it's not like his days as a pop icon. I'm afraid the turn to Islam has been anything but popular. Uh, how did you meet?"

"Some time ago, back in the States, when he was still performing."

My eyes darted back to the hallway, wondering where he was. *Maybe he is in the bathroom.*

"Please," David said, gesturing to a small sofa while pulling up a stool. "I've just been working on *Alpha Omega*, a musical, a bit of philosophy, really."

"Oh? That sounds interesting."

It didn't sound interesting. Besides, the word "interesting" was a red flag.

"Alpha Omega, like beginning and end?" I asked, wanting to sound smart.

"Partially, but there is no real end. It's inspired by the prophets and what they taught."

"A prophet project," I said, the two words escaping like gas.

"That it is," David sighed, leaning forward. "Unfortunately, Yusuf won't be here until tomorrow, late morning. Why don't you return at 11, if it suits you?"

"That's fine."

He could have told me this at the door. We stood in tandem. I couldn't wait to breathe.

"Where are you staying?" David asked.

"At the Ritz, just a short walk from here."

"Frightfully expensive, no?"

"I didn't know where to stay, so I picked something familiar."

"Don't wear anything revealing tomorrow. You know, he is newly converted and following a strict path."

"Oh, gosh," I sputtered, "right, no, absolutely not. Nothing revealing at all."

"Right then," said David, escorting me out.

As impossible as it felt to process, I'd sorted it out once before by parsing the details at JP's. I remembered staring at Steve's hair, noticing how his sleeves rolled up his forearms, how the center of his top lip had a soft point, and his not wanting to let go of my hand. Or was that me?

I felt relieved to have extra time to prepare. I wondered about covering my head, face, ankles, wrists, and neck. Not being a Muslim, I gave myself a pass on the head dilemma, but busied myself by looking for an ankle-length skirt and button-down shirt at Harrod's. I purchased Band-Aids to make my nipples invisible and walked the city of London, passing the time.

Back at the Ritz, I took some time to write in my journal:

I feel so unreal but connected to Yusuf. I feel calm, ready to be myself, to work on whatever I need to work on. I want to live and explore and have a meaningful life. I need to know more about Islam from his mouth. It is drawing me. I will compromise in any way I can. Tomorrow will be our new morning, clear and unruffled by doubt. Am I supposed to learn from him about Allah? To bear his children and make a peaceful home?

The following day I set off under a low, gray sky. Ordinarily, the slurry of slow-moving clouds would seem melancholy, but on this day, they were majestic. My knock on the office door felt like the most important knock of my life. Footsteps. *This was it. Deep breath.*

No, it wasn't it. They were David's feet.

"He should be here soon. Feel free to fetch yourself a cup of tea from the kitchen on the third floor, if you like. I'm on a call."

"Should I get you a cup?" I asked.

"No, but thank you. I am set."

My legs rose and fell on each stair but felt flimsy. I latched on to the doorframe of the long, narrow kitchenette like a tree frog and checked the view below, ensuring the bottom of the front door was visible. I turned off the kitchen light and rested against the doorway, keeping myself in the shadows. I waited. My temples buzzed.

I watched, but mostly listened above the pulsing sound in my ears. The suction of the front door broke and a thin wall of sunlight widened through its opening. A whoosh of fresh air billowed up the staircase as the door thudded shut and I saw the outline of a long skirt. I held my breath. He sailed up the first stairway, and I leaned back, electricity tingling my spine. My throat thickened, and I heard a million droning bees. Inexplicable and breathtaking. *This is really happening. How did this happen?*

Yusuf stayed on the second floor, talking with his brother. I listened to the rhythm of his voice but didn't hear his words. My body felt weighted. *Why did my lips always feel dry?*

The direction of his voice changed, aiming directly up the stairs toward me.

"From America?" he asked.

"Yes, from America."

"Just to see me?"

His unmistakable voice.

"Just to see you."

"Right then. I'll go and meet her. Is she dressed, you know, appropriately?"

"Very much so."

"Good."

CHAPTER 11

Cat Stevens: Part II

Appropriately, modestly dressed, check. In London, just to see him, check. As if that were a lot to ask.

I knew the timing of two stairs versus one, and Yusuf took two up the first set. There wasn't much time. I felt like a starched pretzel. The more I tried to relax, the stiffer I became. The countdown began, and engines roared to life. I was strapped in. Everything around me shrunk like a bad fever dream. My thoughts clattered like magnetized balls. I understood, and then I didn't.

"Where is she?" he muttered to himself.

I tried to say, "Right here, I'm here," but I made a noise like I was swallowing sand.

He was dressed in a white robe, his beard to his collarbone. *Would he pass by? Would he stop to examine the stranger in the kitchen? Was my breath bad?* I stepped out of the blackness into the light with nothing to lose. I presented myself, and all that was disordered about my determination calmed. The world had already told me this was possible.

"Oh! There you are, my American girl!"

I froze. *Was I smiling? How goofy did I look? Did he say, my American girl? How could I possibly be his?* He was boyish and glowing. That smile. He held both hands out to greet me and quickly retracted them. He was jumpy.

"Woman," I said.

"You are lovely, just lovely. I'm so glad you're here. Right, then."

He paused, breathed, and lowered his luminous brown eyes toward the floor. My face heated, and I couldn't meet his gaze. I doubted I could ever get used to seeing his face. Still leaning against the doorway, I felt tipped over. *Say something, Lucy. This is your time. Don't blow it.*

"I am glad I'm here too, and you are there."

Oh, brother.

I looked up, and Yusuf looked down. We did this several times until settling on each other. His eyes flashed. He studied me. The corners of his mouth curved up, and his face relaxed. It was as if he reached inside and found the brightness in me.

"Come and sit so that we can talk," he said.

I sat on the same sofa as the day before, and Yusuf pulled out a rolling stool. The once stunning black curls were shaved close, and he wore a funny, white hat.

"What's the hat you're wearing?" I blurted out my question. "I like it."

Stop talking, Lucy.

Yusuf smiled, still staring.

"The prophet Muhammad, peace be upon him, wore this kind of prayer hat called a taqiya. It keeps my head warm."

"Oh," I barely responded.

Whoever I was, whatever I did, wherever I was from, fell far away and I raced into the future. I would fit into the new world of Islam and have beautiful children with him. I would learn Arabic, wear the proper clothing, and do everything perfectly. I wouldn't break the rules. I would comply. I'd refused to live by others' values and now was leaping into his. Becoming a wholly other person was possible. This was my destination, a new way of being that didn't yet exist. He was all I needed. I would never let him go.

"It's funny to say, but you look familiar. You want to know somethin' else? I've been prayin' for an American girl who'd convert to Islam. Then we could be on the same track, ya know?"

What do I say back to that? His eyebrows raised, and he tilted his magnificent head as if to say, "Of course, you're here."

"It was so easy to follow my heart here," I blurted.

I both surprised and annoyed myself.

"What do you know about Islam?" Yusuf said, emphasizing the second syllable of the word "Islam."

"I don't know anything, but want you to tell me. Tell me everything."

"It was a while after I almost drowned and made a promise to God," he said.

He muttered something foreign I would later recognize as "Insha'Allah," meaning, "If God wills it."

"Really? You almost drowned? Wow," I said.

Enough with the wows.

"I was swimmin' in the ocean, and a wave took me. I went far away and couldn't swim back. I knew I was done, so I prayed to God. I said, 'Please save me, and I'll serve you, do your will.' It worked! I was lifted back to shore. Then, shortly after, my brother gave me a copy of the Qur'an. When I started readin' it, everythin' finally made sense."

"You made a deal and stuck to it."

The book I saw at the Pierre Hotel, later given to me by Yusuf.

The man hardly needs a cheerleader, Lucy.
"Right."

Yusuf stood. My chest sank. Our time was over. My reckless statement created a dead end. He stepped toward me and offered his hand, which, to my credit, I took without devouring.

"Ah," was all he said.

"Maybe you could suggest a book?" I asked, walking toward the stairs, feeling like I would burst into wracking sobs.

"Many books," he smiled. "Let's spend the day together tomorrow. I'll take you to the mosque, and if things go well, we'll have dinner with my Mum tomorrow night."

Spend the day together. The entire day. Mosque. If what goes well? Mum. Dinner. Eating in front of him.

"OK. Sounds good. Will I meet you here? What time?"

"Hmm." He put an index finger to his chin and looked up. "Let's say 11 a.m. We'll have time for me to show you things."

After returning to the hotel, I called my best friend, Timmi, in New Canaan. It took three times as long as the event itself to recount every detail. I needed my feet to land.

"Unbelievable," Timmi said.

"You don't think I'm lying, do you?" I asked.

"God, no. It's hard to believe because things like this don't happen—but, of course, I believe you."

"I don't even know what to say to him, how to have a conversation."

"Maybe don't ask close-ended questions."

"What's a close-ended question?"

"Things that he can answer with a simple yes or no. Do you have any lip balm?"

"Timmi, gosh, it's nothing like that. He's very shy and modest."

"No, I mean, because you generally have your tongue darting in and out of your mouth to lick your lips."

"Ugh. You're right. That's why I can't wear lipstick. I noticed that on the little television show I was on. Thank God for you, Timmi."

"You mean, thank Allah."

"Very funny."

The following day, Yusuf greeted me wearing a dressier ankle-length A-line robe with three buttons at the collar. He looked like a prophet.

"Alhamdulillah," he said. "That means 'Thanks be to God.' That you decided to come back. I wasn't sure and left it in Allah's hands. C'mon."

He showed me to a vehicle I'd never seen, a Citroen.

"We're goin' to Zuhr prayer at the London mosque in Regent's Park. Zuhr is one of the five salah, salat, or prayers. This Friday prayer is mandatory for all Muslim men."

So many strange words. So many la la las.

"Not for women, though?"

"Just obligatory for the men, but you'll still see plenty of women upstairs."

"Upstairs?"

"The sisters pray in a balcony above and behind the men."

"Wait, I can't go with you and stand in back and watch?"

"Men and women pray separately so men's natural attractions won't distract us. Women hold one of two keys to the mysteries of life, and Allah holds the other. Alhamdulillah. Let me park, and then I'll give you somethin' that you'll need."

I guess men didn't have any keys.

He dropped me at the edge of the mosque grounds. At the far end of a vast concrete area, framed on three sides by the mosque buildings, a gold structure shaped like a pencil eraser rose behind the main building. It was topped by a 140-foot-tall minaret with three stacked spheres and a crescent moon.

Yusuf walked toward me in the distance, carrying a small, rolled-up rug. He wore a scarf in loose circles around his neck.

"This place is huge," I said.

"Yes, and recently completed. The dome represents heaven."

In one hand he held a triangle of folded white fabric with knots along its visible edges. "Here," he said, flattening the material between his palms. "It's a gift from Jerusalem; you'll need it to go inside."

I took the triangle carefully. It smelled like musk. I pinched the corners and unfurled it. I looked at him questioningly.

"Now what?" I asked.

"Arrange it over your head and then around your neck like a scarf. You know, loosely, like mine. See?"

I flapped it above my head like a kid about to launch a kite.

"Oh, of course, it's a veil. For the mosque, duh."

"For you," he said, "my American girl."

"Woman," I spoke toward the ground.

"Ah yes, woman. Sorry. You're already teachin' me things."

I continued to finger the veil, known as a hijab, lost in mounting disbelief.

"Right then," he said. "Wrap it around."

He reached toward my face with his hands and paused.

The musk oil scent intensified as I flipped the veil into a billow and found its center. I draped it over my head and accidentally covered my face. Yusuf reached forward and, like a busy tailor, made his way around me, holding one corner of the cloth. I brought the other corner around and back in front. Our hands collided underneath my chin, and I felt the back of his hand against my collarbone.

"Oh, gosh, sorry," I said.

"You look beautiful. It suits you. Ah," he said, looking at his watch, "plenty of time for some lessons. So, when we first enter the mosque, you will go to the right for wudu. The brothers and sisters have separate wudu areas."

"Wudo?"

It sounded like an exotic cocktail.

"No, wudu with a 'u' sound. When it rains, water is collected at the mosque to cleanse and purify our bodies before salah, which means prayer."

"Is it like a communal shower or something?" I asked.

Yusuf looked away and laughed nervously.

"Sorry. No. I got a bit embarrassed. You see, I'm still close to my old life. But back to the lesson. Wudu helps set our intentions. Before every prayer, we perform wudu, or ablution."

"What's ablution mean?"

"Just a fancy way to say washing."

"So this is like church, but on Fridays."

"No, it's a bit more involved. You see, we pray five times every day, at the same time, all Muslims worldwide."

"That's incredible and so organized," I said.

"Yes, I knew you'd be amazed. No other religion has this rhythm where we can all be doin' the same thing."

Yusuf moved closer to me.

"Not only that, but we also face Mecca. Imagine? Every Muslim must be sure they are facing the same spot, which is why I carry a compass."

He reached through a slit in the side of his robe and produced a small compass. "Like this."

"I'm not so great with directions. Why do you have to face a city so far away?"

"Because the prophet Muhammad, Sall Allāhu 'alay-hi wa-sallam, was born there."

"I'm not great at languages either," I said.

"It'll become part of you. You'll see. I just said, 'Blessin's and peace be upon him.' We say that anytime the prophet Muhammad's name is mentioned. Sall Allāhu 'alay-hi wa-sallam. See? Like that. Back to wudu. Once you enter the room, you'll see all the other sisters cleanin' themselves, and you'll pick a spot. Take off your shoes and start by sayin' 'Bismillah,' which means 'In the name of Allah.' Try it."

Yusuf cocked his head.

"Bees miller, or no, wait, Biss Mama,"

"No, here," he said gently, moving his face six inches from mine.

He annunciated slowly, "Bismillah, Bismillah. Just let it come out smoothly, without concern. Nobody's gradin' you."

I hoped my breath was nice. I pronounced my first proper "Bismillah."

"After you say Bismillah, wash your right hand with your left hand three times," he pantomimed.

I imitated the action of left upon the right.

"Then, you'll wash your left hand with the right three times."

Yusuf took my hands and lightly squeezed them.

"It seems like a lot, I know."

The tips of his fingers brushed over the tops of my hands. He looked away and spoke.

"There are simple needs, which is why I was waitin' for an American girl, or rather an American woman, to marry. Inshallah. After your hands, rinse your mouth and the upper part of your throat three times. Gargle, spit, gargle, spit, gargle, spit. Other sisters will be inside doin' the same thing, so you can follow them if you get lost."

I felt far from an adult woman, standing out in the open with the man who'd occupied all my senses for years. Could he find that first night at the Pierre? He was just one man in a world of billions, a man sought after but now hidden, and I found him. Again. Twice, and with relative ease.

"It's like taking a cat bath with extras," I babbled, "and in front of strangers."

I did not just say 'cat bath,' did I? Why couldn't I control what barreled out of my mouth? He did not say 'an American to marry.' He did. It was too late to gulp the words back in.

"I mean, I didn't mean; you know, how cats do that thing?"

I felt slightly disappointed that my gaffe went unacknowledged.

"After your mouth is clean, inhale water from your palm into your nostrils, and blow it out three times."

Inhale water?

"Wait, am I doing this with my right or left palm?"

Yusuf was undoubtedly a good teacher, in fact he seemed delighted to impart the details, but, so far, I imagined entering the mosque bathroom barefoot, finding Mecca's direction, remembering Mecca's direction, gargling, and inhaling water into my airways using a puddle from one of my palms. Nothing about all the confusing details seemed sacred.

"Right, good question. Use your left hand to clean your nose. Your left. Then," Yusuf continued, "put water on your face going from your right to left and ear, and from the edge of your hairline to your chin, yes, three times. Wash your right arm, to the elbow, with your left hand three times, and vice versa, making sure the water touches the whole arm. Wipe your head with your wet hands from front to back and then back to front, but only once. Clean your ears inside and out by putting fingers in all crevices of each ear and a thumb behind it, wiping downwards once each. Be sure you don't touch your neck after your ears. Finally, wash your feet up to the ankles three times, and be sure water goes between the toes. Rinse your hands again, and you're done."

Good grief. Find Mecca, shoes off, gargle, nostrils, face, hairline, chin, right arm, left arm, head, ears, feet, ankles, and hands.

"That must've taken a while to learn. I don't think I'll remember it all. Is that bad?"

I didn't think I'd remember any of it.

"It's only bad when someone knowingly changes the order. When you're doin' it five times every day, it comes quickly."

"Is there a cheat sheet, some visual, step by step? Like a wudu book or a laminated card?"

"We can go into the bookstore after prayer. Once you've completed wudu, using the loo invalidates it, and you'll have to redo the whole thing. So does passin' gas, but only if you can hear or smell it. These are natural things. Let's go inside, shall we?"

I briefly considered Yusuf breaking wind.

He adjusted his shawl, and we walked side by side to the mosque. He stepped back, held the door, and I walked into the start of my Islamic immersion. I fingered the corner of my first veil, wanting to be sure of things. Somehow, one corner ended up in my mouth, and I nibbled it. I quickly tucked the wet corner underneath my shirt near my shoulder. Veil gnawing would be an unattractive habit to acquire and was likely against protocol.

"No need to worry. Allah has us in His hands. Just look at you, bein' here, right now. I knew it. He is guidin' us, Insha-Allah."

"I guess I do feel a little worried," I said, my mouth feeling pasty. "How did you know?"

"I dunno exactly. But look," he said, his face lighting up. "Look over there, at the other end of the prayer room where the gold is. It shows the direction of Mecca, the city where the Prophet Muhammad, peace be upon him, was born."

Yusuf guided me to a door with a universal-looking sign illustrating the profile of a seated woman with her hands underneath a faucet.

"Here is the sisters' wudu," he said. "Whoever comes out first will wait for the other, yes?"

"Absotutely, 'lutely, absolutely, I mean."

I flipped off my Birkenstocks and set them on the shoe rack outside the ablution area. The room was long and narrow. Faucets jutted out over individual cubes, some occupied by women rubbing water on themselves. Two troughs extended the lengths of the walls and carried a continuous rush of drain water. I heard echoed laughter coming from three young women sitting next to one another.

"Asalam alaykum," said one woman draped in peach fabric.

I assumed this meant hello.

"Hi." I waved tentatively and took several steps.

The women's head coverings were settled on their shoulders as they jimmied their pinky fingers between their toes. The woman who first spoke approached me.

"Are you new here?"

"Yeah, it's my first time in a mosque."

"American?"

"American."

"Are you going to salah, the prayer?"

"I thought I'd at least watch," I said.

"You are new to Islam? Please, come over here and sit. We can show you. What is your name?"

"My name is Lucy."

"Mine's Saba. Sisters, this is Lucy, her first time, Alhamdulillah."

"Alhamdulillah," the other two women repeated.

"What does that mean again?" My toes curled against the moist tiling.

"It means, thanks be to Allah. You'll hear it all the time."

She instructed me through the cleansing process: three times this way, one time that way, right to left, left to right, and front to back. I hoped the detailed process wasn't taking as long as it seemed. I was aware of draped figures behind me, waiting. I tried to speed up my water handling.

"No need to hurry," she said, "the room goes on around that corner."

"It's that big?"

"It has to be. The main prayer room holds five thousand men, and the balcony holds half as many sisters. All must wash. Remember, the right hand is pure, and the left is not. Always start with the right, even when you put your shoes on. And no eating with the left."

I snorted water into my nostrils and released it as delicately as possible.

"Yuck. That's just kind of gross," I muttered.

I rinsed my hands and followed Saba past cloaked women chatting like they were in a supermarket line. They smiled as I passed. Saba and the others gathered their rolled-up rugs, and I saw Yusuf wave to me. His eyebrows were raised, and his chin stretched above the crowd of full-length robes. The three helpful women froze when they saw him.

"Ah," he said, a little breathy, "It looks like the kind sisters helped you. Asalam 'alaykum, sisters."

"Wa-Alaikum-Salaam," they replied in unison.

"Could you watch over our new sister here? This is her first salat, insha'Allah."

The women nodded eagerly, looking not at Yusuf, but at the floor. "We will accompany her."

"Sisters, my guest has no prayer rug yet. Could you show her the mosque rugs?"

No prayer rug yet. The story was already written.

Yusuf gave my hand a quick squeeze, and I followed the three women upstairs, where we again removed our footwear and placed them in an orderly line. The balcony overlooked the men's prayer area. There were no furnishings, just a dizzying geometric rug patterned in two shades of bright blue. Calligraphy of Qur'anic verse embellished the domed ceiling, and portholes gleamed like aquamarines. In the dome's center was a car-sized golden chandelier beaded in lead crystal, hanging like a solar pendulum.

A resonant but serene, melodic sound came from the minaret. It was the adhan, the prayer call, beckoning the faithful away from the wild world. It repeated for ten minutes, allowing worshippers to prepare and set intentions. More women streamed up the stairs, unrolled rugs, and claimed sacred space while I stood near the wall, out of everyone's way.

Saba lightly touched the small of my back, and I twitched.

"I'm sorry to frighten you, but I wanted to ask if you wanted to try salat."

"Nope. I don't know why Yusuf thought my having a prayer rug would be helpful. I've never seen anything like this. My experience as an Episcopalian isn't going to help."

"It's OK. When we start, stand against the wall, and I'll pray in front of you. Use me as a guide and do whatever you want."

Just then, a girl with large, bright eyes ran to us.

"Bahija! What did your father say about running at the mosque?" a woman scolded.

The girl presented me with a rolled-up prayer rug.

"The mosque always has extras," the girl said. "It goes in the baskets near the shoes."

"Thank you so much. Everyone is so incredibly kind."

"Islam is a kind religion and welcoming community," Saba said. "Salat is like meditating five times a day, but so much more. It's a moving meditation with certain positions and postures."

I thought about the Ram Dass retreat and how I'd craved a moving meditation.

"You'll see how beautiful it is," Saba continued. "We put the world, the past, behind us."

"There are so many details."

"That is true, and the burden falls away quicker than you'd think."

"Did you grow up as a Muslim?"

"No, I converted after I met my husband. So many people reached out to befriend me and were generous with their time and patience. It's like having a new family. You'll see."

The amplified prayer call stopped, and women stood silently at their prayer rugs. I walked quickly to the back of the room. The women's palms raised and faced forward next to their ears before grasping their knees, bending over like they were about to throw up. They kneeled, bowed, and stood, repeating the process several times while reciting verses of the Qur'an in Arabic. It was calm. Mesmerizing.

"What did you think about your first Muslim prayer?" Saba asked.

"It reminded me a little bit of church, you know? The quiet, the muttering. It was peaceful. Thank you for helping me."

I plodded down the stairs, the only woman not cloaked in fabric. When the ground floor was visible, I searched for Yusuf amidst countless bearded, robed men.

"Asalam 'alaykum," a strange man said, his hands locked behind his back.

It was the person known as the imam, the leader of worship at the mosque.

"You are new here?" He had an accent I couldn't place.

"Yes, it's my first time."

"I'm Zaki Badawi, and I am happy to spend as much time as you'd like answering questions. You call me Zaki, yes? Imam Badawi is a mouthful."

"Thank you." I saw Yusuf grinning across the lobby, pretending to be ensconced in conversation with some brothers.

"You came with someone?" Zaki asked.

"Yes, I came with Yusuf. He's right there."

"Oh, yes, Yusuf. Many people want to speak with him. Here, let's walk toward the prayer room. You have questions?"

"I do, so many. I'm curious about all the details, like for wudu."

"The Prophet, sallallahu alayhi wa salaam, once said, 'If there was a river at a man's door and he took a bath in it five times a day, would you notice any dirt on him?' No, there would be no dirt. He would be pure all day."

"What if you do something that makes you dirty in between prayer times? Like gardening or taking a nap?" I asked.

"Only deep sleep nullifies the last wudu, as does intoxication of any kind, touching one's private areas, and eating camel meat."

"Camel meat, yuck," I blurted, and we laughed. "That won't be a problem."

"Why aren't there any religious paintings or statues?" I asked.

"We believe Allah has no form and is beyond description. The human brain can't conceive of these things. Even though we think we know everything that exists, there is so much more we can't perceive or imagine. Allah is the ultimate truth."

I would later learn that Zaki Badawi, Regent's Park mosque's first imam, was known as a visionary scholar from Egypt. He proposed ways for the London community to deepen their understanding of Islam and was keen on matters of prejudice. He publicly supported women's rights and spoke out against forced marriages. Badawi regularly facilitated interfaith dialogues at the mosque and encouraged imams from afar to brush up on their English-language skills to promote understanding of Islam within Western cultures. Badawi's overall goal was to shrink the gap between East and West before it grew unmanageable.

Yusuf, having visited the bookstore, walked over, carrying a plastic bag.

"Asalam 'alaykum," he addressed the imam. "Here are some books on how to perform wudu and salat."

"With illustrations?" I asked.

"With illustrations."

"Thank you so much. I think I will need these. There's so much to remember."

The imam nodded. "Very nice," he said. "Insha'Allah. I look forward to meeting with you again, sister."

"C'mon, I'll take you to tea at Stavros."

CHAPTER 12

A'isha

"I love that smell, whatever it is," I said, sniffing the inside of Yusuf's car.

"It's musk oil. The Qur'an says that paradise, or heaven, is made of musk."

There wasn't a thought in my head as Yusuf pulled up to the restaurant and parked, guiding the passenger-side tires onto the narrow curb.

"This is it, my first home, where I grew up, right up there," he said, pointing to the floors above Stavros.

Yusuf's father, Stavros Georgiou, and Swedish mother, Ingrid Wickman, purchased a restaurant called The Moulin Rouge, which they later renamed Stavros, in the Soho theater district of London. Yusuf, his sister Anita, and his brother David grew up in the flat above it. All three children bussed and waited tables while attending Catholic school until their parents divorced, when Yusuf was eight. Their mother took them to Gävle, Sweden, then returned to London, where she and Stavros continued running the restaurant together.

Yusuf studied art at the Hammersmith School in London and, by age seventeen in 1965, had written enough music to begin performing at coffee houses and pubs under the name Steve Adams. That same year, he signed with Ardmore & Beechwood and recorded several demos, including "The First Cut Is the Deepest" and the hit single "I Love My Dog." In 1967, Yusuf emerged as a recording artist known worldwide as Cat Stevens.

"I was a bit lonely as a child," he said, "but liked my solitude. Right, then, shall we go in?"

"Sure," I said, scanning the car door for its handle.

"Wait," he said, pivoting, "it's more proper if I open your door."

He steered me to a corner table and ordered sandwiches and tea for both of us. I remembered the plateful of mushrooms at JP's and tried to think of how to keep the conversation going without blundering or veering off in an awkward direction.

"No more music?"

The question lurched out.

Yusuf dotted the corners of his mouth, resettled the napkin into his lap, and looked down.

"You know I've been asked this a few times and don't want to say the same thing, especially to you. Performin' was hard, to begin with, and those vast stadiums. It just was no place for a shy introvert. I was losin' interest a bit, and I started learnin' about Islam, Alhamdulillah, and . . ."

"I'm sorry, what does that mean again?"

"It means 'praise be to God.' In Arabic. Try it. Al-ham-du-lil-lah," he slowly annunciated each syllable.

"Alhamdulillah. Got it. No problem."

Yusuf's eyes sparked.

"The Qur'an allows music, and the imam you met today assured me there was no problem with it. But when I began readin' about Muslim scholars, their opinions were mixed. As a new Muslim under the media's scrutiny, I decided it best to be conservative and keep the strictest path. I released the past, got rid of my guitars, equipment, and reminders, and I'm glad I did."

"Alhamdulillah," I puffed.

"Ah, a quick learner," he said, retreating before speaking again in a softer, more reflective tone. "I'd have gone mad because of the path I was on. You see, Islam has such specific guidance down to every detail. It keeps madness at bay and gives you direction. You'll never get lost. Back then, no one understood me. I didn't understand myself. I was becomin' whom they wanted, a created persona. The image kept people from knowin' me. They told me I was this and that, but I never felt like the person they described. The more famous I got, the more lost and empty I felt. I needed order, a way to understand the universe, and I tried

Before the veil.

many different paths. Finally, I found Islam, Alhamdulillah, this gentle peace. How's the food?"

"Oh, it's good, fine, thank you. I forgot I was even eating."

Cat Stevens was a phantom now. I hadn't expected the performer I feverishly sought for all those years to be gone, or for me to be fine with it.

"I'll meet you at the mosque 'round 11:30 for the midday prayer. Would you come to Mum's for dinner tomorrow? We could go to the mosque again afterward for evening prayer."

"Sure. I'd love that."

Yusuf drove to the hotel and accompanied me inside.

"Thank you, Yusuf. I had a wonderful day."

Distracted, he nodded and approached the front desk. The staff stood at attention and bowed when they responded to him.

"They'll charge my card for your room; meanwhile, let's think of a place you can stay more long term."

"You don't have to do that. I came prepared; besides, I chose to stay here."

"I insist. It's the right thing to do."

About to burst, I hurried to my room and called my sage-like friend Timmi.

"Oh my god, Timmi! Thank God, or Allah, you answered the phone! What a day I had. Yusuf, he took me to the mosque and called me his American girl again! He gave me a veil, showed me where Mecca is, and taught me how to clean myself."

"I think you already knew how to clean yourself, Lu."

"I mean in the Muslim way, where you go into this fascinating bathroom type of place, with all these other women, and do everything three times. Then I went up to a balcony above where the men pray because I guess women really do distract the men, and I watched a whole prayer. It's super complicated, and you should have heard the call to prayer. It was so cool. I met the imam. He's kind of like a pastor or minister, I guess. Yusuf gave me two books; one on wudu, you know, the whole cleaning thing, and another one on how to pray. After the mosque, he took me to where he grew up, and Stavros, the restaurant his parents had. They named it after his father, Stavros. He kept opening doors for me and tried to teach me Arabic words. I didn't know what to say or ask, and when I blurted out some stupid, insensitive question about his music, he didn't even get upset. We're going to the mosque twice tomorrow, and oh my god, you're not going to believe it, but we're having dinner with his mother, whom he calls Mum. So cute. He insisted on paying the hotel bill and said something about staying here, like, long term."

I finally gulped in some air.

"Wait, slow down. How long have you been there, Lu? All of how many days?"

"Three days, and then I met him yesterday. Did I meet him yesterday? Saying it aloud feels weird, like I'm making this whole thing up."

"If you are, you have a mind-blowing imagination. Have you called your mother yet?"

"She hung up on me, as usual."

"Sorry. I remember she did the same thing when you were at the Pierre."

"I do, too. He gave me two beginner books. Hopefully, I can memorize enough to look like I belong."

"Do you want to belong there?"

I paused.

"I might. I'm not sure. I don't want to embarrass him for now, so the least I can do is get the postures down. I had no idea things would go this way, like, I couldn't have imagined this was possible."

"Your life's been like that, making impossible things possible."

I spent that night flipping through the book illustrating every move and phrase of the prayer, but my mind had holes. I moved on to the *Making Wudu for Beginners* and acted out the sequence several times. With the details of Islamic cleansing behind me, I tried memorizing some of the Arabic phrases in the prayer, but nothing stuck.

I stood at the bathroom mirror, laid the books out on the sink, and repeatedly pantomimed the choreography. Once I successfully managed three dress rehearsals outside of the bathroom and without the mirror, I stopped. I doubted this would come naturally and wondered if people used cue sheets taped to their rugs. Besides, I had no idea how to study.

Before bed, I started with my hands by my ears and whispered, "Allahu Akbar." I felt ridiculous. The litany continued with bending, standing, kneeling, more bowing, more kneeling, and prostrating. It was like a game of Twister, but not. I felt no more confident than I had the day before.

After a night's sleep and all matters of Islam still eluding me, I scribbled out the prayer sequence on Ritz stationery. It occurred to me that using notes might be frowned upon, so I copied the prayer onto my left palm.

I arrived at the mosque before Yusuf and marched into the wudu room like a pro.

"May whoever is out there give me the right sequence of events," I said, cleaning between my toes.

I started reciting the prayers and the jumbled words felt eerily right.

With my first solo wudu behind me, I waited for Yusuf in the enormous lobby where I could see the courtyard. I recognized him as a tiny white dot moving toward the fountain. The lower hem of his thobe caught the breeze and billowed before resettling at his ankles. He walked quickly, looking to his left, right, and behind him. I wondered if he was looking for me.

"The name A'isha suits you," he announced, walking toward me in the lobby. "She was the favorite wife of the prophet Muhammad, sallallahu alayhi wa sallam."

My American girl. Long-term stay. Dinner with Mum. A'isha. Wasn't that Stevie Wonder's daughter's name?

We separated as we had the day before, but no one else was on the balcony this time. I guessed Fridays were the big day, the equivalent of Sundays at church. The adhan began its haunting call, and I studied the notes on my palm. Up, down, bow, straighten, right toes, index finger, bend, kneel, straighten, stand, and repeat.

After the prayer, we met downstairs, and I asked, "Who was Muhammad, anyway?"

Yusuf's face opened to the question.

"The prophet Muhammad, sallallahu alayhi wa salam, spent days upon days prayin' in a cave and finally, when he was forty, was visited by Gabriel, who allowed him to receive his first revelation. Muhammad couldn't write, so his companions became his scribes. He was ahead of his time. He forbade female infanticide and said that whites had no superiority over blacks, that all were equal. This was almost fourteen hundred years ago. Nobody thought that way."

Outside, the sun's slant made designs on the ground as we walked.

"I got you somethin'," he said, opening the door to his car.

"You didn't have to give me anything," I said. "You've already given me so much."

He reached into the back and produced a rolled-up prayer rug tied with a frayed rope. "You need one of these," he said.

"My own prayer rug. Thank you."

Before starting the car, Yusuf turned to me and said, "You look beautiful. The veil suits you."

I had a veil that suited me, Islamic how-to books, and a prayer rug.

We entered the suburbs of London, where Yusuf's mother lived. It was a two-level home with lush perennial gardens, a vegetable patch off to one side, and sliding glass doors. "This is my mum's house," he said with an easy smile. "C'mon, let's go inside. She's lookin' forward to meeting you."

I loved how he slipped into a cockney vernacular. He pushed open the front door and called, "Mum?"

An elfish woman whipped around a doorway with her hand extended. "It's lovely to meet you, just lovely. My name's Ingrid."

She grasped my hand and cupped her free hand over it.

"Thank you for having me, Ingrid," I said. "My name's Lucy."

Etiquette came in handy when meeting an ex-pop star's mother.

"Please, call me Mum."

She threaded her hand through the inside of my elbow and walked us both toward the kitchen.

"Now tell me," she said, patting my hand, "do you like sole? Sometimes they've got little bones."

"Oh yes, I do. There's not much I don't like."

"Very good then. A wholesome approach to life. Plenty of things besides fish have tiny bones, if you know what I mean. Perhaps you could take this colander and pick some peas from the garden."

"I'd love to. Just point me in the right direction."

"Ta, ta."

"I'm sorry, what?"

"Ta, you know, it means thank you, in British."

She handed me a colander and reached into a nearby drawer for scissors before opening the door to the yard.

"They are climbing on that little trellis at the end there. Pick the round, plump pods, and leave the flat ones be. You can leave the calyx too since I'll be steamin' them right off."

"OK, will do."

I wasn't sure what a calyx was.

"And get the upper pods. They mature earliest since they've been in the sun the longest. And, please, if you wouldn't mind, snap off a few parsley sprigs."

The garden areas were bound by dark soil. I followed her directives and came back with a pile of peas in emerald pods and deep green parsley.

"Your garden is so pretty."

"Just a cottage garden," Mum said. "Wash your hands first and pluck out those peas, if you don't mind."

"Not at all."

Yusuf came to stand on the other side of his mother at the kitchen counter.

"You two gettin' on then?"

"Couldn't be better," Mum said. "I put her right to work, and she didn't balk at all. This one certainly has good manners. I wonder if she can cook," she said, tapping my waist with one elbow.

"I love to cook."

"One day this week, we'll put her to the test, Mum," Yusuf said, leaning backward and grinning.

"I'm game."

I hurried the tip of my finger down the spine of each pod, releasing peas into the steamer. "I'll set the table if you'd like," I offered, wanting to score points.

His mother used bright yellow potholders, carried a tureen filled with bite-sized white potatoes to the table, and fetched a covered bowl containing the garden peas. I filled the glasses with ice water, and Yusuf set the fish down before taking his seat at the head of the table. He turned his hands up, closed his eyes, and said a quiet prayer.

It sounded like a child's secret language but more graceful than pig Latin. I stared at him.

"Before you ask," Yusuf said, "because I'm sure you will, that prayer translates to 'All praise is due to Allah, who has given me food to eat and provided it without any endeavor on my part, or any power.'"

"What a memory my son has."

Yusuf gently slid the platter toward him and surgically deboned the fish, producing a perfect skeleton.

"It's just like the one on the front of the *Teaser and the Firecat* album."

I winced.

He didn't react but divided the fish, slid a piece onto his plate, and served his mother and me.

"Tasty, Mum. A few bones, but soft enough to eat."

I needed a man who could calmly ingest sharp things like fish skeletons.

Yusuf recited Arabic verses and exaltations softly to himself while Mum and I ate and kept quiet. The unpredictable Bismillahs and Alhamdulillahs weren't conducive to talking, and neither his mum nor I wanted to interrupt his supplications.

I helped clean up, hoped I'd scored more points, and we drove back to London. As Yusuf's car cut through the darkness, the approaching headlights looked like stars floating up the road in pairs. He was so comfortable with silence.

"I've arranged for the flat above Stavros to be ready by tomorrow," he said. "I'll be away with (guitarist) Alun Davies for a couple of days, givin' you time to get settled."

"OK," I said. "That's really generous of you. Have a good weekend."

"Insha'Allah. And the keys to the flat will be at the shop."

"The shop?"

"Sorry. Right. The restaurant."

I stood on the sidewalk and waved goodbye to his disappearing car. I wasn't looking for Cat Stevens anymore. I was looking for the man who gave me my first veil.

Determined to muddle through wudu and prayer with ease, I returned to the mosque the day after moving to the flat at Shaftsbury and New Oxford Street.

"Asalam 'alaykum," Zaki, the imam, said, walking toward me.

"Wa alaikum assalaam," I replied, catching myself by surprise. "I can't believe how easy that just rolled off my tongue."

He smiled briefly and said, "It's important to find some sisters who can inform and guide you, you know, of the same gender."

I loved the word sisters. "I've always wanted sisters."

"You grew up in a family of brothers?"

"No, I grew up alone, the only child. I mean, I wasn't lonely, really, at least I don't think I was, but it was always so quiet."

"Islam will welcome you into its extensive, colorful family."

I gulped. "Oh, right, yes," I stammered.

"Before you go, ask me one question."

"OK, let me think a sec. Everything is all jumbled."

I'd just read about not eating pork, but the notion of giving up hot dogs and bacon seemed too trivial to mention. I asked an equally inane question: "Can you suggest a way to learn Arabic more quickly?"

"Prophet Muhammed, sallallahu 'alayhi wa sallam, said that those proficient with the Qur'an will be with noble scribes and angels, but those who stumble over it and find it difficult reading will get more rewards. Don't overwhelm yourself. Islam is a religion of heart that promotes honor, dignity, and justice, nurtures patience, and encourages curiosity. Acquiring knowledge is compulsory for every Muslim. Did you know that a Muslim invented algebra? Another engineered flight mechanics, and another was the father of modern-day surgery. Islam insists you seek answers, and even more so that you indulge your intellect and curiosity to ask questions."

That type of encouragement was undeniably tempting.

"Wait, I do have a more important question. How do I become a Muslim? Is there a class, an exam, or books to read?"

"It's much simpler. You feel your heart and then speak the shahada, the Islamic profession of faith. Here," he said, offering me a laminated card from his robe pocket. "Look this over, and you will know. You will feel moved, insha'Allah."

The shahada was written in Arabic on the front and translated on the back. It read, "I bear witness that there is no deity worthy of being worshiped but Allah, and I bear witness that Muhammad is His servant and messenger."

This seemed straightforward and clear.

"Thank you for this."

"These are the first words whispered into a Muslim baby's ear and the last words a person hears when he or she is on her deathbed," he said.

"That's intense."

"The proof of God's existence is around you every day, every moment, from science to the infinite beauty of nature and its exquisite order. Did you know if the moon were to move one centimeter downwards, the earth would be covered in water, completely flooded, and we would all perish? And, if the moon moved one centimeter up, the Earth would be torched by the sun's fire and burn for billions of years. We would be ash, and yet, the moon stays. Why? You? Me? No, we do not have these abilities. Only Allah does."

I turned the laminated card over several times and, without a thought, said, "I'm ready."

"Now? Your heart speaks?"

Zaki unfolded two chairs from the wall of the main prayer area and gestured for me to sit.

"There are just a few questions I have for you," he said.

"OK."

"Do you believe there is just one God?"

"Yes."

"Do you believe Muhammad is a messenger of God?"

"Yes."

"You are ready for Shahadah. Repeat what I say."

"Hold on, I think I've got it," I said, closing my eyes and concentrating. "Ashadu an la ilaha illa illa-ilah, wa ashadu anna Muhammadan rasul Allah." I unlocked my eyelids. "Is that right?"

"It is. Now repeat what you just said, but this time in English."

"OK." I closed my eyes again. "I believe, I testify that no one is worthy of worship but God, or Allah, and that Muhammad is the Messenger of God."

"Allahu Akbar."

"Allahu Akbar to you too. Is this where you give me a name?"

"You may choose a Muslim name, but not to rush," said Zaki smiling. "God is great! Congratulations and warm welcomes into the Muslim community and to the Islamic faith. You are within and surrounded by your true family now, and you must get to know your Muslim sisters. No more searching. Your curiosity will be eternally sated."

Sounded like a cure for my temperament. He looked past me, and I heard Yusuf's voice.

"She will be called A'isha, the prophet Muhammed's, sallallahu alayhi as-salām, first and favorite wife."

"Asalam 'alaykum," I replied, stunned.

This seemed like a good phrase to use when thoughts fell short. My legs felt unsteady as I rose from the chair. I was a Muslim.

"Wa alaikum assalaam."

Yusuf's eyes shimmered.

"Weren't you going to say somethin' to me?" he said.

"Well, yes, but it just came over me. It wasn't my plan. Besides, I thought you were away."

"I couldn't stand to be gone any longer because I truly have been praying for a girl, and the girl is you, A'isha. My A'isha. C'mon, I'll drive you home."

Home. I couldn't tell how close or far things were from me. Outside the mosque, everything was sharp and bright. We must have felt the same way about each other. *How was any of this possible in such a short time?* We drove in silence until he pulled over to let me out.

"I'm sorry. I'm a bit speechless, really. Happy. Alhamdulillah. You should call your mum," said Yusuf, "and we'll see my mum for dinner again tonight. There's a K8, a telly box right on that corner. Right then. I'll come 'round to fetch you 'bout five."

He drove off, and I obediently entered the vibrant red box, a prominent crown above the door. Gripping the handset, I asked the operator to make a collect call.

"Yes, that's fine," my mother responded to the operator.

"Hello, Mother."

I paused for indications of irritation or annoyance.

"Oh, hi, Dards. Are you still international?"

"Yup. And please don't hang up. I'm still in London and staying in a flat where Yusuf grew up."

Mother sighed.

"It's time you stop talking about fantasies like they are real. Someone will lock you up in a mental institution someday."

"I'm not making things up. I am with Yusuf."

"You mean Poodie?" she laughed at the reference to our cat and I couldn't help laughing with her.

"No, it's Yusuf now. He changed his name. Remember I told you?"

"All right, Louise. If you say so. No more bacon or bologna for you."

"Yeah, that's OK. My name's A'isha now."

"You could take an interest in my life at some point."

"I'm interested, Mother. What is going on with you?"

"Funny you should ask. You might be interested to know that I'm seeing a man named Bob, an antiques dealer."

"That's great. I'm glad for you."

"And you are the sticking point."

"What does that mean?"

"Lucy, honestly, have you no perspective on what this looks like? I want to have a life, remarry, and enjoy my friends. Think about what a complete embarrassment you are. Is there anything you wouldn't do to get attention? You ruin my life, repeatedly." Click.

The taut, salty heat on the surface of my eyes meant the start of tears. I quickly initiated another call to my father.

"Hi, Dadee."

"Loot! Good of you to call, Sweetie. I am here with Joan Whetstone. You remember Joan. She is the mother to Scotty, Suzie, and Didi."

"The lady that works with Mother? At the Whitney Shop? One of her best friends? Skinny lady with short black hair? We used to go to the

Whetstones' house and sing Christmas carols around their piano. That Joan?"

"Yes, that Joan. Mrs. Whetstone. She sends her regards. And you're still in jolly old London, are you?"

"Yes. I became a Muslim today."

"You became a what, Lucy?"

"But wait a minute. Are you, like, *with* Joan?"

He chuckled and cleared his throat. "Loot, I am not sure what being *with* Joan means. Occasionally I am with Joan, yes, if that answers your question before we move back to a far more interesting topic, which is your Muslimhood."

"I converted to Islam and changed my name to A'isha and have seen Yusuf almost every day since I've been here. Well, three days out of four."

"I see. And this means you are now Princess A'isha? Or is it A'isha Cheyenne?"

My father never hung up on me. He was always warm, even when scolding me. Next, I called Nan.

"Lu, is that you, Lu?" Nan's voice wobbled.

"Hi, Nan. How are you?"

"Ugh! I've been worried sick."

"I'm so sorry, Nanly. I wish you wouldn't worry so much. I miss you. I've missed you since the day we moved away."

"Lu, I've always been a worry wart, and I pray every day that you'd move back so we can be closer, but your mother doesn't think it's important. Now tell me all about your adventures."

I told Nan the story as best I could and promised my next trip in an airplane would be to see her.

"You are a brave young lady, Lucy Johnson," said Nan, with a breathy laugh. "I will call Ellen immediately and insist you come to Florida for Christmas. Promise me you'll come, no matter what."

"No matter what, Nanly. I love you. And you can always call me Lu. You don't have to call me A'isha."

"Call you who? I'll always love you, Lu."

I placed the chunky handset onto its cradle. I loved Nan and Yusuf more than anything.

While savoring Mum's dinner that night in Hampstead, England, a rush of thoughts rose like a mammoth landscape, my emotions not far behind. I'd recorded every transcendent detail of those four days, but I hadn't registered many thoughts or feelings. Fantasy and reality merged into something I couldn't explain.

"Now, how did you meet my son?" Mum asked.

CHAPTER 13

New Canaan, Connecticut

Yusuf looked at his mother, and I studied my plate. He probably didn't remember our one intimate night at the Pierre Hotel. He had so many before and after me. If I answered his mother honestly, I risked my good standing, as well as catching him off guard. There wasn't time to make something up and besides, lying never went well for me.

"Well?" Mum said, waiting for my response.

"I, uh, well, we met at Yusuf's office," I said.

"I prayed for an American girl, Mum, one who'd convert to Islam," Yusuf quickly added. "And, Alhamdulillah, she appeared."

He looked at me expectantly, allowing me to pick up the conversation.

"Yeah, so I spoke with him at his office, and we went right to the mosque."

"Why did you go to his office?" she asked. "Why did you leave America and come to London? Was it for work or school?"

"Something in me needed to find him again," I said.

"Again?"

"I mean I'd met him once, a long, long time ago. Briefly. Very briefly. He probably doesn't even remember."

Thankfully, Mum changed the topic, but Yusuf revived it in the car, after a long silence.

"We met before?" he asked.

When I was in fourth grade, we moved from Lake Forest, Illinois, to 634 Silvermine Road in New Canaan, Connecticut.

I hated this.

"I know you don't remember. Why would you?"

"Tell me."

His car and emotions switched off. He felt impenetrable to me. "A'isha?" he prodded me.

I answered in fragments about JP's, eating mushrooms, flowers in the gutter, the Manhattan skyline, the Pierre, and the Qur'an. I stopped at the holy book. As it turned out, reminiscing in such detail wasn't necessary. He wasn't listening.

I felt something crack open between us.

"Come, I'll see you in," he said, walking briskly ahead of me to the second floor. "I don't like to think back to when I thought of women as chattels. They had to be beautiful, like things, objects, and all. No need to worry. Allah is guiding us," he said.

"I see," I said, even though I didn't.

Yusuf opened the door to the flat and placed a compass from his pocket on the small kitchen table.

"Mecca is here," he pointed. "Best to mark it, and always carry your compass. "Asalam 'alaykum, A'isha." He was cold.

"Wa alaikum assalaam, Yusuf."

Hey, that sounded pretty darn good.

My Muslim toolbox now included a veil that suited me, how-to books, a prayer rug, a new name, and a compass.

The flat was cozy, red, and lightly furnished. It had everything I needed except heat. The next morning while trying to locate the thermostat, someone knocked. An elderly woman dressed in charcoal gray held her folded hands underneath her bosom.

"I'm Stevie's aunt, coming to welcome you. I stopped by yesterday, but you weren't here. I live in a nearby flat if there's anything you need. And you are?" she asked.

"I'm Lucy. A'isha, actually."

My mother was fond of calling Yusuf "Poodie" after our first cat.

"Don't mind if I do," the aunt pronounced, marching into the flat. "Isn't it lovely now that Stevie's letting you stay here?"

"It is. Do you want to have a seat?" I asked.

"That's most kind. Maybe I'll sit for a spell. It can't hurt."

"Would you like some tea?" I asked, opening the tiny cupboards. "I'm sure there's tea here somewhere."

"Upper cabinet, to the left. I'd love some tea; yes, ta ta."

I found the kettle, filled it with water, and set it on the stove. Click, click, click. It didn't ignite. Click, click, click. Still, no flame.

"I'm sorry. I must be doing something wrong here."

"'Tis quite chilly in here. 'Ave you put your coins in?"

"Coins?" I asked.

"Why, coins in the meter, of course."

"The meter?"

"Lemme tell you how utilities work in your mother country," she said, pointing to a cubby by the door. "Go over there and see what I'm talkin' about here. No sense in just listening. Must do."

I obeyed and, inside the cubby, found a metal contraption with several coins on top.

"It only takes a certain number of coins, and then you'll feed the hungry monster again."

"That's different."

"Stevie lived here, you know."

"Really?" I said, igniting the stove and setting up the teacups.

"For quite a time, yes. He was such an interesting child, so unusual. Everything about him was contradictory. Kind-hearted, shy, but not reserved, mind you. He eventually took this flat and painted it red," she said, her eyes darting about. "He was a free spirit, you might say, a curious lad, but wary. Stevie was always looking inside and out for answers to his big questions, and now he's become quite austere, I'm afraid. He insists I call him Yusuf, and that makes me want to call him Stevie even more," she laughed. "Then there was Stevie and his paper bags. He'd take 'em, cut 'em up, and tape 'em to the mirrors. It was the oddest thing. So was his UFO phase. Said he could feel 'em. I wondered if he was going mad, you know. Enough of that. I must go. A pleasure," she said, slapping her knees and standing.

She left before the kettle whistled, and I wondered if she really was Yusuf's aunt.

I returned to the phone box outside and called Timmi to give her the update.

"Maybe it's just me, but he sure sounds strange," Timmi said, "but he's gorgeous to look at."

"Strange, as in?"

"It's probably just me, Lu. So much is happening to you and so quickly. It's kind of hard to put together."

"Yeah. Tell me about it. Am I strange?"

Timmi's laugh led into her reply.

"You aren't strange. You just do strange or unusual things that most people would be too afraid to do. On the other hand, he is strange and does strange things. Plus, he sounds moody. Yuck."

"I feel strange a lot of the time. Mostly because I do strange things like you said."

"Am I strange?" Timmi asked.

"No," I said, both of us laughing. "How do we know anything about ourselves? I mean, I say I'm strange. How would I know?"

"This whole thing is unbelievable. I don't know how you're doing it."

"Me either. I feel like I just stand in front of him, totally awkward, not knowing how long to make eye contact or when to cross my arms. Then on top of it, I want to make myself interesting enough for him."

"Is he interesting or what?"

"I couldn't tell you. It's hard to know him."

"Well, don't overthink it, Lu. And try not to analyze everything so much."

Timmi was right. It was better not to examine the magic too closely. There were more grown-up things to work on like letting go of the fantasies I'd projected onto him. Yusuf, the man, was not his music, nor his pop-star status. I didn't even know Cat Stevens, and Cat Stevens didn't know me. We'd only brushed up against one another, and now Cat Stevens was gone. The man whose face lit up when he talked to me was Yusuf Islam, and he was the man with whom I was falling in love.

Over the next week, Yusuf and I spent almost every waking moment together. We helped his brother, David, put his album together and Yusuf worked on *The Fantasy Ring*, a fan club booklet explaining why he left music. He asked for my opinions on colors and layouts. Because of contractual commitments, Yusuf was releasing a greatest-hits album and asked me to help choose a photograph for its cover.

Whether at the office, mosque, or his mother's house, our conversations were mainly about Islam. He still knew nothing about me, and I knew little about him. Islamic details overwhelmed me, but as I read the Qur'an and asked questions, things started to fall into place. I was learning oversized concepts I'd yet to think through. My knowledge was rudimentary, but Islam made sense.

Proving God's existence by observing the order of nature was more plausible than the God I learned about in Sunday school. Allah was simply beyond our comprehension, whereas a Santa-type man sitting on a throne beyond the gates of heaven was absurd to me.

I wanted to learn more and followed the imam's advice by connecting with other Muslim women. Saba, who helped with my first wudu and salat, introduced me to Hafsa and Nuriya. They were kind, inviting, and tolerant of novice questions.

"Why don't you eat with the men?" I asked.

"It's more comfortable this way, right, sisters? We can remove our hijab, relax, and talk."

"What about praying behind them? I don't entirely get that."

"So their weaknesses won't cause trouble."

"You mean we're responsible for their weaknesses?"

"For our reactions to their weaknesses."

"So that's why we cover up everything? To hide what men are weak to?" I asked.

"Yes. But remember that it's a choice. No one orders us to do it. Only three of six thousand verses reference dress in the Qur'an, and the word hijab means barrier, not veil or clothing. When I wear the hijab, I feel protected. It shows that I know my power. It tells people that my body is not available to be consumed by a man's eyes, for fantasy or otherwise. Men cannot help the need to look, so we help them. Their instinct is to breed. Besides, it's a relief not to be stared at."

Islam was rooted in qualities I lacked: common sense and self-control. Much later in life, when I knew myself better, I regretted not going into the military because of its hierarchy, protocols, and guidance. Despite my proclivity for freedom, having order, limits, and schedules suited me. Islam taught that freedom and self-control can coexist.

I was excited to have new Muslim friends, but Yusuf disapproved.

"Even the imam told me to get to know some Muslim sisters," I said. "Everyone needs friends."

"You don't see me runnin' off to be with friends."

"You have your brother, sister, and mother. I don't have these things. Besides, this is your home."

"You're home now, A'isha, with your family. You don't need friends," he said. "I want to be all you need."

I was stunned, and sent spinning.

"I'm not sure what to say or what you mean. Who doesn't want the person they care about to have friends?"

"I need to look after what is so precious to me," he said, crescents of water forming at the bottoms of his eyes. "You know I've waited for you, a girl just like you, and that girl, she . . ."

"Woman," I said.

Yusuf laughed and continued. "Right, then. That girl, that woman, I've waited for and prayed for doesn't need, that woman doesn't want friends. You know that day you showed up? I was so shocked I felt numb all over. And, A'isha, you must understand, this is all so new, and I'm tryin' hard to follow the strictest interpretation of the Prophet's sallallahu alayhi wa salam words. I want it to be right, insha'Allah."

I considered what his aunt had told me, and assumed Yusuf retreated when facing strong emotions. My best response was to tamp down mine.

"I see how sensitive you are, Yusuf, and love that you want to protect me, but it's not something I'm used to. This is probably the wrong thing to do, but I'm going to do it anyway," I said, touching him by interlocking our fingers. "There's so much to say and I'm keeping a lot in. You are beautiful."

I wanted to wrap myself around him and knew that soon, I could.

"A'isha," he said, tracing my hand with his finger, "we shall be married in Allah's name. Take one step, and Allah will surely take hundreds. We can be patient, knowin' what's ahead. We have until the end of our lives on earth to be together."

I opened my mouth. Nothing came out. I was paralyzed, my senses stumped, but I heard clearly. *We shall be married in Allah's name.*

The day before I returned to Boston to prepare for my new life, I went to the mosque for early prayer. Saba, Hafsa, and Nuriya greeted me.

"We missed you yesterday," Hafsa said, touching the outside of my arm.

"Yusuf didn't want me to come. He doesn't think I need friends."

The three glanced at one another.

"He's a nervous sort, that one. A'isha. We have something important to tell you," Saba said. "Come, let's walk outside. You need to know this before you leave for Boston."

"Is everything OK?" I asked.

"Yes, Alhamdulillah. Please take this at face value. The sisters and I talked about it and feel it's important to tell you because we can see where your heart is leading." Saba took a big breath. "A respectable Muslim father is determined that his daughter, Fauzia, marry Yusuf."

I assumed many respectable Muslim fathers wanted their daughters to marry Yusuf.

"That seems normal," I said. "I mean, he is quite the catch."

"It's more than just a want, A'isha. Fauzia and her family have met socially with Yusuf," Saba added.

"Oh? Thanks for telling me. How long ago was that?"

"Just before you arrived."

"Oh, phew. Because he said we are getting married!"

The three women covered their mouths and jumped up and down a bit.

"Get back to London quickly," Hafsa said.

"You bet I will. I'll get rid of my things, let go of my apartment and come right back. Well, after he meets my parents."

Yusuf and I visited with his family after I left the mosque.

I met his niece, Rebecca, and his sister Anita. Yusuf rearranged rocks in his mother's garden until prayer time when we took our places in separate rooms. Then I cooked dinner and passed another one of Mum's tests. The following morning, May 28, Yusuf drove slowly to Heathrow Airport.

"I hate leaving you," I said, "and all of this."

"You see how, if you drive at a reasonable speed, the cars go past, and there's no stress, no race at all."

He had a handy way of sailing past things.

A small pick-up truck with a sapling held steady by four straps whizzed by. It reminded me of a scene from *Harold and Maude*, the movie that featured his music."Did you see that truck with the tree in it?"

"I'll get you a return ticket for July 10th," he continued, not answering me, again.

"I don't want to leave."

"That should give you time to put things in order."

"Everything is here, with you."

"I'll come to meet your parents in a couple of weeks."

"Can't we change the ticket, so I can stay a little longer?"

I rested my hand between our seats to bridge the gap between us. Maybe nonverbal communication worked better. He cupped the top of my hand and it felt warm. "Sweetness," was all he said.

Before leaving the car, Yusuf handed me a heavy orange book. I recognized it as the Qur'an I'd seen at the Pierre Hotel, the Qur'an his brother David brought back for him from Jerusalem. Another divine intercession. He walked me into the airport, took my hands and, for the first time, studied my face without looking away. People rolled their suitcases past us while we stood facing each other in some kind of force field. The corners of his mouth curved up as he squeezed my hands.

"There's so much my heart wants to say, A'isha."

The plane rose into the pure blue sky and cruised high above the wrinkled Atlantic Ocean. The water looked soft and powerless from so far away. I felt blissfully indifferent. Compliance was comfortable, almost freeing.

The cross-Atlantic flight gave me time enough to think, but thoughts darted and bounced too quickly to catch. I reviewed my past—our past—starting with the fiercely consumed sixteen-year-old on a quest to find Cat Stevens. Our first meeting was deceptively simple, and it was easy, then and now, to make sense of its parameters. This time, we'd fallen into something so profound, so quickly, there was no sense to make.

Only weeks before, I'd heeded the call to London. That call came from Cat Stevens, a persona that evaporated while we had tea at Stavros. But was I sure? Could an idea be loved with this intensity? Were we both loving ideas of the other? Was I trying to anticipate his desires so I could promptly deliver them? It would be detrimental to blow up both of our lives for my childish illusions, but I had to keep going. The dream was too convincing to abandon. It was all I ever wanted.

After a restless flight, I learned my luggage was missing, so I carried my wallet, prayer rug, compass, and Qur'an through Logan Airport and found a taxi. There wasn't much time to change my life, but I knew what to do first and called my mother.

"Hi, Mother. I'm back, and guess what?" I pushed out my question before she had time to hang up. "We're getting married!"

"Lu-Lu. You're very bright. Assuming this story is true, and I'm sure it isn't, kindly explain how you can possibly know him well enough to get married."

"I don't know how to explain anything that's happened, but it doesn't matter because I belong with him. It's like we've always known each other. But you can grill me when I see you."

"I admit a visit would be nice."

"Would it be OK if Yusuf visited at some point and stayed with us in New Canaan? He needs to meet you."

"Poodie? Stay here? On Marshall Ridge Road? Gracious! I better take those posters down."

"Seriously, though, Mother. The posters are down. You know they've been down for a long time."

"I'll go along with this for now. At least it's entertaining."

"You can finally make that meatloaf," I added.

She didn't hang up. Another miracle.

Yusuf called to say his visit to New Canaan would be delayed, but that he would be there soon. He changed the date of my one-way flight to London from July 10th to the 17th, and I didn't have time to wonder why.

I cheerfully gave my landlord notice, assessed the contents of my little apartment, and brought food to the man in the dumpster. He wasn't there. I hoped he was OK. I didn't like being around other reminders of the "old me" and my "old life" and went to New Canaan where I could wait for Yusuf without distractions.

"Louise, why are you wearing all that clothing? It's June, in case you haven't noticed," said Mother, pecking me on the cheek.

We had some catching up to do.

"Why on earth did you bring a rug? I have plenty of rugs here."

"You know that Yusuf converted to Islam, right? It only made sense for me to do the same."

I held my breath, waiting for an explosion.

"From stripping to burkas? You are a piece of work," she said with a hint of affection.

"I changed my name to A'isha and pray five times daily."

"What about your last name? Or is A'isha just one word like Prince, or Cher?

"It's 'Abdul Kabir' and means servant of the great."

Mother held her hand against her mouth, trying not to laugh.

"And who might 'the great' be? Would that be Poodie? Poodie the Great? You are the servant of Poodie the Great."

We both laughed. I could only take myself so seriously around my mother.

"That's funny, Mother, but please promise to behave when he's here. You know, like, don't call him Poodie. Oh my god, I will die if you do. Promise?"

"I promise to try very hard, Lu," she laughed.

"Remember, I'm not Lu, Lucy, or Dardle; I'm A'isha. Please just try."

Several days passed before Yusuf called—collect. Mother had a fit.

"Honestly, Lucy. It's not like he doesn't have plenty of money. Please instruct him to refrain from calling collect ever again."

On June 6th, I asked to borrow her car to pick Yusuf up at the Darien bus terminal. When she didn't answer, I searched her face for doubt and knew she thought I was making the whole thing up.

"I'm not kidding, Mother, really. I'm not wearing this stuff and asking you to call me A'isha for no reason."

An hour later I pulled into the driveway with Yusuf in the front seat, Mother held the door open.

"Look who's here," Mother said, gleaming. "It's Poodie Stevens."

"Mother," I whispered tensely, "please."

"Now, Lu-Lu, keep your sense of humor. Don't be so serious," she said, turning to Yusuf with her hand out. "Must I wear a veil to shake your hand?"

Her eyes twinkled, and he smiled.

"Not at all," he said, shaking her hand. "I'm pleased to meet you, Mrs.?"

"Good grief, don't you know my child's last name? It's Johnson, but Ellen is fine. Let me show you to the guest room." Yusuf handed her a piece of luggage.

"What's in this thing? Rocks?" Asked my mother.

Yusuf glanced down. "I brought my typewriter. You know, I'm always thinkin'."

"I'm glad you did," said Mother. "I'd make a wonderful topic for some lyrics."

They went upstairs, chatting all the way, and I started dinner. I heard Mother tell him it was nearly impossible for her to call me A'isha after knowing me my entire life.

"A'isha, it's time to pray, Maghrib."

"OK, I'll be right up," I called from the stove.

"You aren't really praying five times a day, are you?" Mother asked.

"I am."

"Can I watch?"

"Mother, no, you can't watch."

"He sure is pretty, even with no hair. But that beard's gotta go."

I served Mother's meatloaf in the dining room and took my place at the table.

"Allahumma barik lana fima razaqtana waqina athaban-nar," Yusuf said.

"What on earth does all that mean?" Mother asked.

"The literal translation is, 'God, bless the food you have provided us and save us from the punishment of hellfire,'" Yusuf said.

"That's ominous. I don't like the sounds of that," she said. "It reminds me of Catholicism, which my mother tried to force down my throat. Thank God my father was Episcopalian. Can we come up with something more positive?"

"You have to remember the culture within which it was written and practiced. It's a supplication, or du'a, to remind us that all blessin's come from Allah. It is a way to communicate with Allah and feel connected."

"Like saying grace before a meal, but with a threat," Mother said. "Too much unnecessary information."

Yusuf didn't submit.

"No, not really. The du'a is a private moment with Allah and is not said communally. I say it quietly, to myself."

"Great dinner service, Lu," said Mother. "Oops! A'isha. You know, Poodie, Yusuf, I think it's quite funny that Lucy had posters of you all over her bedroom walls growing up. I took them down before you arrived. Her father bought musical books and let her choose which photographs to blow up. Ruined the wallpaper. She never listened to anyone else's music and ran away to find you, which I see she finally has. Again, if her first story was true."

I shrunk. Yusuf didn't respond, but quietly recited to himself. Mother kept talking.

"What kind of music do you like? I adore big band music, which you know nothing about. And I am quite fond of Stevie Wonder, the Rolling Stones, Elton John, and the Allman Brothers. Do you ever listen to your own albums? That must be strange."

Yusuf finally looked up.

"I've nothin' much to do with music anymore," he replied blandly.

"How depressing," my mother said.

Over the next week, if we weren't taking a walk, praying, or eating, Yusuf was on his typewriter in the guest room. After we walked around downtown New Canaan, acquaintances, friends, parents, siblings, and strangers found reasons to "pop over." Mother entertained the throngs and served cucumber finger sandwiches. If we weren't there, people waited in the driveway. If Yusuf was holed up in his room, they stayed until he came downstairs. We visited Timmi at the Ox Ridge Hunt Club, where she worked, and walked through the stables. Young girls in beige jodhpurs dropped their equine tasks to steal a look. The horses nuzzled Yusuf's neck and investigated his fingers with their velvet muzzles. "They're so sensual, really," he giggled.

We walked at Waveny Park the day Yusuf left and sat on the grass against an old oak.

"Are you sure you want me to come back to London?" I asked.

"If you are serious about bein' my wife. You must be patient with me, A'isha."

"I have been, for longer than you know. I've never kept so much inside. I just hope I've shown some of what I feel."

"You have. Have I?"

"Yes."

"I feel so much for you," he said, stroking my back with the palm of his hand. "I honestly never thought I would fall in love with my wife. I thought I'd marry a Muslim woman and love would come with time. This is magical. And right."

Yusuf was off to Greece, and I stretched out on the empty guest room bed. He'd left a wadded pile of damp towels on the floor next to the night table. I picked one from the top, lay it over my face, and counted the days before returning to London. I smelled musk oil.

Mother came in, with a bottle of Pledge and a soft piece of fabric, to clean the room.

"For God's sake, the man didn't lift a finger. He couldn't even bring his water glass down from the night before."

CHAPTER 14

Fauzia

It was as if I'd never stripped. What was the Naked i and who was Princess Cheyenne?

Back in Boston, I found a mosque and continued with daily prayers, which kept me grounded and focused on marrying Yusuf as a Muslim woman. In preparation for living in London, I started saying goodbye to people and giving things away. Any leftover time was spent increasing my running distances until I felt a gripping pain in my lower ribcage. Thinking my body needed to move and stretch, I started taking dance classes at the Joy of Movement Center, veil and all.

Yusuf called daily, usually more than once. He inexplicably changed the flight back to London several times and said he planned to return to New Canaan to make a formal proposal before my mother but didn't say when. Mother said Poodie could visit again if he promised to bring his empty glasses to the kitchen.

Yusuf and I spent hours on the phone. He seemed more himself and relaxed. Maybe it was the distance between us. His mother was recovering from surgery in the hospital the day he started fretting about my being in Boston. He said a city had too many temptations for a new Muslim woman.

In my journal, I wrote, *Things to remember in England—I am me; I want to explore, I have a life ahead of me, I have goals, it is not a sin to live and experience life, take time to think before acting, keep it slow and in perspective.* Not that I knew how to heed my own advice.

A couple of days later, while Yusuf was making jam, his mother got on the phone for a chat.

"Fauzia?" she asked.

"No, it's me, A'isha. Soon to be your daughter-in-law."

"Stop teasing, now. It's Fauzia."

Who the fuck is Fauzia? I repeated the name slowly to myself. I didn't like the name but didn't know why until I recalled the sisters in London telling me about the father who wanted his daughter, Fauzia, to marry Yusuf. I remembered his being unnaturally perturbed when I'd made friends at the mosque. Then there were the constant date changes.

I leaned into the wall. The phone made rubbing sounds as Mum handed the phone to Yusuf. I hung up and fell onto the couch.

Yusuf called back immediately. We didn't mention his mother's cognitive lapse and I was silent. Over time, our conversations grew shorter.

One media outlet's version of how my relationship with Yusuf ended.

While enjoying Gay Head Beach on Martha's Vineyard, I shed the hijab and wore only my birthday suit.

I couldn't bring myself to ask for clarification but couldn't ignore the hurdle.

When my cousins from Greenwich invited me to Martha's Vineyard for the last week in June, I was relieved by the distraction. I shared my plans with Mother and she asked why Yusuf hadn't set a date to officially propose.

"The writing's on the wall," she said. "Besides, you can't marry a man with no sense of humor."

She was right. Yusuf had no sense of humor. Had we laughed together? I couldn't remember. For him, I could live without laughter. He was subdued, logical, and focused, exactly what I needed.

I stayed at Aunt Audrey's guest cottage in Edgartown. My cousins and I had picnics with warm brie and white grapes, went to the movies, body-surfed, and rode horses bareback on Katama Beach.

They noticed the constant trans-Atlantic calls, sometimes at three in the morning. They took turns answering the phone just so they could hear his voice. Yusuf was audibly tense when I mentioned going to the beach. He said it was anti-Islamic. I didn't divulge that I'd visited Gay Head and gone nude into the clay pits.

His calls lasted just long enough to ask where I was, who I was with, and what I was doing. Nothing about how I felt or what I was thinking. One day he called eight times, each call lasting less than three minutes. He was tracking me. Even my cousins got sick of him.

Back in Boston, I started interval training on the MIT track and took long, slow runs at 2 in the morning. If I didn't answer late-night calls, he became suspicious. I told him I was running and that too was "anti-Islamic." If our calls were disconnected, Yusuf blamed me. One time the song "Hard-Headed Woman" played on the radio when we were talking. I turned the volume up so he could hear it, and he told me that's what he thought when we first met. Maybe Yusuf said that to other women, too.

By mid-summer I still had no definitive plans. I sensed an opening during an unusually relaxed conversation and knew I needed to take the plunge and ask about Fauzia, his coming to New Canaan, and my anticipated trip back to London, but I didn't. I shared something about myself instead.

"I am afraid you won't accept me, that I won't be good enough," I said. "You act like you don't want me as your wife anymore."

He ignored my conversational foray. I wanted to scream into the phone.

"There's a Muslim brother who will be callin' you. He's new to Boston," he said,

"Why is he calling me?" I asked. "That's creepy."

"He's just arrivin' and doesn't know the city."

"Then tell him to find a man to show him around."

I felt cast off. Rather than rock the boat, I distracted myself and ran further and harder. I thought about my Wonder Woman alter-ego, Mildred Schwartz, and how funny she was, and left my hijab at home for the first time. Looking to provoke a reckoning, I told Yusuf what I used to do for work, hoping the disturbance would shock him enough to come back to me, his future wife. He went on about how we all have pasts.

I stoked the fire.

"In case you want to know what I do all day, I'm taking dance classes, like ballet and jazz, and training for the Boston Marathon."

It didn't register.

"Your suitcase was returned to London yesterday. I want you there with it, A'isha. The ties aren't broken and never will be."

His loving words were brilliant, but our reality was empty.

"Then what is our plan? Everything's dangling and unknown."

He wants me in London, and his heart wants to be with me, but his actions contradict his wants.

I vowed to pin him down whenever we talked.

"My mother wants to know when you're coming to New Canaan to propose."

"Insha'Allah," he said.

"It's hard living with this uncertainty, Yusuf; let's set the return date now."

"Insha'Allah."

"I was supposed to come back on July 10th, then the 17th, then the 21st, and now next month. I'd like to come back next Thursday."

"Insha'Allah."

It was tiresome, and soon became infuriating.

I hated my incompetence. I lacked the skills to successfully negotiate the impasse. I berated myself for hiding questions about Fauzia and not being myself and confronting him head on. I didn't know how to prepare countermeasures against anonymous adversaries. Yusuf offering my companionship to the "Muslim brother" should have prompted fierce objection rather than cowardice. I'd not managed the red flags well. I never did.

"I used to be a stripper." I enunciated, this time in a stand-alone sentence.

He said he was shocked, yet within minutes spoke lovingly, reiterating vague promises for our future. I decided to choose measured anger over helplessness. I told my story to a freelance journalist I'd met, and she sold the story to *People* magazine.

Lucy Was Cat's Meow but When She Bared Her Soul She Got Scratched
By Nancy McMillan
August 20, 1979

Can a rock star turned Muslim turned recluse find wedded bliss with a hippie turned vegetarian turned stripper? It is not an idle question.

Consider the case of Cat Stevens, who two years ago began to embrace Islam, stopped touring and adopted the name Yusuf.

In 1976 Stevens had met Lucy Johnson, a 16-year-old fresh-faced blonde who was tossed out of New York's exclusive Emma Willard School for smoking marijuana. Backstage at one of his concerts, Lucy slipped Cat a poem ("really tacky," she remembers) and he took her to dinner. "It blossomed," as Lucy puts it, "into a one-night stand." Cat went back on the road and Lucy joined a commune, later settling down to become a stripper named Princess Cheyenne in Boston's famed Combat Zone.

Lucy met Cat again in May. Now deeply religious, he entertained her for a month in London, where they had frequent dinners with his mother. They studied Islam at his mosque (where she took the name A'isha) and talked of marriage. Lucy did not mention her showbiz career.

In June Cat visited Lucy's mother in Connecticut. Lucy, already a non-drinking vegetarian, took to preparing Muslim meals in her three-room Boston flat. By July Cat was telephoning her regularly from London. "One night we kept getting disconnected," recalls Lucy. Cat told her it might be some sort of omen.

Late in July Lucy thought it was time to tell Cat everything and called him to describe her now dormant career as one of Boston's better-known burlesque queens. There was a sharp intake of breath, then silence. Lucy remembers Cat's next words: "I'm shocked."

"He made some noises about my past being past," Lucy recalls, "but when I told him I wanted to continue with acting lessons, he really freaked out. I don't want to give up things like backpacking, horseback riding, acting and dancing. He thinks we should give up everything pleasurable."

For his part, Stevens (who still uses his stage name) acknowledges that he is looking for a bride, but at the moment Lucy isn't the one. "It would take a long time before she could become a good Muslim wife," he says, adding that he is courting a woman in London who fits those requirements.

Lucy says she's still getting trans-Atlantic Cat calls. "He'll ask me to come over right away, and then call back and say we shouldn't see each other. He changes his mind when it comes to music, too. I don't know how he's going to reconcile his religion with performing, at least for money. He says we should give up everything, but he flies to Washington, D.C. just to get his teeth capped. Basically, he's a bundle of contradictions."

I'd only skimmed the article when I called Mother. She hung up. I preemptively reread the article dozens of times before bed, trying to assign the words between the quotation marks to Yusuf. I wasn't the one and didn't fit his requirements.

I called him.

"You lied to me over and over. You convinced me that everything you said was true, that you loved me and that we were getting married. How could you do that? You must have lied to her too."

At first, he sputtered, unable to put a meaningful sentence together. Then he coldly stated that a written letter would suit his needs better.

Oh, well fucking excuse me.

Over the next few days, I developed a fever and it hurt to breathe. I went to the emergency room at Beth Israel Hospital and waited in a scooped-out plastic chair. I left my headscarf at home. A doctor with dark, arching brows and an impeccably trimmed beard sauntered my way. He looked as though he belonged on an ancient throne atop a windy cliff, at least until he fidgeted with a clipboard.

"Miss?"

"Yes, hi."

"You're Louise?"

I nodded.

"This way, please. Name's Guy."

He walked ahead of me like a Muslim man.

"Dr. Guy?"

"You can call me Guy. I'm actually a hand doctor. Saw you waiting and had some time on my hands."

"Hardy har. That's a terrible joke. I don't need a hand doctor; I need a lung doctor."

We entered a cubicle walled off by curtains, where he asked me about my symptoms before prescribing antibiotics.

"Do you live in the area?" Guy asked.

"Back Bay."

"I live in the Back Bay as well. What street are you on?"

"Marlboro and Mass. Ave."

"Two blocks away."

I didn't recall giving him my number, but he called me the following day.

"Hey, it's Guy, the doctor who saw you at the ER."

"I remember. Hi, it's Guy? Poor guy, having to say, 'Hi, it's Guy' your whole life."

"What? Is this Louise?"

"You can call me Lucy. I was commenting on the rhyme you've lived with your entire life."

"Uh-huh. I called to check on you and ensure you pick up that prescription."

He sounded stern, a real take-charge kind of guy, the antithesis of Yusuf.

"I'll pick it up. Thanks for calling."

"How about brunch and a movie when you feel better?"

"I don't know. Not right now. Just dealing with stuff."

"OK. I'll check in next week. Gorgeous photograph of you in *People* magazine, by the way."

The ramifications of sharing details of my love life in a national magazine didn't occur to me. While Mother and Yusuf were burning the article for different reasons, Nan called from Lake Forest to see about getting a framed print of the photograph. Mel offered me $110 a night to return to work, and a man alleging to be a film producer from Warner Brothers called to cast me in three movies. I hung up on him. Several local TV talk shows, including *Woman 79*, booked me as their guest and I forgot about Guy.

Yusuf's beautifully penned, emotionally barren letter arrived on August 21st. It took him four pages and seven words to confirm the truth: "A Muslim woman was introduced to me."

Was he ever going to tell me what I was up against or give me a chance to prove myself? How long had he planned on stringing me along like a toy? I considered his possible motives, but stopped. It was only guesswork. He was locked away inside himself until he decided to peek out. I had lived for those moments.

"There you are my American girl!" "I truly have been praying for a girl, and the girl is you. It is you, A'isha." "I want to be all you need." "There's so much my heart wants to say, A'isha." "We shall be married in Allah's name." "I want officially propose in front of your mother." "All ties aren't broken; they never will be." "My heart wants to be with you." "Sweetness." Words. Anyone can use them.

Several days before he was to marry Fauzia, I set the alarm for 1:30 a.m., 6:30 a.m. Yusuf time. After telling him I was happy for him, I admitted to the lie. I said I was confused and that I missed him and our future. Thoughts streamed from my mouth without pause or filter.

"How did I let this happen? I should have pressed you on things as they came up, but I was afraid I'd ruin it. I'm not exactly powerless or weak. I can stand up to things and have—plenty of times. Not that you would know since you never asked me anything about my life. Do you even know what happened? Or remember how we started? No and no. You don't remember because you had different women every night of the week, and I was just one of them. I knew that."

I didn't know if he was still on the phone, but I kept going.

"I'm the one that gave you that stupid rose in New Haven, waited for you in New York City, at JP's, where you asked me to have dinner with you, like you expected it, or for me to be there, waiting for you. I may have been only sixteen, but I knew exactly what I was doing. We ate a plate of mushrooms, dealt with the flowers outside the limo, went to the Pierre, and then, to cap things off, I lost my virginity to you. From the time I knew anything about sex, I refused to get near boys. Why? Because I was saving myself for you. Saving myself. Imagine that? Who does that? When Jay Sanderson tried to kiss me at choir practice, I refused. I wouldn't even kiss anyone. You knew I was a virgin because you sensed it and asked. I didn't lie. We made love again in the morning, and twice I went to your dinky little altar and looked at the Qur'an, the one I have with me now, the same one, Yusuf, the one David gave you. You didn't even know my name because you never asked.

"Then I waited three years and two months to come back to find you again, on a whim or something. What are the odds? Tell me, what are the odds? There's no statistical formula on the planet that would predict this happening, none. I didn't know you were waiting for an American to convert and marry. How would I know that? It felt so natural to be with you. I forgot about the whole Cat Stevens thing within a day. You were Yusuf. Obviously, we both felt strongly, and you confirmed everything; you said we were getting married. You still haven't told me we're not.

"Can you begin to imagine what this has done to me? Changing the dates, committing, promising, assuring, and not following through, playing me so I'd tag along? What am I, just in case? A backup wife for you? A second or third wife? And what was with trying to hand me off to some Muslim stranger? Really? I'm a baton in a relay race? A cow up for auction? We love each other. We are not strangers. So go ahead, marry little Miss fucking Fauzia, who you don't even know. See how great that is. And you know I would have made a really great Muslim fucking wife!"

I was out of breath and broken. Silence.

"Yusuf?"

I thought he hung up.

"A'isha, I, uh, well, anything can happen in the future. I know we'll be together. I know it from the deepest parts of myself."

Although ill-equipped to sustain a relationship and very self-centered, I was learning to pivot into other perspectives. I knew a lifelong Muslim woman could teach him, hold him on course, and answer his questions. His was a practical decision based on fear, not love. He'd distanced himself, narrowed his vision, and considered the functions he needed rather than love and its possibilities. I imagined Fauzia excelled at cooking, housekeeping, praying, procreating, keeping up appearances, and complying. That dirty word, comply.

Yusuf continued to call and write long after he married. Early on, he wrote, "Being married satisfies a lot of innocent needs, but she gives me quite a headache." Eventually, his communications faded.

Whatever quirks of fate or wrinkles in time caused us to meet twice, and with such immediate familiarity and intensity, were mysterious. As was I. I needed to learn who I was, and a return to Princess Cheyenne was a good start.

CHAPTER 15

Princess Cheyenne

It was as if I'd never stopped being Princess Cheyenne. I packed away my long skirts and hijab, and bought spandex pants in red, blue, and black. I stayed in constant motion and ran more than sixty miles a week. I returned to weight training, took at least one dance class a day, and, for variety, added yoga and swimming to my repertoire.

The YWCA in Cambridge was located across the street from the Joy of Movement Center and had daily nude swims. I used the opportunity to become a better swimmer and, within two weeks, was completing 40 laps per day in a full-on, naked crawl.

I took a shiatsu class, started exploring macrobiotic cuisine, and learned how to write about feelings in my journal. I considered the future, thought about college, and tried to forget about Yusuf. I decided to visit my friend Beth in Boulder around Christmas to explore the options for an ex-Muslim, high-school dropout at the University of Colorado.
My relationship with Mother shifted. Maybe it was my newfound interest in college that brought us closer. I seized the opportunity and invited her to Boston and an Elton John concert for her birthday. She accepted.

We spent the afternoon exploring the high-end shops on Newbury Street before changing into concert attire. Mother wore green espadrille shoes, a wraparound skirt, turtleneck, and cardigan sweater tied loosely around her shoulders. She didn't comment on my spandex pants, pink satin shirt,

My stint in London sparked many changes in me personally, and Princess Cheyenne was on fire.

or cowboy hat. We sipped champagne in the back of a Phantom Rolls Royce on our way to dinner and headed to the Music Hall to see Elton John from fifth-row seats. Mother insisted on bringing the two dozen long-stemmed roses I gave her.

"It's what fans do," she said.

Halfway through the show, something unexpected happened. She clutched the huge swath of flowers and rushed the stage. My jaw dropped when Elton John took the roses from her hands and smiled.

On our way home, Mother insisted we drive by the Naked i. We slowed to a stop in front, and she peered out the window at the marquee and photographs.

"I see the Princess Cheyenne status is intact despite your slip into Islamic life," Mother said, clearing her throat. "Cute picture, Lu, if you weren't naked."

When I returned to work, the Naked i had completed a second-floor dressing room. Aside from that, and the departure of a few dancers, it was—quite literally—the same familiar grind.

Dancers frequently quit and returned. Most women started stripping, not on a whim, but as a temporary solution, a time-limited gig, a means to a supposed end or an adjunctive, monetary uptick. Compared to other jobs, the parameters and rewards were unsurpassed. Stripping was loaded with vocational charm: we worked in perpetual adolescence, were guaranteed adoration, and most irresponsible decisions were forgiven or rewarded. The Naked i's revolving door was always in motion.

It felt good to be home, talking and listening to people's reflections in the mirror while sitting naked on a plastic chair, eating Guddler's freshly caught lobster. There was always fresh drama brewing.

As I adjusted to my reentry that first night back, a new dancer fidgeted with her labial piercing. The dressing-room committee prepared to weigh in, with Dori at the helm.

"Dang. No magnets around you. How many you got goin'?" Dori asked.

"Let's see. I have two labia piercings, a clitoral bar, a tiny little diamond, it's real by the way, on the in-between part, and a fake one near my anus. Lemme see now, that's five. Two nipples make seven, belly button makes eight. Then one on my tongue, one under it, and both nostrils make twelve."

"At least you can add. What's your name?"

"I'm calling myself Thyme, like the seasoning, if it's not taken. I love my mother's thyme chicken casserole."

"Nobody will know it's not related to a clock," said Wilhelmina. "Tick, tick, tick."

"Right. Good point. Unless the DJ spells it."

"No way will that work."

"Yeah, no."

"Uh-uh."

"Up next on our front stage is Thyme, spelled with a y, m, and e."

"Please welcome the herb, Thyme."

"Pick another herb."

"Ok, then. Anise."

"Nope. Sounds like anus."

"Catnap?"

"-nip."

"What's that red powder that tastes like nothing and goes on top of white fish and potato salad and shit?" Dori asked.

"Lawry Salt?"

"No, not Lawry Salt."

"Paprika?"

"That's it. Paprika. I love it. Thank you."

Paprika's metal collection flashed unexpectedly, like glass on pavement. You never knew when or from where she might sparkle. She spent most of her earnings on additional piercings until, one night, she staggered off the stage slurring her words and lost consciousness. Sepsis put Paprika in the hospital and a damper on piercings.

While arranging things inside a locker, I responded to stray greetings of "Hey, Chey." I noticed a water-filled glass bowl sitting on the makeup table. Something moved inside of it.

"What the heck is that thing?" I asked.

"That's Bernie," answered Jazz. "One of my customers gave me a fish."

"It's eyeballing me," said Dori. "It's creepy."

"Hello lonely little Bernie fish," Jazz laughed, tapping the bowl with her fingernail.

"There's nothing in his bowl. Shouldn't he have, like, plastic leaves or something?" asked Dori.

"That's dangerous. Bernie could shred his pretty fins on sharp plastic leaves."

"You could also blow his eardrums out by tapping on the dang glass. He looks cold, wet, and depressed to me," said Dori. "Can I pet it?"

"Jesus, Dori, no." Jazz walked protectively toward the fishbowl. "I mean really, when was the last time you pet a fish in a bowl of water, or in anything?"

"I did, at some water park where you paid to pet the dolphins," said Udon, in the midst of a Downward Dog yoga posture.

"Dolphins are mammals, not fish," said Wilhelmina.

"OK, guys. Sorry, just asking. I'm not touching your dang fish; I'm just taking my makeup off the table."

Dori removed the bag between Bernie and the mirror, and the tadpole-sized fish jumped up and out of the bowl, a trail of water beads in its wake.

"What did you do?" Jazz yelled, corralling the dark wiggling fish against the mirror and into her palm.

"Shut the fuck up, Jazz. I didn't do nothing," said Dori. "I moved my makeup bag is all. I dare you to swallow it."

"That would be mean. Come on you guys, really," I said.

"Oh Princess, stop being so sensitive. You eat that nasty old sushi too," said Dori. "What's the difference? I'll give anyone 100 bucks just to see it."

Jazz slipped Bernie's torquing body into the bowl and Lauren sauntered over. She was relatively new but already known for losing her wig on stage due to a significant alcohol intake. Before Jazz could whisk the bowl away, Lauren plucked the fish out from between two fake fingernails, popped him in her mouth and swigged some champagne. Bernie was no more and Lauren was $100 richer.

"Lauren! No, you didn't! Fuck you, what the fuck? Barf it up. Who does that? Who swallows a live fish?" Jazz yelled, going for Lauren's neck.

Lauren backed away, made an exaggerated gulp, and smiled.

"Opportunists do," Lauren said calmly. "Now back off. It's too late, babe. Dori, gimme my hundred bucks so I can buy this girl a new fish."

"You're batshit crazy," Dori said, counting out the money. "Now come get me when you poop, and I'll give you another $50."

Most antics weren't as cruel. I shook this one off as I felt familiar cramping. I remembered having tucked away the diaphragm Giselle gave me and decided to take it for a test drive. I also chose to perform in a black velvet dress, just to be safe.

Mel was at his usual post and I picked out a floor-show song to surprise him. A respectable floor-show song had a melody that built, like an orgasm, but never brazenly so. "You Shook Me," by Led Zeppelin, fit the bill. I crawled down the runway on all fours, feeling like a foolish, oversized toddler. Not knowing what else to do, I made some tentative leg spreads.

"Whoa, you better check yourself," one customer yelled out.

"She must've cut herself on a piece of glass."

Blood being body temperature, I felt nothing. I assumed they were referring to someone else. Giselle leaned against Mel with crossed arms and grinned. We made eye contact and she walked away.

"Nice to see you back, Princess," she hissed over her shoulder.

Numb with embarrassment, I flew into the bathroom to rinse myself off and removed the diaphragm. I was about to throw it away when I saw the hole of light in its center and, upon further inspection, spotted dozens of smaller holes. Birth control barriers didn't have holes and, apparently, one dancer's jealousy knew no bounds. A trip to Sam's Joke Shop was in order.

I would have acted on my revenge immediately, but following the article in *People* magazine, publicity soared. It seemed like every day there was a new request for an interview or guest appearance on a talk show. One thing fed into the next, and the next, until it became never-ending.

I was named "The Best Dressed Bostonian" by the *Boston Herald American*. *Boston* magazine labeled me "Noblesse Oblige Overachiever," when comparing me to "Underachiever Caroline Kennedy." I had to look up the words "noblesse" and "oblige." Profiles were done in every local paper, and Norma Nathan, the *Herald*'s feisty gossip columnist, featured something about me at least once a month.

Nathan and I got on so well that we had a standing lunch date at Legal Sea Foods, even when I had nothing juicy to report. I was glad to be on her good side. Any move I made was fodder for her column, "The Eye," including my wearing running shorts to a restaurant opening or refusing to wear stilettos.

Local and national talk shows invited me to be their guest, sometimes requiring that I be flown out of state. DJs at the iconic rock station, WBCN, 104.1 FM, wanted to nominate me for mayor and I became a frequent visitor to WBZ radio, where I sat with David Brudnoy and Norm Nathan. I was invited to dance on Harvard Lampoon's 30-foot banquet table and asked to write a review of male strippers at the Golden Banana.

Every time I was in the public eye, I gained more power to change things at work. The exchange of public relations for privilege was a loose equation, but one I understood well. I chipped away at perceived inconveniences, negotiating music volume, show schedules, and drink hustling.

Not only did Mel agree to set a show schedule, but he also printed it in the *Boston Globe*, the *Herald*, the Boston *Phoenix*, and in the back of *Boston* magazine. My 7, 9, 11 p.m., and 1 a.m. shows were also listed out front. When I decided that the 1 a.m. show was too late, we moved it to 12:40 a.m.

I no longer had to mix with customers and could leave the premises between my shows. Mel still forbade me to touch the music volume and refused to change the name of the Pussy Galore Stag Bar because he said it was named after a James Bond character. Even so, it felt like working in a different club.

More of the club's customers came in to see me and the crowds gathered before show times. Twenty minutes later they drained out like bath water.

Dressing room unrest increased as more onlookers wondered aloud about "The Princess," in reaction to every new piece of press about "The Princess," and to every change to club protocol initiated by "The Princess." Dancers moaned, with good reason, about dancing behind me on the back stage while I performed on the main stage. They whined to management about having to follow me on the show schedule and perform to an emptying room.

I found out who my friends were, like Jazz, who confronted me differently. She made it easy to discuss things and I didn't get defensive. I loved her laugh, and how she added the words like "burger" or "meister" for comic effect.

"The worst thing they did was publicize your schedule," she said, holding an eyelash curler steady. "What are they, stoopid?" she asked, feigning a Providence accent.

"You mean because of the marketing part?" I asked sincerely.

"Aha!" Jazz laughed her exclamation. "Clever girl."

"Woman," I said.

Jazz enjoyed calling me by my given name. "Oh, Louise, really. Don't take yourself so seriously. Hold on. Let me switch eyes."

She trapped the opposite eyelid with the metal clamps and continued.

"Sort of. Why drive people in and out so quickly? Keep them guessing. Let them wait around and order more alcohol. Seems like a complete no-brainer to me. Wait, wonder, and drink. Maybe then you wouldn't have to deal with so many holes in your diaphragm."

"Should I suggest it to Mel or Ray?" I asked.

"Louise, you can be so brilliant and then so idiotic. God, no, unless you want to backtrack and give up your gains and risk mine."

"I'm confused. You just told me it's bad, but now say not to change it."

"Because, selfishly, I have a plan," Jazz proclaimed, thrusting a round hairbrush toward the ceiling. "I will make use of my fabulous voice," she said, followed by a perfectly toned scale of notes in her highest soprano voice. "I will ask Mel for a microphone that no one else can use! And, whilst I have your Ladyship's ear, I'd like some say in your musical choices from this point forward, since I, too, must dance to your heinous lineup on occasion. Think of it like a piggyback on your power. No Vivaldi. Forget Mannheim Steamroller, as well. Renaissance Fair music doesn't work for me. Now, what is your solution for my following you on the front stage? For keeping the crowd here?"

"I don't know. What's in this for me?"

"It's good will, Louise. Maybe you won't be targeted. Talk me up through spread legs."

"OK, announce through the legs only. Should I also ramble on about you, pass out flyers that highlight that tedious old evening gown you like to wear?"

We both laughed.

"Once I sing like a little bird, nobody will notice."

Within a week, Jazz procured her own microphone (not to be touched by anyone else), along with recordings of instrument accompaniment. She debuted with "Wind Beneath My Wings." Her efforts birthed a new stripper subset called the "co-feature," which Mel and Ray both agreed to. This tamped down everyone's complaints but Giselle's, and dancers focused on creative aspirations that would result in their being "co-featured."

Privilege afforded me a cushioned version of stripping. It set me apart, so I was only partially absorbed into the Naked i culture. As much as I wanted to be part of the whole, I more enjoyed the royalties that accompanied being The Princess.

A strange thing started happening. Every time I danced, the music became softer until finally, it dropped to barely perceptible levels and all I heard were conversations. I insisted Giselle was behind it and Mel assured me this wasn't the case, that people wanted to hear their own conversations. I took matters into my own hands by increasing the volume, only to have it disappear seconds later. I walked off the stage in my first stripper snit and Mel fired me.

I moped and penned a sappy, pleading note: "Dear Mel, I apologize for turning the music up, and I know that apologies, sincere apologies, don't include the word 'but,' but, I can't dance if I can't hear the music. I can't dance to conversation. There must be a solution."

When he didn't respond right away, I squeezed into my new spandex pants and kept dancing. Udon and I went to a club on Lansdowne Street called Boston-Boston. I was happy no matter where I danced.

While taking a dance-floor break, I flounced my hair up and down, hoping to dry the sweat, when a young man with vines painted on his face started playing with my hair. Bertrand was from France, on MDMA (the drug commonly known as Ecstasy, or Molly), and lived with a couple at the Piano Factory, where artists rented affordable loft space. He worked at the Coolidge Corner movie house, and the couple provided housing and a stipend. Udon sauntered over as Bertrand explained that they paid him as a sort of sex slave, or toy. Because he was breathtaking, it sounded intriguing, but also a bit strange. I'd never heard of that type of arrangement.

While Udon and I hung on every word, the club's manager, Patrick Lyons, introduced himself. He was a nice-looking man, like a stretched version of Donny Osmond with green eyes and a stronger jaw. Within minutes, Lyons convinced Udon and me to co-host an upcoming Halloween party at the club, along with a contingent of drag queens. I'd never hosted a party and didn't understand why he wanted us in on it. Udon spread the word among her European Back Bay friends and I went to my press connections. We both weighed in on the event decor.

Before the party, Mel called.

"I wouldn't have considered rehiring you five days ago, but since I read your note, I'm thinking about it."

He probably meant, "I'm thinking about putting up with you for the publicity." Two days later he told me not to come back, but to what end I didn't know. I put it out of my mind as I busied myself with the party.

Timmi came up from New Canaan with a couple of other friends, who wore my Naked i costumes. I concocted an ice costume out of beads and metallic body paint. Pat Lyons greeted us at the door, excited to show off the club's transformation. There were leaves two feet deep, silver pumpkins on pedestals, smoke, monsters, and hanging vines. The enormous club was a fantastical space that became filled with hundreds of fantastical people. Among the crowd of shimmering revelers was Poison Ivy, green skin and all, a man in a stag's head studded with rhinestones, the Pope, countless nuns, some with beards, a few Dolly Partons, and a giant Quaalude. We danced until our feet burned. Then I went home with Pat.

It was the first of many parties, and he was the first of many men.

Guy, from the ER, resurfaced.

"Come watch a movie and have some breakfast."

"When?"

"In two hours."

A rational person would have refused. I sprinted to his apartment. He buzzed me into a fragrant foyer with dark wood and stained glass. Lox, bagels, and cream cheese were arranged on a low coffee table with an ornate silver tray displaying hairbrushes.

Hairbrushes? No popcorn? Seeing hair in close to proximity to food caused my upper lip to curl.

"Bad association to bagels?" he asked.

"It's the whole hair/food combo."

Guy moved the tray to a stately desk and scooped me against him. He smelled like nutmeg and lemon.

"Yikes," I blurted.

"Is that bad or good or both?" he asked, gathering my hair around his forearm.

He went on, not leaving a breath for me to answer. Not only was Guy a hand surgeon, but according to him, a film director, soon to be in Paris to see Samuel Beckett. He went to Harvard, Yale for fine arts, BU med school. It didn't occur to me how much time that might take, or that he was lying. I wanted to unbutton his shirt.

"Uh, uh, uh," he scolded me, wagging one finger. "You know what really gets me off?"

"Isn't it kind of soon to start with that?"

He put an arm underneath my legs and whisked me into his bedroom. I felt a tickle of dread, or was that excitement? Given I could count my sexual partners on one hand, I didn't know. Sex so far had been mindlessly straightforward.

"If you're a good girl, I might feed you."

"That's absurd."

The statements just fell out as he plopped me onto a mammoth, manly bed.

"I didn't take you as shy," he said.

"Shy? No, I meant your statement sounded ridiculous."

"Is this part of your game?"

I was lost.

"Is there some kind of theme here you want to tell me about?"

"I like the word cock when a woman says it."

It sounded painfully cliché, and I laughed.

"Maybe we could get to know each other first."

I thought this was a reasonable way to slow things down.

"Now take off your clothes and get the brush tray! You've been a naughty girl."

"Woman," I said, still laughing.

"What?"

"Nothing. Don't worry about it."

I got off the bed and walked away slowly while unbuttoning my jeans, shaking a little to force them to the floor. I returned with the tray and no thoughts about what a hairbrush had to do with sex.

"Nobody's ever brushed my hair before, well, except for my mother, of course."

Guy ignored me and selected an oval wooden brush. He tapped the back of it against his palm.

"Don't worry, I have ice."

"Ice?"

"Silence!"

He sat on a chair without arms. "Come here," he said, removing his belt.

I turned around so he could brush my hair.

"No," he said. "Stand before me and remove my shirt. Then carefully hang it on that hanger," he pointed.

"Hang up your shirt? Oh my God. You've got to be kidding me. Hang up your own shirt."

Even though Guy was catnip, my desire evaporated. I couldn't find anything sexy about fetching a tray of hairbrushes and being ordered to hang up a stranger's shirt.

"Turn back around and sit so I can brush your tresses."

"Now we're talking," I said as he first put his fingers through my hair.

Guy started brushing and I sunk like melting putty onto his lap.

"Now lay across my knees."

I did as he said and when I faced my body down onto his lap it was clear how much this aroused him. He stung my rear end with the bristle side of the brush, causing me to buck and squirm to escape. One of his arms was anchored against my lower back, but I reached the ground with my feet, splayed my toes, and rose against the weight of his hold like a giant frog.

"I'm good," I said.

"I could be much better," he said, brandishing the brush in one hand and adjusting his crotch with the other.

"Not my thing."

I got back into my jeans and left. Clearly, I had a lot to learn. Men consistently showed me they were more complicated than they looked.

Yusuf called to invite me to a concert he was giving in London, but I tamped down any latent optimism.

"Here we go again. I thought music was taboo," I said.

Rather than respond directly, he told me he'd had an amazing, powerful dream about me, one that I would have been happy about. I knew enough not to ask for details.

"You're very much still in my consciousness," he said.

He would always be in mine.

CHAPTER 16

The Pussy Galore Stag Bar

The tail end of the Sexual Revolution was the perfect bronco for me to buck. In the late 1970s and early 1980s, sex was as common as saying hello. After I'd been spurned as a suitably demure wife for a devout Muslim male, I became the antithesis. I ran wild and unchecked. And, in fact, casually screwing several people in a day had no repercussions. No one expected monogamy. It was stifling and unnecessary. Sex had nothing to do with making babies or world peace. It was its own reward.

Erotic escapades were gleaned from magnetic passings and stray glances on Newbury Street, meeting friends of friends of friends, press opportunities, nightclubs, grocery stores, gallery openings, museum exhibitions, and performance art parties, but never, ever at the Naked i.

Art, sensuality, and exhibitionism converged in dark loft spaces where performance artists entertained at "open house" parties. It seemed as if everyone in the city of Boston was invited and included without question. If you didn't like one performance, you walked less than a block to the next. Overcrowded and dimly lit, anything could happen. It was impossible to avoid touching. No one wanted to avoid it, anyway.

At one performance, I stood against a kitchen island and rested my foot on the bottom rung of a stool. It was jammed, yet people still nudged through the door. Things got so tight that a stranger's erection pressed against me from behind. I felt its warmth through my flimsy, calf-length skirt but didn't bother turning around. I wasn't wearing underwear. I didn't believe in underwear. For fun, I moved my foot to the next highest rung, leaned forward, and rested my forearms on the counter. As I stretched out, a hand landed on my shoulder, and I felt him slip underneath my skirt. I took his hand and led the man through the wide hallway into a large, slow freight elevator. After pressing the roof button, I looked at the shirtless man in painter's overalls with rags of black hair and blue eyes. We scrambled to the floor, and when the elevator doors rattled open, I was on top of him. His name was Brad, and I never saw him again, but not because I wouldn't have. It's just how things went back then.

There were plenty of men I saw regularly. Like Bertrand, the French sex toy from the Piano Factory. He had a knack for visiting just hours after my being with Patrick from Boston-Boston, or Marty from *Evening Magazine*. I met Hillel running, which was the same way I met Thomas, Johnny, two Michaels, and three Joes. I met Glenn as he careened out of a deli on rollerblades while, at the same time, biting into a sandwich named after me. The eponymous "Princess Cheyenne Sandwich," featured in a Newbury Street café, had grilled chicken breast, honey mustard, and Boston lettuce between broiled, buttered bread.

"Hey, you're eating me," I said.

It was a great pickup line. Off we went.

While shopping for tofu cheesecake ingredients at Erehwon, the natural food store on Newbury Street, I fixated on an aproned man arranging daikon radishes in the produce section. His 45-minute lunch break was plenty of time before a professor named Christopher taught his last class across the river at MIT. I didn't know anybody's last name. It was unnecessary.

I liked men. I embraced them wholeheartedly, some for a few minutes and some for weeks. No matter how brief the encounter was, I learned something new. Like how most men rarely had more than one orgasm. Poor things. I could easily have fifteen.

I wondered if I might like women and found out the night Trish and her boyfriend joined the Naked i clan for a night of dancing at Boston-Boston. She'd recently taken to grazing her nipples against my back at work or leaning into me while we were naked. I could always appreciate a beautiful body, but felt more tingly than merely appreciative. Her boyfriend was on Quaaludes and stayed crouched in a corner, drooling, fighting to maintain consciousness. Once he lost the battle, we booked it to the ladies room and kissed. It wasn't the last time. The boyfriend thought our subsequent rendezvous included him, but he graciously ingested enough Quaaludes to pass out every time. After a few encounters with Trish, I wondered why women weren't all over each other at work. Soon, we were.

After some press about the Boston-Boston party, Mel asked me to return to work. I did, which led to my hosting several females-only get-togethers. My apartment became a den. I borrowed several futons and embellished them with plush comforters. I dispersed candles, wine, and breath mints and set fires in both fireplaces. I invited my friend Claire as an assistant/coach. She designated my living room couch as her "classroom."

After the eighteen guests arrived, the initial dithering didn't last long. Everyone wanted to jump right in. One woman undressed another who undressed another until everyone ripped off their clothes. Some took breaks from the action to watch other women or visit Claire's couch. Every futon was occupied, and an erotic tangle of who knows how many women poured over the sides of my bed. One naked body branched into

The Pussy Galore Stag Bar was a small room with a floor-level stage that adjoined the Naked i.

another on the floor in between complex acrobatics. When Claire's couch was empty, she gently wandered the rooms and offered wine, water, towels, and suggestions. Everyone was pleasant and respectful. "Can I join you?" "Is there room for me?" and "Is it OK if I touch you?" We laughed and talked until the morning. So civilized.

That first odyssey broke things open. At work, we felt freer to explore possibilities, and we did. A few of us took a field trip to Plato's Retreat in New York City and watched soup-to-nuts kink. It was less threatening than I expected. When something wasn't your thing, you moved on to a different sandbox or stage. Those with no interest in actively participating, but who simply wanted to watch, were respected.

Dancers became more open about their experiences. Linda was one of the few married women at the Naked i. Her Czechoslovakian husband often visited, eager to discuss their elaborate sexual adventures. They hosted weekend-long role-plays and started inviting dancers from the club. One of their kinks was Linda coming home with welts of some sort.

"Hey, Cheyenne, would you mind whipping me with the thorny sides of these roses?"

It was a simple request, like asking for a cigarette.

Once I decided to go to college, my father started visiting me in Boston.

We came onto each other without restraint. I felt comfortable when dancers came on to me and free to approach those I was attracted to, like Sativa, who was built like a colt and wore dainty anklets. Her biker boyfriend was none too pleased. Shannon, a shy woman with wheat-colored hair and aquamarine eyes, pressed me against a locker like a storm out of nowhere and kissed me. It was all fine.

During my frolicking phase, I considered a trial of prostitution for a dizzying amount of money from a short, older Jewish man named Pops. He reminded me of a shrunken, grayer version of Jerry Lewis in his role as the absent-minded professor. Pops had an enduring interest in strippers and took us shopping and to fancy dinners. He treated his favorites, like Krystal, to tropical vacations, furs, and jewels. It was hard not to like his friendly, straightforward ways, even when not one of his chosen.

Pops owned multiple taxicab companies but given the barely foldable wad in his pants pocket, I suspected other cash businesses were at play. Although he said he was too old for cocaine, he kept a supply in his other pocket and provided significant amounts to the dancers most likely to distribute it.

By 1979, cocaine was widely available and touted as a harmless, nonaddictive substance. It was used for sexual enhancement and as an antidote to sleep, boredom, overeating, and drunkenness. Adverse reactions were believed to be nonexistent. Nobody knew about its reinforcing potential and how rats with unlimited access to cocaine preferred it to food and water.

Dancers liked to do a line before hitting the stage to revive tired routines or counteract the effects of alcohol. Women scurried into the bathroom stall, laid out a line of coke on the top of the toilet tank, and snorted like rooting pigs. When cocaine drifted off the slippery surface it was scooped up from the bathroom floor. The cocaine ritual required a meticulous, mindful approach to ensure nothing was wasted. One breath in the wrong direction dispersed the powder and rendered it unrecoverable from a carpet.

Even though I was prescribed amphetamines at age six, I didn't take to cocaine. I noticed an improvement in focus when I used the drug, but dancing didn't require my attention. That came naturally. If anything, cocaine made me anxious.

Cocaine came in paper packets that were emptied into pill bottles or vials. Strippers were frugal regarding their coke and licked the packet so every particle was ingested. Some vials were shaped like fairies, dragons, or upright vacuums, and hung from necklaces. We gathered around a coaster-sized mirror or, in a pinch, the mirror from an eye shadow palette, or, in a desperate pinch the make-up table. The coke's owner tapped out the powder, divided it according to the number of users, and, with a steady hand and razor blade, drew the lines. We took delicate snuffles and patted our noses with toilet paper squares to avoid coke remnants glowing purple in the black lights. Any powder haze left on the mirror was swabbed with a fingertip and applied to the gums.

Men thought their drug paraphernalia reflected status. The use of credit cards, ornate spoons, or miniature shovels was preferred over single-edged razor blades, unless they were gold. A platinum American Express trumped a MasterCard, and a gold spoon outperformed silver, which far surpassed the tip of an acrylic fingernail. A slice of polished agate eclipsed a beveled mirror, and both were better than a tabletop. A percale-crisp $100 bill trumped a soggy $20 bill, which outdid the McDonald's spoon stirrer or a hastily cut milkshake straw. A carved ivory tube topped them all.

Pops didn't care about impressions. He carried a discreet bullet-shaped contraption that pressed underneath one nostril and neatly delivered cocaine.

I thought if I could demo prostitution with anybody, it would be him. Pops was enjoyable enough, and his looks represented what I might expect of a client of his caliber; friendly, frumpy, and hygienically stable. Realistically, even by changing a well-heeled frog into a handsome prince, I doubted I had the mental fortitude to approach sex transactionally. But I wouldn't know unless I tried. So, I did. Once.

Pops offered me $5,000 to spend the night with him at the Park Plaza Hotel. Back at the hotel after dinner at Maison Robert, one of Boston's best restaurants, he unceremoniously unzipped his pants. Spotting his spindly legs underneath the canopy of blue boxers triggered my urge to laugh. I didn't want to be rude, so I held my breath to stave off the giggles.

But his silly little legs and the absurdity of the situation set me off. There was Pops, his bowels gurgling, sucking on obscenely white dentures, and puffing out his hairless, freckled, sagging chest, waiting for me to say or do something to initiate the deed. I apologized for my lack of courage and for causing him any embarrassment. We watched Johnny

Carson in separate beds, and the next day he took me shopping at Bonwit Teller.

"You're a good kid for trying," he said, handing me a $1,000 consolation prize. "If you ever change your mind, I'll be around."

I was happy to keep sex separate and in its proper place.

"DB's Golden Banana," named for the club's owner, Louis DiBella, who had a booming produce business, hosted the first male-stripper extravaganza of its kind. I was invited to write a review of the event, which I wrongly assumed would be comparable to my own line of work.

The club was in Peabody, a suburb on Boston's North Shore, whose sprawling interior was adorned with go-go cages and teemed with vocal middle-aged women screaming as if they were being murdered. Nonetheless, seeing women publicly ogle men was invigorating. It was something new.

I was shown to a table at the front of the stage where "The Panther," barefoot and glistening with inexplicably thick oil, struggled with a paunchy, aggressive woman in sweats. One of her hands hooked around his jockstrap and the other clenched the back of his head as she tried to kiss him. I saw disgust underneath his smile as he twisted out of her grip.

"Lucky" was called to the stage next, and the crowd erupted, pumping their fists with wild enthusiasm. It was like a sporting event. Lucky bounded out in a resplendent but modified white tuxedo and inched toward the women's outstretched arms. He squatted down to their eye level, and within seconds his formal attire was blood-stained from scratches on his neck and upper chest.

I endured the indomitable "Master Blaster," the enigmatic "Rod Rammer," and the camouflaged "Semper Fi," who wore rounds of ammo crisscrossed against his enormous torso. One performed pushups, another thrust across the stage like a wind-up toy, and another flounced around in a zebra thong that sported smiley faces.

All the men were pectorally gifted. They had striated shoulders, plump biceps, and chiseled abs, in stark contrast to woefully neglected legs. They were slathered in oil, perhaps shielding themselves, ineffectively, against assaults from the unhinged audience. They never stopped moving; none could dance.

But the women's madness stole the show. They howled, clawed, ripped, frothed, pinched, and bit. Even if the age-old sexual script of repression drove their savage hunger, it was nefarious.

Ironically, neither the Naked i nor its strippers would tolerate a fraction of that behavior. The event review ran in *Boston* magazine.

Playboy called, wanting to include me in a piece called "Sex in Boston." I hardly considered myself Playboy material, but there was yet another adventure to be had. The photographer, Richard Klein, confirmed the date, and I hustled to Hedy Jo's to pick up the Southern Belle costume.

"Well, I'll be. Get over here and let me give you a big old hug. And here we thought you'd forgotten us because of some wild ride."

"Which wild ride?" I asked, as Hedy Jo slammed her arms around me. I was always happy to see her.

"Buzzy, get on out here," she yelled into my ear. "The Princess herself is back."

He walked out quickly, smiling. I'd never seen him perky.

"We wondered where you disappeared to," he said. "Then we found out in *People* magazine. Hey, did the wife tell you?"

"Lord have mercy! Buzzy, she just walked in the door."

"We're moving. No more winters for us. Off to Las Vegas."

"That must be why you're full of beans. When?" I asked.

"Before hell freezes over, anyway. After Christmas, we'll be gone. Hopefully. We'll see."

Hedy Jo looked at my expression and said, "Honey child, Las Vegas isn't that far in a big old airplane."

"I might be gone, too! In college in Colorado. Then I'll be close by."

"College? But you just started gettin' all famous and such. And these costumes . . ."

"Mel will fly me back for long weekends and school breaks. So, what made you decide to leave Boston?"

"There's a lot of business out there and I'm old, we're old, and truth be told, I've got some minor health issues that the cold doesn't help."

"You're OK, though? And, by the way, you aren't old to me."

"Born in 1920, with a penis!"

"I'm sorry, what?"

"I've been fixin' to tell you, but you up and left. You in a rush?"

"Don't torture Her Highness. Shorten the story, dear," Buzzy said.

"My parents named me Carl Rollins Hammonds, and I was the oldest boy of seven kids."

"You go on, dear. I know this story better than I know the sky's blue. I'll go get some work done," he said.

I didn't want the consolidated version and I wasn't in a rush, so I settled in and listened.

"I grew little boobs when I was twelve, but the doctor said I'd outgrow it, which I didn't. I was impatient, like you, and persistent, also like you, so back we went. He told my mama that the good Lord made me half male and half female. She took to her bed for weeks, just like your mama did, and when she came out, told me that no matter what, I'd be getting into heaven and not to worry myself none."

"You're not getting into heaven. Too late for you," Buzzy yelled from the back.

"Mama was worried plenty, though, because other doctors told her I'd have a short life and end up in a mental institution. At seventeen, I went and did what you did and left home. But back then, I found the carnival, and they put me right into the freak show as a half-man, half-woman. I felt so relieved, like I was born again. Because of that freak show, I got hormone shots and danced a little before I was drafted. I even performed as a female impersonator while I was serving. Ha! After the war, I produced my own dance shows at state fairs and, in my free time, hounded every doctor I found. A group finally agreed that I needed sex-change surgery. But, do you know, the damn New York State Medical Society refused? Why? Because you could take a man's penis off, but not his balls. It was against the law. Imagine that as a look! I didn't have the money Christine Jorgenson had and couldn't fly off to Denmark, so I saved my money and did things in pieces, like Frankenstein style. I was already making costumes by then and had a list a mile long of performers who wanted my things. Finally, when I was forty-two, plastic surgeons, regular surgeons, a urologist, and a psychiatrist, of course, got me through seven hours of surgery. After two weeks in the hospital, I left feeling exactly like myself for the first time."

Hedy Jo looked away and fanned her face.

"I still get emotional. I legally changed my name, married my Buzzy, and here we are. Now you know why I can talk out of both sides. It comes in handy."

"I can't begin to imagine what courage that took. One woman at the i had that surgery, too, but more recently. I've never heard anything like what you just told me. It's amazing; I think amazing says it all."

"It doesn't feel amazing when it's your life. It just feels like your same old life."

"I think I know exactly what you mean."

I felt happy having the costume Hedy Jo first imagined me in, and when she finally moved to Las Vegas I felt sad, like when I moved from Lake Forest, away from Nan, Roberta, and Poomp.

The Southern Belle was a $3,800 spectacle with a corset bodice; short, billowed sleeves; and a wide-brimmed hat curled up on one side, with a spray of tall feather plumes. Its voluminous hoop skirt was bright white, embellished with sequin roses, and meant to exaggerate the hourglass silhouette I'd never have. The thing begged for a bubble machine and, like the Indian ensemble, required its own liquor cabinet for storage.

When the opening "ooo-bops" of Manhattan Transfer's "Tuxedo Junction" played, the bartenders knew to hunker down. To defend against the spinning, oversized hoop, they plastered themselves against the bar sinks with every pass I made. They relaxed once the bubble machine stopped and the whistle in "Sweet Georgia Brown" started. At that point in the show, I dropped the hoop, did a little Charleston, more if the audience clapped, and finished the set with Pink Floyd's "Great Gig in the Sky."

An unusual request came from the Cambridge Center for Adult Education. They asked me to teach a class called "How to Strip for Your Husband," and I immediately accepted. The course was limited to twelve women, and I wondered if I'd get three. To my surprise, there was a waiting list by week's end. I requested an extra chair for the class, and the Center took it upon themselves to tape black construction paper to the classroom door window. All twelve middle-aged women arrived early and sat in a circle staring at me. I felt more nervous than I had on any live television show.

"Hey, everyone. I'm Lucy, and I dance as Princess Cheyenne, but as the same person. Does that make sense?"

The group of women smiled but said nothing.

"I've never taught before, so maybe you can tell me what you expect from the class."

One woman raised her hand halfway.

"Hi, yes?" I asked.

"Can you strip out of those jeans?"

"If I wanted to, sure. When I first auditioned, I wore jeans just like these. I had no idea."

They laughed and I told them the story about auditioning for Anne Diamond.

"What's it like to have all that power and attention every night?" another woman asked.

"It's a blast," I said.

I realized the best I could do was impart the kind of fun I had at work. In the first of the four sessions, we discussed what rules were necessary to make everyone comfortable. Making nudity optional was my only rule. Then they told me what they wanted from the class.

"I want to learn how to strut," "Teach me how not to be a spaz," "Did stripping start in the Sumerian times?" "I want step-by-step, detailed instructions, like meeting minutes." We took a field trip to Downtown Crossing for stripper clothing and visited the Naked i. We discussed music, props, and outfits. They practiced walking in spiked heels or decided on bare feet. We went over pubic hair shaving and power dynamics and practiced different moves. The last class was a dress rehearsal.

They'd continuously surprised me, but something bigger was in the works.

On the last day, I cracked open the classroom door and was startled by a man sitting in the empty chair designated for the performances. He didn't see me, so I quietly returned to the office.

"There's a strange man in the classroom. Just wondering what I should do."

"A strange man?" asked a woman in the office. "That shouldn't be. Here, let me walk back with you."

When we entered the room, the twelve women leaped out of a storage closet laughing and hooting. I was thoroughly confused and delighted.

I didn't know that the twelve industrious women gathered the week before and constructed a male dummy to sit in the empty chair. They stuffed pantyhose with cotton batting, ran wire hangers through the sections, held him together with more hose, and dressed him in a sports coat, trousers, and bow tie. His head was made with the toe of a pantyhose leg filled with socks and crumpled-up brown paper for a nose and chin. They named him "Nuthatch."

Nuthatch patiently sat through twelve five-minute performances as the women gave each other feedback.

"Love, love, love the over-your-shoulder look." "Here, take this garter. It matches." "How about a top hat?"

As for how their performances went with their individual audience(s), I would never know, but I had those students to thank for developing the curriculum I repeated several times in Cambridge and at the Boston Center for Adult Education.

Before spending Christmas in Florida with Nan and Mother, I made the planned trip to Boulder, Colorado, and it was love at first sight. I found the man I'd met three years prior at the CU admissions office and applied. I was accepted, rented a house, and registered for my first college courses in January of 1980.

CHAPTER 17

Boulder, Colorado

An article once called me "the thinking man's stripper," not to be confused with "the thinking stripper." I knew nothing about the mechanics of college and didn't consider that I'd entered nontraditionally, without test scores, a high school diploma, or knowing how to study. Clueless about the rigors of academics, I saw no problem commuting from Boulder to Boston to keep working.

Classes started the third week in January, giving me plenty of time to work, pack, and seek revenge for a pin-pricked diaphragm. I easily forgave but rarely forgot and visited the joke shop before work one night.

"Well, hello there," Sam said, a newspaper sprawled before him. "I wasn't sure I'd ever see you again. You're getting awfully famous. How about some fart spray?"

I'd started laughing the moment I saw his face.

"Fart spray? You crack me up. I just think about you and laugh."

"Hey, get this. The squirting ketchup bottle just got Best of Boston for pranks. I'll get you one on the house. I bet you can put it to good work," Sam said, stepping out from behind the counter. "Oh! I think you dropped some money by the door," he said.

"That's weird," I said, walking over to pick it up.

The moment my finger touched the bill, it zipped into Sam's hand. We both laughed so hard that we cried.

"I should have known."

"I'm sure you didn't come here to be startled."

"You have itching powder, right?" I asked.

Sam nodded.

"Can you tell me how it works?"

"It's a powder, naturally, with tiny fibers that make you itch. You put a tiny bit on anything that will come into contact with skin, and voila!"

"Does it hurt?"

"Do you want it to hurt?"

"No!"

"It's temporary and completely harmless."

"Great, I'll take some."

"So Princess, what are some of your most memorable pranks?" he asked.

"Oh gosh, there are so many. Probably nailing my mother's shoes to the floor. I ruined her loafers, and she wasn't amused. But my father took the hit for me. All my other pranks are disappointingly common. But I'm young yet! Thanks for this. I know the perfect opportunity for your award-winning fake ketchup. I'll try that for fun when we order out."

At the club, food choices had evolved away from submarine sandwiches, pizza and french fries. They couldn't compete with the allure of sushi and sashimi. We opened the red-and-white soy-sauce packets with our teeth and mixed the sauce with wasabi, like chemists. Forks were for the uninitiated, so we achieved mastery over chopsticks. It was the cool way to eat. The bravest among us ate quail eggs and octopus legs and Jazz always had a quip about the "giant clam," or "clam-meister." Larger sushi orders arrived in table-sized wooden boats with umbrellas, edible orchids, and tangles of daikon root. We were exotic dancers eating exotic foods. Mouthing buttery fish chunks and dropping salty ginger folds onto each other's tongues was nothing like teasing cheese strings from pizza slices. It attracted men's attention, and they watched. Then they asked to join us and paid for our dinners. Sushi became a stripper's ideal power food: free, low calorie, low fat, non-drowsy, and with minimal bloat.

One night, I ordered onion rings and french fries when the other dancers ordered their sushi boat. I knew no one could resist the pull of fried food. I set the trick ketchup bottle in front of me and hid the packets. The food arrived and Giselle unexpectedly sat across from me. I considered her.

My Saab turbo was the first large purchase I made. I loved that car.

True, she was magnetic, but not turn-around-on-the-street pretty. Her warm smile defied her brittle eyes, insentient like stone. One never knew where her cajoling was leading or what she wanted, because she appeared to need nothing. She was all set. Giselle was inscrutable and unassailable, yet it irked me how compelling she was. I wanted to figure her out and be on her good side. I wished I didn't care.

"Push over, bitch," said Dori, carrying her mixing-with-customers dress balled up in one hand. "I'm fuckin' starved."

She'd come from the stage wearing a bra and jock. The hanging gold beads rolled softly on her ass when she gestured. There was nothing not to like about Dori. She was bold, authentic, and kept to the same baseline. Her eyes were the color of celery.

When people asked where she was from, she said, "I'm from Georgia and Alabama."

"You can't be from two different states."

"Fuck all y'all. I can be from wherever I dang well please."

Her mother waitressed at the Naked i, and Dori went to a hairdressing school in addition to working at the club. When she became a "co-feature," she was called Dori Dixon.

Giselle rolled her eyes and made room for Dori. Jazz walked over and sat next to me.

"Louise? Fries and onion rings? For you?"

"I was in the mood."

"Must be getting your period. Mind if I have some?"

"No, please. Want some ketchup with them?"

"Nah, I don't like ketchup," said Jazz.

"Oh man, those onion rings smell so good, I'll have some, but I need ketchup," said Giselle.

Perfect. Giselle took a paper plate and skewered several fat onion rings on a fingernail before plopping them on a plate. I stood up and pretended to futz with the cap on the ketchup bottle.

"Shit, hold on. Something's wrong with the top," I said, shaking it. "There."

"They gave you an entire bottle of ketchup with your order?" she asked.

Shit.

"Yeah. Said they ran out of packets."

She held it over her plate and shook the bottle. When nothing came out, she squeezed it in between both hands and a glossy red string poured onto her lap.

"Jesus Christ! I just got this gold lamé dress."

Giselle shot up in smoke. She would have turned over the table if it hadn't been bolted to the floor. Jazz, Dori, and I laughed, and Giselle fingered the string.

"Not funny," she said, coolly. "If that's the best you can do, tell me where the ketchup is."

I handed over the packets and decided to wait on the itching powder. I didn't have to wait long.

On Friday night, Giselle snidely inserted herself into a conversation I was having with Alan Dershowitz, a well-known defense attorney. She was keen on reaping any potential benefits from notable Naked i patrons, especially those I was friendly with. I always enjoyed bantering with Alan, and this night he was interrogating me about feminism.

"Are you a feminist?" he asked.

"I have no idea."

"A feminist probably wouldn't work here or agree that any woman should work here."

"If being a feminist limits what I do or don't do with my body, then no, I must not be a feminist."

"Are you oppressed?"

"Meaning pushed down?"

"Trapped by circumstances, or people within those circumstances."

"No way! I feel completely free. I'm hardly a victim."

"OK. Are you objectified?"

"I don't know. Am I?"

"Are you an object of desire, letting men use your appearance to get off? I'd say yes. You're a commodity."

"Why is it up to me whether or not I'm objectified? It's the customers doing the objectifying, not me."

"You're the one dancing naked for them."

"You're the one looking and deciding what I am to you. I don't have to care what you make of me. I can't turn myself into an object. The viewer does that."

"But you invite people to do it."

"How do you know that? I mean, you'd have to be in my head. I don't come to work thinking, 'I hope all the guys I invited in to objectify me are here.' That's ridiculous. You got me going on this one."

Alan smiled and said, "I know. It's what I do."

"Well, who do we have here?" Giselle asked, snaking her way next to Alan at the bar.

"Alan, Giselle. Giselle, Alan," I said. "Nice chatting, Alan. I'll leave you two. I have to go get ready."

I couldn't wait to zip into the dressing room and see if Giselle had left any articles of clothing out. Sure enough, her locker was partially open from costume pieces hanging out the door. I sprinkled itching powder into the cups of her bra and inside her shoes, ensuring I spread it evenly. I couldn't bring myself to do the same for her G-string, primarily because

I didn't want to touch it, and secondarily because it seemed over the top mean.

I got into my costume and, within seconds, felt hot pinpricks on the sides of my hips and the back of my neck. *Shit! I didn't rinse my hands off after applying the powder.* I asked the DJ to get me a glass of ice and, in between songs, stood behind the curtain, scratching furiously. At least I knew what Giselle would feel.

I had no idea how long it would last, so I brought the ice on stage for my floor show, hoping to cloak the debacle in an ice gimmick. Not only did it numb the urge to scratch, but it also became part of my floor-show routine on occasion. No matter the many ways a woman's nipples become erect, men attribute it to one thing and one thing only, even if the culprit is right in front of them.

I dumped my costume pieces in front of my locker and stood behind the DJ naked. I'd suffered too much to miss out on Miss Composed squirming like a silverfish. And squirm she didn't. I watched like a hawk as Giselle undressed on stage and re-dressed in her mixing gown. She didn't even flinch. Maybe she had reptilian skin.

Meanwhile, I iced my red splotches until I got home and applied calamine lotion. So much for pranks. I was heading off to college at a good time.

My college plans seemed to make my parents more available. My father even came to visit me before I left. We took a long run along the Charles River and went out for dinner. Afterward, he insisted we drop by the Naked i, where he charmed and humored my colleagues while also getting to know Ray, Mel, and Ricky. Dancers and management would continue to ask when "Skip" was coming back, which he often did, every time I came to Boston.

My father was intrigued by the Naked i's Lola situation. Each time he was there, it was a different Lola.

"What's with the merry-go-round of Lolas?" was his opening question.

I locked up my costumes in three liquor-cabinets, to be deployed on long weekends and school breaks, and flew to Boulder a few days before the term began. By the time I figured out what registration day entailed, the classes I wanted were filled. I signed up for Great Books, Introduction to Fiction, and Experimental Psychology, which met the requirement for some prerequisites, and saxophone as an extracurricular. The woman taking my information put me on waiting lists for the two classes I wanted and handed me a laminated sheet, telling me to choose my major. She had to explain that a major was an area of focus for my degree. I chose religious studies, journalism a week later, and psychology a week after that. Working at the Naked i gave me a head start in psychology. I also delivered pleading notes with one rose each to the professors of French and Native American Religions. It worked and I was admitted to both classes.

College life was an abrupt shift. Having to pay close attention, take notes, and learn how to study were new skills in the context of learning. Part of my being admitted nontraditionally meant I was placed on academic probation for two semesters and couldn't let my grade point average go below 3.0, if I made it that far. I also needed to gain my high school General Equivalency Degree by the end of my second semester.

I trained for team soccer, the cross-country ski team, and the Boston Marathon. Sometimes I headed out at 3 a.m. to run the Royal Arch Trail into the Flatirons, those mammoth slabs of rock aimed upwards like satellite dishes. When the sky showed a hint of light, I reversed to run downhill and watched the tiny gold dots of the city switch on.

After soccer practice, we ran long distance as a team. It made no sense to run the streets of Boulder when there were so many beautiful trails nearby, so we trotted into nature. Keeping our shirts on in the heat was silly, so we tucked them into the backs of our shorts. This progressed to a more competitive challenge where we tried to get as close to home as possible without wearing shirts. Some of Boulder's retired police officers likely remember this phase as we were occasionally stopped and gently reminded that the distraction could cause accidents. They never told us to put our shirts back on. We did the same thing at a road race, and I happened to cross the finish line proudly carrying my shirt, alongside the shirtless men. *Running Times* ran a photograph of the minor spectacle, which Norma Nathan at the *Boston Herald* naturally picked up on.

College effectively tapered my raucous sexual experimentation phase. When my stints with men lengthened, I became either overly attached or disinterested and trapped. There was still fun to be had.

I had a brief frolic with the cross-country ski coach and we often stayed to ski recreationally after team practice. Just as he was becoming a drip, he challenged me to a naked trek around the Eldora cross-country track where we practiced. I guess he'd heard about the soccer runs. I clicked into my ski bindings and looped the pole straps loosely around my wrists. He was in a spandex racing suit, and I, not anticipating a serious workout, had changed into recreational knickers with snowflake socks.

"OK, let's get naked," he said, steamy plumes rising over him. "Whoever skis the longest without getting dressed wins."

"Let's warm up in our clothes first," I said, pushing off on one ski. "And socks allowed."

"Sounds good," he said. "One loop. Let's do it."

The ski tracks were deep, and the recent snowfall made them slippery and fast. Everything was blue in the moonlight. We completed one loop and dropped our clothing before sprinting away. He was much faster, and I eventually lost sight of him. I assumed he'd started another lap when he'd actually booked it to the car. Panting and sweating, I ran the edge of a wide downhill trail, and snow sprayed between my legs.

"You did it. You are too much," he yelled up to me from his car. "My balls disappeared. You beat me fair and square."

I swished him with snow.

"I want my prize," I said.

He wrapped me in a fleece blanket and drove to "Time Out," the grooviest hot tub facility in Boulder, where we lounged in rooftop cauldrons as snow melted on our heads.

That was as interesting as things got between us.

I hung out with a chiropractor who looked like a male lion. He introduced me to tantric sex and we played Monopoly while doing coffee enemas. We were lovers until he told me we weren't until he told me we were. *Couldn't men like this be fixed?* Nothing worked: manipulation, pity parties, loving, chasing, hating, gnashing, or forgetting. I wondered why men said they didn't want things when they did.

Sometimes it was simpler to meet, greet, and leave.

I met Bear at a natural-food restaurant during a long weekend in Aspen. I wanted to braid his hair, preferably while inside his tipi, naked, and told him as much.

"Everyone wants to braid my hair," he said, eyeballing me for two seconds. "OK, fine. You can braid it. Let's go."

"Can I brush it first?"

I didn't brush or braid anything. We ended up on a pelt inside his well-appointed tipi, and he told me I was a "tornado."

There were many men I fell for and didn't have sex with. Like Davide, the professor of Native American Religions at CU. I excelled in his class and experienced the first glow of clothed, intellectual approval when he recognized me as a good student with decent ideas. I noticed him watching me run intervals on the track one day, but assumed I imagined it until he asked me to stop by his office for no academic reason.

"Drop by anytime," he said.

So I did. With increasing frequency. It felt intense. Then Davide asked me to meet him in the chapel one afternoon for some drumming and dancing. He played the congas and I danced like a lunatic. I started leaving him notes, embarrassing notes about wanting him. It felt childish until he opened up to me about his personal life and gave me a book called "It Does Not Die; A Romance about Mircea Eliade." That was quite the title.

Ram Dass came to Boulder and, desperate to get a grip, I asked if he'd have tea with me.

"Of course I can't," he said, which made perfect sense. He was, after all, a guru star.

He placed his hands on my shoulders and said, "You know, sometimes, when we feel real connections, we want to capture them, put a time stamp on them instead of just being there, like we are now. It's so beautiful in this very moment." Good, old Ram Dass.

Toward the end of the semester, Davide came to my house, and I gave him a ceramic drum I'd made. He said he wanted to stay in touch over the summer. Rather than jumping into bed, we talked about our shared physical attraction.

"Don't overanalyze it," he said. "Making love is an expression rather than a means to something."

When the semester ended, no one was as surprised as I was when I came close to having a perfect grade point average. Unfortunately, I didn't know I had to formally withdraw from the saxophone class. That mistake would take three years to erase from my GPA.

The *Playboy* article came out and *The Real Paper* called to interview me for a 1980 article:

"Anatomy of a Stripper"
Celebrated striptease dancer Princess Cheyenne reveals a thing or two to Gerald Peary.

We talked to Princess Cheyenne, Boston's most famous striptease dancer at the Naked i club in the Combat Zone. It was there that the blonde, blue-eyed, Brahmin stripper made her reputation strolling down the ramp like a pristine Miss Teenage America.

Cheyenne has now given up the hedonistic life that made her the toast of Boston and gone back to school as a journalism and psychology major at the University of Colorado. But to the delight of her fans, she recently returned to the Naked i to work during her spring vacation.

What is your real name?
Lucy Johnson. Cheyenne used to be my nickname, but they added Princess when they wanted me to be a star. I had an Indian act that I burned out on. I no longer use it. My head dress is hanging in my living room in Boulder, Colorado.

What was your life like before becoming an entertainer at the Naked i?
I was born in Illinois, raised in New Canaan, Connecticut. Both towns were rich, nasty, and confining, with false security. I went to four high schools before I was 16. I said, "Forget it." At 16 I moved to Vermont and lived with 12 other people for about eight months. I met an attorney who is divorced, twice my age, with four children. We decided to travel around the country and live in a tent. We covered 5,000 miles, and then we came to Boston. I started dancing, out of curiosity. All of a sudden, there was great interest in me.

How were you discovered in the press?
Boston *magazine was the first to do a story on me. Then* Evening Magazine. *Marty Sender and I had a little thing.*

Can we quote you on that?
Sure, he doesn't care. It was very short and fun; we're still very good friends. Norma Nathan loves to write about me. Nancy McMillan, a freelancer, asked if she could do a thing for People *on my relationship with Cat Stevens. When she did that,* Playboy *asked me to send pictures. I'm in the May issue, with photographs of my party at Boston-Boston.*

About three months from now, Playboy *is doing a whole article and spread on me individually.*

Who else in Boston has adopted you?
A few of the Red Sox. The one I know best is Dennis Eckersley.

Anyone else?
The Paul Winter Consort. WBCN.

What's the story on you and Cat Stevens?
I had a mad crush on Cat Stevens since I was 12. When I was 16 I met him once, never to see him again. Or so I thought. The year after I started dancing, I went to England in the summer and bumped into him again in London. I became a Muslim and we were going to get married. Then I decided I didn't want to get married and I came back here.

So the romance is over?
He's married to a Turkish Muslim woman. We still write each other all the time. He calls me now and then, and he came over to meet my parents. So we don't want to sever all connections just because we have a difference in religion.

You're not a Muslim anymore?
No, though nothing negative happened. Everything positive happened. It's just that I'm not really ready for that kind of life in America. If I was in Iran, I have no problem being a Muslim. I still read the Qur'an and do the Muslim prayer instead of meditation.

What was your role as a Muslim woman?
Not much.

Was there any pleasure?
There was pleasure in knowing I was safe. For the time I lived in the Muslim community in London, I felt really consistent. Praying five times a day makes you go on a straight line. The women were really tight, the

men were really tight, but the two weren't really tight together. Yes, it was neat for me to feel I could be open and not critical of it. Now people are giving the Iranians such a hard time, but we haven't lived in a totally religious country. Who are we to judge? I hear people saying how fucked up Muslims are. I can say I don't think so. I've been thinking about writing an article on Islam for New Age magazine, but I've been procrastinating on it.

Were you comfortable behind a veil?
It felt good. When I first came back to America, I was still wearing it. I felt strange but also safe because people couldn't really look at me. It was nice not to have men drooling at me.

And yet you went back to stripping?
It was hard but I realized I had to follow my heart. My experience with Cat Stevens had ended. It was not something to hold onto. So I came back here, as before, to the Naked i. This is not your normal run-of-the-mill strip club. I visited them all over the country. And every other club, whether in Denver or Los Angeles or San Francisco or Boston, I felt somewhat threatened. I thought, this is really sick. This is really gross. The vibes were so bad that I didn't stick around. But the Naked i is very tame, nice, comfortable. The women that work here are fantastic and have really good hearts. I'm spoiled by the place.

What is special about your dance act?
I love getting into costumes. It's a real high. My costumes are the Pink Panther, Southern Belle, janitor, country girl, and ice. Ice is a costume of beads worn all over my legs and everywhere. In a day I try to put on all the costumes. Also, I don't wear makeup. I don't wear shoes. I smile. I really try to project what I'm feeling. I try to remain open and vulnerable. I think a lot of women who dance try to close themselves off. I've seen other blondes. I've seen women with 10 times better bodies and faces than I have. But I think success is what you project. I want the people to feel, "Wow, that's great."

And when you are depressed or angry?
The show must go on! But dancing can really get me smiling, no matter what.

You also don't mix with the customers?
  I didn't for a while in the beginning. I was freaked out and scared. But sitting in the dressing room gets very boring. So I tried it, and realized the customers are just people. You don't have to do anything you don't want to do. If someone attacks you verbally or physically, all you have to do is say, "I'll see you later." Or get him thrown out.

Are the customers at the Naked i unhappy or lonely people?
  Not at all. It's a very normal group. To tell you the truth, I don't think I've ever met a man who hasn't been in a strip club. So that's what a variety there is.

What do the men want, those who pay $7 for a drink to sit and talk to you?
  To sit and talk to me. If they want more I can walk away.

What was the most amazing proposition?
  $5,000. But I didn't take it. No way. There are times I've thought about it, but it's like contemplating suicide. You don't really get close to acting on it.

What's the most money you ever made in a week of dancing?
  The standard six day week. $720.

Did you pay for your publicized parties at Boston-Boston?
  No. I was going with Pat Lyons, who ran Boston-Boston for a while. We're still friends. The first one was a Halloween party, with 2,000 people there and outrageous outfits. It was done in collaboration with Pauline Goulet, who works there also, and a transvestite whose name I can't remember. Pat saw that this was very successful, and we had another, my going away party. 1,000 people. By invitation only.

Why did you decide to leave Boston and go back to school?
  I'm not a serious person, but I want to do something. I don't want to strip the rest of my life. I'd like to get a trade down, and I like living in Boulder. I have a neat house and neat friends. I go to school three hours and then come home. My boyfriend is 31. He's a chiropractor, very bright. If I lived in the dorm I'd probably lose my mind.

Do you write?
I have a journal that I've kept for a couple of years. But there's so much that I kind of have to wait until I calm down a bit, so things come out in pieces instead of a big ball of yarn.

What year are you in school?
A freshman.

How old are you now?
20. But I always say, "If I die today, I'll be satisfied." That's very true. I almost died the first half of this year, falling off a cliff in a car. The first thing I thought was, "OK, I feel really good about what I've done." I feel I've really lived.

CHAPTER 18

Andy Kaufman

While I was on a semester break from the University of Colorado in 1981, NBC Studios in New York City agreed to land-transport the Indian costume's headpiece ahead of my flight as taking it on a plane risked damaging its ostrich feathers and lavish decoration.

I arrived at LaGuardia and quickly found my driver holding a "Princess Cheyenne" sign. He whisked me to 30 Rockefeller Center, where I would be a guest on *The Tomorrow Show* with Tom Snyder. I had a tour of the *Saturday Night Live* set before Candy led me into her stylist room and faced me away from the mirror. She got to work in fast motion teasing, gelling, spraying, and curling my hair and then smeared my face with something that felt like Cool Whip. She applied liners, powders, shadows, and mascara. When Candy spun me around, I met my smoldering, slightly exotic twin.

As Tom Snyder looked on from his seat, I danced in full regalia in front of a live band. I must have been nervous because without thinking, I removed my heavily beaded vest and swung it like a lasso above my head. I thought throwing it over the hovering monolith camera would be adorable on the air. Its weight and momentum propelled at lightning speed toward Tom Snyder. He ducked. The vest grazed the top of his head and took his toupée with it. Candy hurried out, reseated the hairpiece, and I stepped down to take my seat.

I went on the road with Andy Kaufman and PBS Soundstage recorded *The Andy Kaufman Show*. It aired in July 1983.

After my first national television show, *Playboy* flew me to Chicago for a test shoot. Another lengthy makeup session ensued before I was trotted out to the studio, where legendary photographer Pompeo Posar (I didn't know he was legendary) stood atop a ladder threading film into a camera. The assistant brought baskets of props and a cooler filled with cold soda cans that, they made clear, were to refresh my nipples. Pompeo rattled down the ladder to introduce himself and pose me on the mattress before dashing back to his roost.

"Raise the back of your head toward the ceiling. That's it, yes, and deep breath in, drop your shoulders now draw them back. Yes, exactly, now exaggerate your lumbar curvature."

"My what?"

"Your lower back, make it curve. No, the other way, out. That's it, yes. It makes everything better."

The assistant ran back and forth like a ball boy, swapping strands of fake pearls and opaque scarves and rearranging swaths of draping fabrics and silk pillows.

After eight hours of being poked, brushed, and bent, I felt like a reupholstered chair. While *Playboy* spreads may seem effortless, producing one is anything but. By the end, we were all exhausted. I was ready for bed, solely for a good night's sleep.

I made best use of that trip to Chicago and visited with Nan, then spent the rest of school break back in Boston, working at the club.

The rugged little package that was the waitress, Susan, clomped up the stairs to the dressing room while calling me.

"Oh, Purrrrrincesss. Some wicked annoying foreign guy is asking for you. I can't understand a word he says. He's doing all these crazy charades. He's super hyper."

I pulled my eyeballs under my brows.

"Puh. I'm not in the mood."

"Ha! Just wait. This guy'll put you in an even worse mood. He talks with a really soft voice and keeps repeating, 'Pleencess, Pleencess.' Fucking hysterical. Just come down so he shuts the fuck up and stops bugging me."

I found the foreign man sitting at a round table, one leg dangling from the stool. He spotted me, grinned, stood, and clapped loudly. Everyone around us looked and I wanted to crawl under something.

"Theez way, theez way, have sit, have sit," he squeaked. "You sleep?"

"What? Um, no. I was relaxing upstairs."

His eyes expanded. He had a child's face, unruly dark hair, and the most alarming blue eyes I'd ever seen—cobalt blue with silver flecks. Even in the semi-darkness they weren't of this world. He wasn't exactly handsome, but his face sparkled.

"You veddy, veddy beezy. Yes. Veddy beezy. Time for de lunch?"

"What? No, never mind. What brings you to the Naked i?" I asked.

He opened his mouth as if to say something but didn't.

"Where are you from? Are you visiting?"

"I from zee vest, zee vest, uh, how you say? Uh, uh, thataway," he pointed.

"I have no idea what you're trying to say. I'm sorry. I really should go. I have to get ready."

"OK!" he straightened and clapped again. "Vee have zee, zee lunches. Yes. I come next day, ven you heppy."

I hoped he didn't. Did he say lunch?

The odd man made good on his promise and five nights in a row walked in like a penguin with his shiny, expectant face and alien blue eyes. He sat at the same table and presented the same loops of non-conversation in the form of charades. The man never stopped smiling.

When I asked him for details about his life, he said, "I no understand vut you ask. I no stop coming ven you have zee lunches."

I explained that I didn't go out with customers.

His face dropped. "I no understand zee no lunches."

I pointed to the men sitting in the club.

"See all these guys, these men, sitting down, walking around, staring at us? They are customers, customers," I annunciated, "like you. It's against the club rules to see zee customers outside zee club."

"Yes, but, but, vee are in zee loves," he said, sparkling and practically on his tiptoes. "I want zee lunches weeth zee, zee, Pleencess. Yes. And you are, are zee Pleencess."

I wanted to get my hackles up, but felt too sorry for the lost, timid man. He was infuriating and dazzling. Strangely, he drew me in.

"You do know who that is, right, Louise?" Jazz asked in the dressing room.

"Know who he is? How could you know who he is when you can't understand a damn thing he says?"

"It's Latka from Taxi."

"Jesus, now you sound like him. Who?"

"Andy Kaufman. He's on a sitcom."

"He's always on *Saturday Night Live*, like, constantly," added Trish. "He's supposedly wicked funny, but I don't get the humor. He's just weird, and better not steal you away from me."

The name Andy Kaufman wasn't familiar. I worked at night and didn't own a television.

"I think you guys are mistaking him for someone else. He can't speak any English. Don't you have to speak English to be on an American sitcom? Have you seen him carrying on, waving his arms, trying to make a charade? He couldn't possibly be on television."

"I say we all gather round The Princess's table tonight when he comes in," threatened Giselle. "We'll get to the bottom of this."

She made good on the threat, and a throng of dancers and customers surrounded our table.

"Hey, are you Andy Kaufman?" "Are you that guy on Taxi?" "I love your Mighty Mouse routine!" "That's Andy doing the Foreign Man." "Why do you wrestle women?"

More people gathered to see what the ruckus was and leaned in closer. The man's body stiffened, and his hands became fists. He looked helpless and I felt the urge to shoo everyone away. After he cleared his throat, the man released a stream of word salad in a strangled, frail voice.

"No beat up!" he yelled. "Pleases, go vay, go vay. I vunt to be with zee Pleencess."

Satisfied they had the wrong man, the crowd dispersed.

"Nah, that's not Andy Kaufman. It couldn't be." "Andy's more put together than that guy."

I agreed to meet the nameless man for lunch at The Seventh Inn, a natural foods restaurant in Park Square.

"I so heppy you meet for zee lunches," he said, blinking.

I searched his face for comprehension. There was none.

"You don't know where the Seventh Inn is. OK. Hold on a sec."

"Pleences, don't leaves me."

"Oh my God," I stammered.

I walked to the bar for a pen and napkin and drew a map. I wrote '1:00 pm' at the top. He stood, edged closer to me, and shook his head no.

"What? Look, this is the best I can do."

"Pleencess no good draw. Ha ha ha. Ha ha ha. Ha ha ha."

I started laughing so hard the pen fell from between my fingers. He waited for me to resume, but when I looked at him, I laughed harder, like a crazy person. My face was wet with tears, and my nose was running. The man's expression didn't change.

"No cry. No cry. Heppy, heppy, like thees," the man said, hopping up and down.

"OK," I said, catching my breath. "I'm sorry, I don't know what that was. Phew. Not sad laughing, funny laughing, heppy laughing. Anyway, here's the map."

I counted on him not following but when I arrived, he was sitting at a table, his eyes eagerly pinned on me. He sprang from his seat and barreled toward me.

"Hi. Hi. Good. You like me. Now, you do!" he proclaimed. "I, I, uh, I tink we fall in zee loves, yes?"

"I don't know your name, and we can't communicate. Can we start with lunch?" I asked, walking to the table.

"Yes, yes, English good and better, no? Yes. Movies, fight, make zee love, een boy and girl style."

"You're ridiculous."

"Vait, vait. You say I zee best? Oooo," he said, clapping his hands frenetically.

I sat, and he didn't. He removed a napkin from the table, snapped it open, and tucked one corner into his shirt collar. Then he turned toward the dining area and back to me, like he'd forgotten something.

I guessed he wanted the men's room.

"The bathroom's over there," I said, pointing.

He took a glass and spoon, turned, and tapped on the glass, louder and louder, until he had the restaurant's attention. I felt like I was on acid.

"Ladies and gentlemen," he said in a perfect New York accent. "I'm sorry to interrupt everyone's lunch, but this lovely little lady and I plan on falling in love. Isn't that great?"

I barely heard the applause or saw the nodding heads because I'd come close to leaving my body. He was beaming and talking like an American from New York.

"Are you OK, Lamb Chop? You look pale."

"Wait, sit the eff down. You're not from another country?" I asked through my teeth. "What the fuck. Who does that? And fuck you with your Lamb Chop crap."

"Come on, Lamb Chop. It's not so bad. I can explain."

Our server bustled over with her pad and pen, ready to take our order. I took a breath.

"I'm so sorry to bother you, but, oh my God, I can't even believe this! I love Latka so much," she gushed. "And Taxi, too! Can I have your autograph? Please?"

Andy's gigantic blue eyes danced.

Andy Kaufman was born in 1949, the oldest of three children from Great Neck, New York. Neighborhood kids thought he was bizarre, and adults took him for multiple psych evaluations. Andy made the conscious decision not to care what other people thought. Instead of going out to play, he happily stayed in his room, where he broadcast "live" shows for an imaginary television audience. When he was eight years old, he started entertaining at children's parties for free before charging $5 and, later, $50.

Captivated by the theatrics of professional wrestlers on television, Andy imitated their techniques with his younger brother, Michael. Andy accidentally injured Michael's neck while performing a "piledriver," causing his brother to spend three weeks in traction.

As a teenager, Andy wrote poetry, plays, and stories like "Hamburger," "Lost Thumb," and "The Shameless Bohemian." He performed some of them at coffee houses in Greenwich Village. He later enrolled at Boston's Graham Junior College to study television and radio production and hosted and produced *Uncle Andy's Fun House* on WCSB-TV, the college's closed-circuit television station. While at school, Andy hitchhiked from Boston to Las Vegas to meet his idol, Elvis Presley. Andy also discovered Transcendental Meditation, which helped him overcome his shyness. Later, he trained as a TM teacher in Majorca, Spain, and attended advanced training at Interlocken, Switzerland, and Vittel, France. Andy said that TM was the only thing he took seriously. He meditated twice a day for the rest of his short life.

After graduation, Andy took his show on the road, confusing, irritating, and entertaining audiences. He opened for The Temptations in Northampton, Massachusetts, performed at the Improv in New York and Los Angeles, and at Catch a Rising Star. After making his television debut on Dean Martin's *Comedy World*. Dick Ebersol from NBC invited Andy to audition for what is now *Saturday Night Live*. On its inaugural broadcast, Andy lip-synched to "The Theme from Mighty Mouse" and returned to SNL a dozen times. He appeared on *The Tonight Show Starring Johnny Carson*, The *David Letterman Show*, Dick Van Dyke's weekly variety show, *Hollywood Squares*, *The Dating Game*, and countless others. He rode a float in the Macy's Thanksgiving Day Parade, started wrestling women, and proclaimed himself the "World Intergender Wrestling Champion," a title he made up. Andy was most widely known for his role as Latka Gravas on the ABC sitcom, *Taxi*.

During lunch, Andy explained that he immersed himself in a character until it wasn't just a part; it was real. He meant that literally. As for why he maintained the foreign character for so many days, he said, "I've read all about you and want you to be my girlfriend but had to work myself up to asking you. Will you?"

We walked through the Boston Common and Public Gardens and continued talking. I noticed people snickering as they passed us and realized

Andy was wearing a dinner napkin tucked into his shirt. He told me about growing up in Great Neck, how much he loved amusement parks, especially Coney Island, and a museum with sideshows and a flea circus that he frequented as a child.

"I skipped school and went every chance I had. They all became my friends. There was the Turtle Girl, the Elephant Skin Lady, the Sword Swallower, um, let's see, a snake charmer and tattooed lady, of course, but my all-time favorite was the flea trainer."

"Flea trainer? With real, live fleas? No way."

"Yes, way. This wonderful man was a flea circus ringmaster."

"What on earth did he do? Or they?"

"You've never been to a flea circus before? I can't believe this. Seriously? They dance, and they pull chariots and cannons, wear costumes. I think it's fake now, but not back then at good ol' Hubert's Museum, my favorite."

We spent the next four days touring Massachusetts to visit amusement parks: Lincoln Park in Dartmouth, Paragon Park in Hull, Whalom Park in Lunenburg, among others. We rode bumper cars, scramblers, tilt-a-whirls, carousels, and roller coasters. Each attraction was a fresh opportunity for mischief. Andy's entire world was an amusement park and tickets were never in short supply.

On roller coasters, just as the cars unhinged from their positions and the gears started, Andy would nervously unstrap his safety belt, stand, and wave his arms.

"Excuse me, sir?" Andy called.

"Where are you going?" I asked. "Sit down."

"Sir, please come help me," he begged. "I need help."

Several tattooed men rushed toward us.

"I'd like to go home and have my ice cream now," Andy said, the cranks churning underneath us. "I left it out on the kitchen counter."

"Just sit down, man," one guy said as they turned to walk away.

"I don't really want ice cream," Andy sputtered. "I'm too afraid to have ice cream now. This car feels loose and tippy. We're all going to die! Let me out of here!"

The men quickly unlatched our car to get the screaming, sobbing Andy away from the customers.

"Whatever you people do," he said, passing the waiting line, "please, PLEASE, don't get on this ride. It's broken! Badly broken! And I won't have your blood on my hands!"

On our way home, we always stopped for ice cream.

"Hi, emm, I want zee ice cream, but don't know veech vun? You have so much, uh, veech is zee bestest?"

"I'm sorry, sir, what?" asked the young woman in cutoffs minding the ice cream window.

"I, I not know. Ehhm, may I have tastes?"

Fortunately, there were only a few people in line.

"Oh, sure. What do you want to try, sir?"

"Thees," Andy said, pointing to the chocolate chip. "An zen thees one, and zen thees one."

Andy sampled a dozen flavors and the line behind us swelled with impatient people. I cringed inside. Finally, he decided on vanilla.

The more I watched his face, the more attractive he became. He was painfully, tearfully funny, mirthful, and unflappable. I admired everything about this man.

The charm of his humor hooked deep.

Once Andy started staying with me, he didn't want to have sex right away because he said he was falling in love with me. He explained how his libido often got the best of him and that the Maharishi, the man who developed Transcendental Meditation, said that sex released energy forever and it was best saved for love.

"I want to try it," Andy said. "But you have to promise to tell me when you fall in love back. Then we can make love."

Andy donned a floor length nightshirt and instead of making love, he sang Fabian's "In This Friendly World":

In this friendly, friendly world with each day so full of joy
Why should any heart be lonely?
In this friendly, friendly world with each night so full of dreams
Why should any heart be afraid?
The world is such a wonderful place to wander through
When you've got someone you love to wander along with you
With the skies so full of stars and the river so full of song

> *Every heart should be so thankful*
> *Thankful for this friendly, friendly world*

After "carnival week," we went to a natural foods store for groceries. While I groped a cantaloupe, testing for ripeness, Andy lurched toward me and wrestled it away. I wrestled it right back into my arms and he started sobbing. Loudly. An employee marched toward me with fire in his eyes, followed by two others. They huddled around Andy, comforting him.

"It'll be OK, sir. We'll give you as many cantaloupes as you want." Then the one talking turned to me. "What kind of woman are you, picking on this poor man? Look at him. He's shaking. You traumatized him over a piece of fruit."

"He stole my cantaloupe, and I took it back. Isn't that right, mister? What a pathetic bag of soggy beans you are."

Andy cried harder and didn't speak.

"Ma'am, it wasn't yours unless you paid for it, am I right?" asked the clerk.

Shoppers gawked. The store was on pause.

"This women's rights thing has gone way too far," one man yelled in an accusatory voice. "Enough!"

"Oh my God, I cannot believe this! It's a piece of fruit. Fruit! He can keep his stupid cantaloupe. I hope there's a worm in it."

I shoved the cantaloupe into his hands, and one of his fingers inadvertently pegged a soft spot.

"Sir," one of the clerks said, patting Andy's back, "it's going to be OK."

Andy looked up at the clerk lovingly, a large, orbed fruit stuck on one finger and cantaloupe juice dripping onto the floor.

"Oh, please. Hey, mister," I said, "knock off the crying and be a big boy. Be a real manly man and grope your own damn cantaloupes from now on. Don't wait for women to do your dirty work. You probably don't even know how to wash your own underwear."

"He's more of a real man than you'll ever be, and he's fighting for his rights," said the man who'd yelled at me, "and isn't afraid to be emotional."

I didn't dare look at Andy.

"Hey, Bud! Listen up. First, I'm a woman, not a man. Second, I was just robbed. Third, he's fake crying. He's full of shit. Why don't you invite him to your next drum circle or whatever."

"Leave him alone. Go on your way."

"It's probably best," said the clerk, "before we have to call the police."

"The police? For what crime?"

"My finger, I think it's broken," Andy whimpered.

"Fine," I said, handing Andy my shopping basket. "And Snookums? Here's the grocery list. I'll wait for you at home."

Andy came out with a bag of groceries, and we gave each other congratulatory looks.

No moment was too mundane for improvisation or provocation, and I was always game, no explanations needed. He hatched schemes at the speed of sound so I couldn't articulate in my mind what he was doing or where he was going, but I stepped into it anyway. I didn't mind. If I missed the beat, he just played with that. Andy Kaufman was the person I trusted the most.

We perused Boston's high-end Newbury Street for hours, Andy skulking behind me as a lecherous man and following me into stores. His behavior raised the concerns of retail workers and customers alike. He hid in racks of clothing or grabbed a scarf or sweater and posed with the mannequins.

"Excuse me, Miss," said a freshly perfumed salesclerk. "Are you OK?"

"Am I OK? Why? Is something wrong with me?"

"Not you, but there's a man following your every move."

"What man? I didn't notice a man. Where is this man?"

Andy had already vanished.

"He's right over, um, right by the . . ." she said, turning in a full circle. "He was just there. I swear. He has dark hair, big eyebrows, kind of hunched over."

Another store wasted no time calling the police. Cops roared up the crowded street, sirens blazing. Mark Parenteau, the drive-time DJ from WBCN, pulled over for the cruisers and noticed me outside, speaking with the officers. He double-parked and rushed over. I explained to the cops I never saw a man following me. They urged me to contact them should the need arise. The cops left and Andy strolled out of the store.

"Princess," nodded Mark. "In trouble, as usual? Wait, is that Andy Kaufman? *The* Andy Kaufman. Nice to meet you, man. Love your work."

We spent the rest of the day at the radio station.

New York was Andy's favorite city to play in. We walked all day and night, initiating playlets and romantic dramas. Without warning, he'd sprint away behind me, then race back, get on his hands and knees, and grovel.

"Please, please come back, Honey Pie. Don't leave the kids for him! Or me! We have no food, water, or shelter."

I kept walking, ignoring him. He crawled along and started appealing to passersby.

"I can't raise seven children by myself! He's not worth giving up the kids and me for!"

After several blocks and a lot of dirty looks, we switched roles. He walked quickly, glancing over his shoulder repeatedly as I struggled to keep up. Then, usually in front of a busy department store, Andy stopped.

"I told you; you are not allowed to follow me around all day like a pathetic puppy. It's over. Get it through your dumb blond head. Over! Now, your day pass is about over so I suggest you get a cab back to Bellevue."

"But I can't stay away, darling. I have nothing but you. Please, I'm begging you. I'll behave. I promise. You'll see."

We ate at a macrobiotic or vegetarian restaurant before embarking on my favorite Andy antic: serial movie-viewing. We'd buy tickets and popcorn, take our seats, and wait for the movie to run long enough for people to get involved in the plot. Then, Andy stood and admonished me in a Southern twang.

"But my Honey Pie, delicious little Lamb Chop, don't accuse me of such unspeakable sins. Only the good Lord has the right to name our sins. What did you say? Say it again. Go on. I dare you. Say it louder. Go on. I'm a what? Satan swine?"

"Mister, sit your ass down and shut the fuck up," was the general audience response in Manhattan.

But Andy never backed down and finished everything he started, no matter how uncomfortable. Eventually, the house lights came on, and a manager escorted us out to the sounds of applause.

"I want my money back for the popcorn." Andy refused to leave until the refund was in his hand.

We walked a mere 15 feet to the next movie theater and repeated the scene. One night we visited seventeen different theaters.

Every waking moment was a carnival of mischief. During our escapades and nights spent together, we learned about some commonalities.

He barely graduated from high school, and I still hadn't. We both made the dean's list our first semester in college, we were macrobiotic, took LSD when we were young, danced to music in our rooms, hitchhiked, didn't get picked for teams or have many friends, and couldn't go to sleep without having ice cream.

I remember the exact moment I fell in love with Andy Kaufman. He was the "Foreign Man," standing stick straight on a stage, arms at his sides, softly fidgeting his fingers, and waiting for a record to play from his portable turntable. "Here I Come to Save the Day," the theme song from the Mighty Mouse cartoon, played, and Andy looked unsure, helpless, and lost. His fingers constantly twitched while he searched the room for whatever got away. Suddenly, he swept up his arm with swagger, bent one knee to the beat and mouthed the first line of the chorus before retreating again to his original stance. Andy's eyes darted from side to side like a boy trying to get the edge on a starting gun as he waited for the next chorus. Then, he started "singing" at the wrong time. That's when I fell for him.

The Foreign Man dressed how he acted, like he didn't have a clue. He wore his father's old sport coat, a button-down shirt over a black turtleneck, loafers, white socks, and pants that were too short. His comedic aspirations clearly exceeded his abilities, yet he tried so hard, stammering his way into a supposed joke that wasn't a joke at all. He attempted "eemeetations" of Jimmy Carter, Muhammad Ali, and Archie Bunker, among others, all in the same meek voice. Thin, nervous laughter came from the audience.

"You're laughing at me," he sputtered with wet eyes.

The audience shifted in their seats and started conversations with their neighbors. They booed, yelled, and walked out. Inevitably, one audience member admonished people for being so cruel.

Andy's singular life goal was to have fun. If the audience didn't have fun with him, that was fine. He didn't need their approval.

The Foreign Man made a final offer.

"Now, last but not to be de least, I vud like to eemeetate de Elvis Presley. Tank you veddy much."

He turned away from the audience, ripped off the sides of his pants, shed his coat, donned a rhinestone Elvis jacket, combed his hair three times, and strapped on a guitar. When he looked over one shoulder with his upper lip lifted, Andy was fully transformed. He was Elvis. The crowd went nuts.

When he was done, he took off his guitar and coat, leaned tentatively into the microphone and said, "Tenk you veddy much."

Andy's Foreign Man personality inspired the creation of Taxi character Latka Gravas, the mechanic at Sunshine Cab Company, which Andy played for 144 episodes, from 1978 to 1983.

Andy and I became inseparable. When he was traveling or at home in Los Angeles, we talked on the phone several times a day. When he wasn't staying with me in Boston, he was staying with me in Boulder, stirring things up on and off campus.

He went to classes with me, and we swam at the rec center every day.

"Let's go for a sweem!" he'd say.

Andy introduced me to Haagen-Dazs ice cream at the mall in Boulder, where a shop had opened. I remember how excited he was watching me try my first spoonful. We'd sit outside and stir the ice cream into soup and watch the street performers.

The fun insanity of being with Andy made life in Boulder seem dull. There were plenty of good schools in Boston; I could work when I felt like it and see Andy more often. His traveling from Los Angeles and New York to Boulder robbed us of precious play time. I moved back in December of 1981 and was accepted to Boston University's School of Communications for the 1982 Spring semester. When Andy asked me to go with him on the road, I withdrew before classes started. College could wait.

The most memorable show was at the Park West Theatre in Chicago in March 1982. Andy insisted we invite my grandmother, Nan.

"Hi, um, is this Mrs. Reeves? My name's Andy, and I love my grandmother Pearl as much as Lucy loves you, and I told your wonderful granddaughter, Lucy here, that if my grandmother Pearl lived near Chicago, I'd pick her right up in a snazzy limo and bring her to my show. Hi, yes, no, that's right, you don't know me. Yes, I'm the Andy she talks about. Wait, hold on, don't hang up."

Andy held the phone away from his ear and looked at me.

"Lamp Chop, is there another Andy in your life?"

"No, no, of course not. Hi Nan! Can't wait to see you," I said.

Andy wore his "I Love Grandma" shirt when we picked her up from the North Shore in a limo. Nan had quite the surprise when, during the show, a hypnotist put me under and I started taking off my clothes. The Chicago police came rushing down the aisles to squelch the illegal activity.

Wrestling became Andy's focus. He'd always loved it but couldn't see himself wrestling men and winning, so he started wrestling women in the 1970s. The first televised match was on *The Tomorrow Show* with Tom Snyder in 1979, followed by *Saturday Night Live*. Andy was determined to defend the self-awarded title, "Intergender Wrestling Champion of the World."

He offered $1,000 to any female audience member who could beat him and goaded them with derogatory sexist comments. Women got so worked up, they fought each other for the honor of attacking the odious man. Andy won every match.

In April of 1982, Andy was invited to wrestle the reigning Southern heavyweight wrestling champion, Jerry Lawyer, in Memphis, Tennessee. Andy was pile-driven by Lawler, causing injury to his cervical vertebrae. In an eerie repetition of the wrestling incident with his brother, Andy spent three days in traction before coming to visit me in Boston. I was worried.

CHAPTER 19

Stripper Parade

Andy arrived in a neck brace. I was frantic.

"You look awful. What did the doctors say?"

"My neck. I'm not supposed to turn my head, not even once. It could make me paralyzed."

"Jesus, how is that supposed to work? Can you sit down? Do you need a wheelchair? What can I get you? Oh my god, I am so sorry."

I was close to tears.

"Takeout from the Seventh Inn would be nice. Is the menu still in the desk drawer?" Andy asked, turning.

"You just said you could be paralyzed if you turned your head."

"Oh yeah. You're supposed to remind me. What kind of girlfriend are you? You're fired."

Andy's eyes bounced around, and he ripped open the neck brace.

"Andy!"

Then it dawned on me. Of course.

"I even had you going. Ha!" laughed Andy.

"I don't think it's the least bit funny."

"I swear, I'm not trying to be funny. You're not breaking up with me, are you? Will you still be my girlfriend? I'd be nothing without you."

"Yes! No! You just fired me. I can't believe you planned this, like, faked the whole thing, and didn't think to tell me. Did you ever think I might worry about you, Andy? I'm leaving. Fuck this shit!"

"But you live here. What about dinner? I'm hungry."

"I'll have dinner by myself."

"Fine. Get out! No dinner for you. And no lovemaking! Or ice cream before bed!"

I was so confused I was letting him kick me out of my own apartment.

"Fine. I have to get my coat. I can't believe you did this to me."

"Nope. No coat for you. Now get out."

I slammed the door, forgot my keys, and tried opening the door. It was locked.

"Andy," I said, banging on the door.

He kept the safety chain intact and cracked the door. I saw one sapphire eye and a set of long black eyelashes.

"Aw," he said. "You look upset. You need to meditate."

"I need my fucking keys is what I need."

"No. You don't need keys. You're leaving."

Andy smiled and unhooked the chain.

"So glad you're not paralyzed, you asshole. Yes, I'm still your girlfriend."

"I can't believe you bought it. It's a first! Aside from my manager, Bob, you're the only person who thinks like me."

"No one on this planet thinks like you."

If I wasn't with Andy, I was working. When he visited, we shoved my furniture against the walls and hosted wrestling parties for friends and neighbors. We attended lectures at the Kushi Institute for Macrobiotics, danced at Dance Free in Harvard Square, and drank wheatgrass juice at the Hippocrates Institute on Exeter Street. I learned how to make him laugh. He learned how to be vulnerable.

One night, stretched out behind me in bed, he sobbed in between my shoulder blades and, when he was done, talked about his past until the sun came up. It was the closest we would ever be.

After two years together, our romance evolved into more of a friendship. I always knew he wasn't lifetime partner material. We stayed close and spoke on the phone four or five times a week. Sometimes, it sounded like he had lost his breath. One time I asked him if he was masturbating during our call, and he said no, the pollution in Los Angeles was getting to him.

Public backlash against Andy's wrestling mania resulted in fewer bookings and his being voted off *Saturday Night Live*. David Letterman was the only late-night host who still invited him for guest spots. *Taxi* was canceled, and Andy wasn't allowed to participate in a TM instructor training. He pretended to be fine but asked me to visit him in Los Angeles. He said I could cheer him up.

I'd started Emerson College, and Andy booked me a round-trip flight to Los Angeles after the fall semester ended in December 1983. Before I was set to leave, Andy told me everyone was worried about his cough and that his arm hurt, even though he couldn't remember injuring it.

"I told you I had cancer," he said. "Remember the things on my back? In the beginning?"

I remembered feeling them before I saw them. When we first met, Andy liked the lights out, and after we made love, I moved my hands gently over his back while he rested on me. I felt domes the size of golf balls half-buried in his hairy back.

Andy stiffened when I touched them.

"Sorry," I said.

"No, I'm sorry. Are you disgusted with me?"

"Andy, no. Come on. They're only bumps. Do they hurt?"

"I don't know," he said. "I don't think they hurt. If terrible things are growing out of me, then terrible things are growing inside of me."

"What does that mean?"

"That I have cancer, and it's getting worse."

Andy kept delaying my flight to LA, but I should have gone myself. He confirmed his premonitions and had terrible things growing inside of him. It was getting worse. My heart locked. It took my breath away.

There was a tumor, an exceedingly rare, large cell lung carcinoma, blocking his airway, causing pneumonia. Cancer cells crowded the hollows of his bones, making his arm hurt and displacing tissue in his magnificent brain. He had palliative radiation, and we talked when he could. Only once did he tell me he was scared. He changed my flight to LA six times.

"I'm going to see a psychic surgeon in the Philippines in three days. It's all I have left to try," said Andy in a quiet voice.

"What about the Kushi Institute? I'll go there today, right now, and talk to them."

After exhausting conventional methods of treatment, Andy only had the strength and time for one more trip. He had "psychic surgery" in the Philippines, where they pretended to remove things from his body. Andy said he was cured.

A publicity photo for the Naked i.

It was harder to reach him, and after several days, I assumed he was back in the hospital. I knew how to track him down and called his room. A nurse answered and said he was too weak to talk.

"Let me write your number down," the nurse suggested.

"Oh, he knows my number. It's OK."

"Give it to me anyway. Just in case," she said.

Because Andy's brain was disintegrating.

The phone rang. It was the nurse.

"He told me to tell you, Lucy, not to miss a day of fun," she said.

Tender, sweet Andy died at Cedars-Sinai Medical Center in Los Angeles on May 16, 1984, at 6:30 p.m. He was thirty-five years old and the first person I'd lost to death. He escaped.

I graduated summa cum laude from Emerson College.

Looking back, I'm glad I'd never heard of Andy Kaufman before I met him. I got to know him without preconceived notions and listened to his stories without trying to fit them into an explanation of who Andy "really was." He was beyond genius, beyond self-actualized, beyond any way I've heard a person described, the archetypal free spirit who invited me into his childhood bedroom and let me stay and play.

The night I'd heard that Andy died, I sat under the spotlight at the Naked i, watching the smoke and musing that I was a selfish coward for not going to LA. Everything about his death mattered, but I couldn't say what or how.

"Hello, young lady. It must be a first."

A familiar elderly man the width of a stick tottered sideways toward me, smiling. He couldn't know what I was feeling about Andy.

"A first?" I asked, not wanting to engage but feeling gentle toward the frail man.

"A stripper writing a magazine article. Well done. Come have a drink when I get settled in my spot."

I'd said hello to him several times before and received a silver dollar for my efforts, but hadn't taken the time to know him. Dancers didn't sit with him. He always smiled and stacked silver dollars at the bar.

"What's a Nice Girl Like You Doing in a Place Like This" was an article I put together for *Boston* magazine and included photographs by Roswell Angier, a brief narrative, and dancer interviews. It was published a few weeks before Andy died. I'd forgotten about it and a lot of things.

"They Have Their Reasons"
Interviews by Lucy Johnson

Dori Dixon
Naked i Cabaret

> Dori, 23, grew up in Georgia and Alabama, where she completed high school. She studied psychology at Pensacola Junior College, in Florida. Dori has also attended hairdressing school and plans to open a salon that would offer both beauty services and clothing. Dori's mother has been a waitress at the Naked i during her daughter's six-year stint there.
>
> "I like the spotlight. You feel appreciated when you dance because it's not nasty—it's an art. People don't yell at you, like they yell at a

waitress if their eggs aren't done right. The girls are really off-the-wall in here, so you can get along with them, most of them anyway. It's a nice atmosphere to work in. It's loose. I'm just trying to make it on my own, to put myself through school, pay my own bills, and at the same time live comfortably and do what I want to do. I have to have a job that pays me enough to do that. Who else is going to pay you to get drunk?"

Kendra
Naked i Cabaret

Kendra, 25, was born in Washington DC, where she attended an all-girl high school. If the skirt of her plaid uniform was more than three inches above the knee, she had to go to school on Saturday as a punishment. Kendra went to college for two years to study English because she felt she had a knack for writing. She has danced at the Naked i for two and a half years.

"I like the raunchiness, it's a kind of reality. Sometimes I look at it as a strange kind of reality, but it is reality. I'm here because I choose to be. Stripping gives me a lot of freedom. I can take time off or I can work a lot. My salary changes depending on how much I want to work. I can be my own person and choose my own styles and show off to other people. I don't have to play a role, not as if I was a secretary or a businesswoman."

Diana
Naked i Cabaret

Diana, 19, graduated from high school in Framingham and attended Framingham State College, where she studied psychology and business. She's been a stripper for six months.

"Stripping has built up my confidence in a lot of ways. I have learned so much about people and myself here. The money was the thing that brought me here, but I think I like it. In any other job, I was more or less in the background, but here it's like I'm the main attraction. I feel like the people are coming here to see me, rather than that I'm working for them. You do meet a lot of weirdos. But I come to work, I do what I can while I'm here, and when I leave I have a normal, average, everyday life. Usually takes me a good hour and a half before I get adjusted to the scene. I relax, sit downstairs by the stage for a while, and watch the whole situation."

Gwynnedd
Naked i Cabaret

Gwynnedd (pronounced "Gwenneth") is 22 and studying to be a hairdresser. She graduated from the Cambridge pilot school, spent a few years in California, and did some acting in Cambridge. Gwynnedd has worked as a stripper for one year and nine months.

"Stripping makes me feel absolutely high—it's exhilarating. I've always been really afraid to reach out and talk to people. Deep down inside I'm shy, but on stage I tend to ham it up. I'm here basically for the money, but also for the sheer thrill of performing. My boyfriend thinks I'm gonna turn to prostitution. He met me in here. He's extremely jealous if another man sees my body. We fight every night. I wouldn't leave dancing for him. I meet regular working-class people, lawyers, doctors, stockbrokers. I like it. We're not whores. Just because we take off our clothes, it doesn't mean we're out for a fast buck. A lot of us are serious performers. We really put thought into our shows and into our costumes. I love to be seen."

Linda Lamia
Naked i Cabaret

Linda Lamia, 21, from Winnipeg, Canada, traveled alone for three years instead of completing her high school education. After she gets her GED, she intends to go to college and study interior design. Later, she plans to retire to the south of France. Linda has been stripping at the Naked i for two years and expects to be there for another five.

"I'm an exhibitionist. I think almost anyone would have to be somewhat of an exhibitionist to get on stage and dance. As jobs go, it's much better than waitressing. You don't work so hard for the money you make. I enjoy meeting some of the people. It doesn't really interfere with my lifestyle at all. I can come to work and know that I'm not going to have to punch in and do something terrible that I really don't want to do. I enjoy dancing. I think the Naked i is a good place to work, so it's not that much out of character for a woman like me to be here."

Chenelle
Naked i Cabaret

Chenelle, Kendra's roommate, is 21. She started working at the Naked i as a waitress. Born in San Jose, California, she was raised in Lexington and Marblehead.

"I think I've learned more here than I could anywhere else about the way people deal with themselves or other people. Dancing is easy; it takes a very little of my time and my energy. It pays well. I guess it's kind of exciting, it's an adventure, and fun in a way. Stripping isn't like working; it's more haphazard. It's easier than any other job I've had. If someone had told me two years ago that I'd be working here, I would've been very shocked, but now that I'm here it doesn't seem that shocking or strange."

Lona
Naked i Cabaret

Lona, 20, was born in Atlanta and later moved to Boston, where she attended Hyde Park High School; she graduated from Brookline High School. Lona, who wants to be a professional dancer, has worked at the Naked I for two years.

"I love stripping, turning the men on when they can't touch me. I like to see their tongues pop out. I just like to see the expressions on their faces. And I like the tips. It's not a sleazy club, it's not cheap, it's not too dirty. We have a nice, clean, comfortable dressing room and we get a better crowd than the other clubs. I can save a lot of money to go to dance classes. Oh, all kinds of crazy stuff goes on in here. You're always partying or something, and there's always something exciting happening. With all the clubs on Washington Street, if I didn't like this one I'd go to work in another one. But I see a lot of girls in here who are almost pushing 30. I hope I'm not gonna be here like that.

Rikki Harte
Golden Banana

>*Rikki, 23, grew up in the blueberry capital of the world, Cherryfield, Maine, where she picked blueberries every summer and pulled lobsters in the fall. She took classes at the Actors Workshop in Boston. She wants to breed blue Persians and to live next-door to Johnny Carson on Malibu Beach. Ricky has been a stripper for four years.*
>
>*"I like being a woman. I like putting on makeup. I like getting applause. I like to make people happy. And I like the money. Great presents, anything from stuffed animals to $100 bills. I love the hours—you can sleep all day. You never know who you're gonna meet. When someone asks me why I'm here I usually say, 'because I'm making more money than you are.' And then I just walk out and get in my Corvette and split, and they figure it out."*

I sat next to the man and his magazine, a pen acting as a bookmark for the article's first page. He would become, by far, the most bizarre customer friendship I'd have.

"Oh, there you are, you rascal," he said in a wavering voice. "Name's Nate and it is an absolute pleasure. You wouldn't mind signing this for an old man, would you?"

"Hi, um, no. It's a first, but sure."

"That's N November, A alpha, T tango, and E echo. Nate."

Nate ordered an old-fashioned with a twist of orange and two maraschino cherries.

"There you go, Nate. My first autograph."

"Certainly not your last, either."

Nate produced three rolls of silver dollars from his navy-blue blazer pocket and scored the brown paper with his thumbnail.

"You'll pardon me a moment while I get my coins in order," he said.

"Oh, of course."

I watched him inspect the coins in his palm and align the edges, building three stacks on the bar. He explained that waitresses and bartenders got slightly discolored coins, and the brightest went to dancers. Nate talked about his aging German shepherd and his career in strategic air defense and microwave radar technology. He reminded me of Nan, so pleasant and calming.

I saw him regularly and looked forward to his stories. Eventually, he talked to me about his wife.

"It's a grisly situation. I suppose it's improper to tell you this, but no one else knows and it's been a lot to keep in."

The stripper: a repository of secrets, confessions, and unmentionable things.

"She's afraid I'll leave her, which I never would. But she got it in her head, you see, and her solution was to make herself helpless. Now I do everything for her. She can't drive, bathe, cook, do laundry, anything. Without me, she'd perish."

"I'm sorry," I said. "But you can go out? I mean, she won't starve or get hurt without you there?"

"Oh," he guffawed, "believe me, she already hurt herself."

"While you weren't there? Did she fall or something?"

"In a manner of speaking, yes. She didn't fall until her hands did."

I considered Nate's age and assumed he wasn't finding the right words.

"How could I leave her alone with no hands? Leave anyone alone with no hands?"

"I'm sorry, I'm not following you. By hands, do you mean, like, a symbol of something?"

Nate turned to me and held up one finger.

"No." He lowered his voice. "She cut off both of her hands while I was away on my last business trip before retiring. It was a bloody mess."

The notion was logistically impossible.

"Not to be rude, but how can anyone cut off both hands when the first hand is gone? How can anyone cut their hand off, period?"

"With great determination, a wily temperament, a touch of mental illness, vodka, and pills. She clamped my old miter saw to a worktable in the garage, tied tourniquets on both arms, and called 911 before proceeding. She didn't want to die, she wanted to get back at me for mostly imagined affairs. She fainted when the saw jammed from bone chips and ligaments on the second hand. They brought the hands to the hospital, but they were a mess and couldn't be reattached. That really would've gotten her! Having working hands after all that. Now she wears colorful scarves over the stumps. Said it smelled terrible but didn't feel a thing."

I didn't completely buy the story until Nate's declining health made it impossible for him to visit the club. He'd given me his address, and I sent him a Christmas card with my return address on the envelope. He then sent back an early Easter card with his phone number and a check for $20,000. I called to tell him I couldn't accept his gift.

"You must, you absolutely must. Not only is it a gift for you, but it is also a gift to me. You'll never understand the importance. Please," he begged. "Our friendship has meant the world to me. The regard you've shown me doesn't have a price, but this is the least I can do. It's almost my time to go, and I have more money than I know what to do with."

I deposited the check and sent him a thank you note. Within weeks, Nate sent an additional $40,000. He told me he was worn out and had stopped taking his medications. Then, he stopped answering and, eventually, the phone was disconnected.

Nate named me as a beneficiary to his will and I inherited a summer house in Kennebunkport. I chose not to defend my position in probate court.

Following Nate's death, I was audited by the IRS and hired Morris Goldings, the attorney who represented the Naked i. Morris successfully argued that I received gifts, not tips, from Nate.

By the end of 1984, I'd purchased and renovated a two-family Victorian on Ashmont Hill in Dorchester, a residential neighborhood that felt worlds away from my toney former digs in the heart of the city. I'd completed my third semester at Emerson College and had a literary agent pitching a manuscript to Little, Brown and Houghton Mifflin. The agent ultimately negotiated with Warner Brothers for the rights to my story.

As I thawed from the shock of Andy's death, his indomitable spirit became more evident. Every unusual person or situation I found myself in caused me to wonder what he might have done—like the stripper parade, in which I pictured him leading us, like Mr. Peanut, through the streets of Boston.

The parade came to be because the *Boston Herald*'s gossip columnist, Norma Nathan, introduced me to Legal Sea Foods in Park Square. I ate there as an alternative to The Seventh Inn and became friendly with the employees. I enjoyed the workplace stories, my favorite being how the owner, Roger Berkowitz, allegedly infused Legal's ice cream bonbons with laxatives to prevent the staff from wiping out the popular restaurant's supply. How the clientele avoided receiving them is a mystery.

One night, Captain Katie, the floor manager, called the Naked i looking for me.

"It's his highness's birthday coming up," she said in an Irish brogue, "and we want to do something special. Nothing normal like a cake or candles. That wouldn't suit him. Something shocking. He gets such a kick out of you, we decided to invite you."

"Thanks, Katie. Of course, I'll be there."

"But wait, I have a small favor to ask."

"You want me to dance on a table?"

Katie laughed.

"No, no. There'll be people having lunch. But if you could make an entrance in your costume, you know, surprise the life out of him, maybe sneak up from behind. Lord knows the man always has surprises up his sleeve. Now it's his turn."

I brought some friends along, and we discussed where to get into our costumes.

"Louise," urged Jazz, "why don't we walk from here? It's not that far."

At 12:15 p.m., five massive, glittery costumes, too fantastic to be part of the ordinary world, paraded in sneakers eight blocks from the Naked i to Legal Sea Foods. The moving visual elicited streams of hoots and honks. The Park Plaza hotel attendants saw us coming and opened both doors to accommodate the breadth of our feathers, hoops, wings, and tails. We snuck up behind Roger, accomplishing even more than Captain Katie imagined.

CHAPTER 20

Motorcycle Cop

"Well, well, well," Phil Donahue smirked, shaking his head dubiously. "What are the fine residents of Lake Forest, Illinois, saying about their debutante, Princess Cheyenne?"

"I'm sure my mother's friends are all calling her," I said. (I didn't know then that, by the time her friends had their say, Mother and I wouldn't speak for five years.)

"What do we think about our Lake Forest native, here in her red dress and feather boa?" he asked, arms spread.

Dozens of hands shot up, and Donahue jogged up the aisle with his microphone.

"You don't look like a stripper," said the man.

Donahue surveyed the audience while moving.

"What does a stripper look like?" I asked.

Before I finished my response, Donahue had returned to the man.

"They sound uneducated, wear lots of makeup, you know, rough around the edges, and not from a town like Lake Forest. The typical stereotype."

"Sir, I actually don't know. Stereotypes are lazy and inaccurate. The dancers I know don't fit your description."

"Why is it OK to be used?" asked another.

"I have every right to use myself. My body, brain, and performances are commodified with my consent. That's not being used; it's a mutual exchange like any other job."

Donahue jogged the microphone over to yet another man.

"What about your past do you think made you start stripping?" He winked.

"Definitely not trauma or daddy issues. I never meant to become a stripper. It was accidental, something I stumbled into and was good at."

I winked back and took a breath.

"If I was a man," I continued, "would you wink at me? Would you ask the same question if I worked at a dry cleaner?"

I loved talking against the tide, touting my firsthand experiences, and dispelling the stigma of strippers on television. It felt important.

A self-appointed male "expert" in the audience made a long-winded introduction before spitting out a question.

"What's it like to be a sex worker?"

"A sex worker? I'm not a sex worker. Isn't a sex worker a prostitute or someone who performs sexual acts for money? I don't have sex for money. I prefer free sex. Why do people assume strippers are prostitutes? Stripping is performance, not sex."

"It's manipulative," he continued, trying to save face. "You manipulate men to make money."

"I just show up to dance, and men come in by choice."

"OK, but you're objectifying yourself."

"Jeez. From my being a sex worker to manipulating men to turning myself into an object, you're all over the place. I don't know how to objectify myself."

Finally, a woman spoke from the audience.

"Hi. People like you ruin marriages."

"I'm sorry you see it that way," I said.

Later in the show, my friend, one-time colleague, and intellectual sparring partner, Lauri Lewin, joined me underneath the blazing studio lights. She'd written a cautionary memoir called, *Naked Is the Best Disguise: My Life as a Stripper*.

Lauri and I appeared on several talk shows together to discuss our disparate experiences and theories. In my view, dancers had all the power. Lauri felt stripping was oppressive. During the commercial break, a Donahue producer came to the stage and encouraged us to argue more.

"It makes for good television," she said.

I should have gone into television. Instead, I landed on the radio.

On the back porch of my two-family in Dorchester with future husband Donny Wightman.

After graduating from Emerson in May 1985, I hosted a sex advice radio show on WBCN, opposite Dr. Ruth Wertheimer's NBC syndicated show. I presented the latest sex research, fun facts, relationship tips, and sexual advice. I opened the show with something like this:

"Dr. Ruth, push aside. Hi, I'm Princess Cheyenne, and you're listening to 104.1 WBCN Boston. I'm putting my years of experience working as a stripper at the Naked i to help you find better ways to cope with anything about sex and relationships. Give us a call at 617-536-8000, where my colleagues, Haley and Sharon, are waiting to take your questions. You can also write to me with questions I'll discuss next time."

Dr. Ruth wasn't provocative, and I was. She didn't talk about her experiences, and I did. Sex was still a taboo subject in the mid-1980s, and the show stood out enough for *Playboy* to include me in its March 1986 feature "America's Sexiest DJs."

Excitement about the upcoming photo shoot, my radio show, and various talk-show appearances outstripped the Naked i's banal, grinding routine. My time on stage started feeling uninspired and mechanical. If a customer was rude, I turned his drink upside down over his head. I complained about the club's air quality and the dancers who used "my" songs.

Mel noticed my discontent and installed the pole I'd been asking for. He raised my nightly pay to $145.

"It's only my pole, right? Like, no one else can use it. Or touch it. It wouldn't be hygienic."

"Only your pole," Mel smiled. "The Princess Pole."

He twirled a slender bottle of Tabasco sauce on the tabletop between his thumb and forefinger, three times one way, three times the other, over and over until depositing it into the breast pocket of his Oxford suit jacket.

"Why do you put hot sauce in your pocket?" I asked.

"Because most restaurants around here don't have it," he said. "I like to be prepared."

That was the last curiosity I found living inside the Naked i Cabaret: Mel's Tabasco sauce.

The pristine Princess Pole was erected within a week. I'd barely mastered hanging upside down like a sleeping bat when other dancers put their grubby paws—and other body parts—on it. The surface was flaky, and I refused to touch it. I wanted to wrap the pole in crime-scene tape.

At my behest, Mel installed yet another pole. I told everyone I had genital warts, which made my nightly pole inspections unnecessary as colleagues kept their hands off. The replacement had an outer tube that spun with me, and I whirled around pole number two like it was a carnival ride.

I lacked gymnastic ability but managed slow descents from the ceiling in full pole-straddle. This was a crowd-pleaser. After a week of hearing "pole, pole, pole" chanted to other dancers, I felt like a heel and relinquished my exclusive rights to the prop and left rubbing alcohol and paper towels behind the curtain. Besides, the pole didn't cure my boredom.

Mel handed me an article from a San Francisco newspaper that was based on an interview I'd given after starting the radio show. I read the article while he stared at me.

"Stripper Johnson: 'Attitudes are changing'"
by Ken Franckling, UPI Feature Writer

BOSTON—*By day Lucy Johnson is a 25-year-old aspiring writer studying at a small liberal arts college. She has a girl-next-door look of innocent charm and is a stripper in Boston's adult entertainment district known as the Combat Zone. Under the stage name Princess Cheyenne, her wholesome looks and vivacious charisma have made her one of Boston's highest-paid strippers.*

In an unofficial way, she has become the grimy Combat Zone's unofficial public relations representative as the subject of numerous regional newspaper and magazine articles. Born in Lake Forest, Illinois, and raised in New Canaan, Connecticut, Johnson said she became a stripper as a "rebellion against my upper-class upbringing and the desire to see other facets of life."

She is one of dozens of stage-struck exhibitionists who dance in the all-nude bars in Boston's four-block zone. At the Naked i Cabaret, the tamest of the lot, up to thirty-five young women take off their clothes— three times for those on the night shift, four times for daysiders.

"*People's attitudes are changing a lot toward nudity and sex. There are so many shocking things in the world, it's kind of innocent these days,*" *Johnson said.*

She is adamant in her defense of the Combat Zone at a time Mayor Raymond L. Flynn wants it shut down to make way for economic redevelopment. "*If Ray Flynn tries to close this place up, he'll have to deal with me first,*" *she said.*

Johnson calls the Naked i "a fun place."

"It's harmless," she said. "It gives a lot of women a place to work where they are paid fairly—better than other jobs—where they are treated fairly and have control over their jobs. They don't have to empty wastebaskets, get coffee, or flirt with their bosses."

Johnson, dressed in crimson, whisks down the Naked i's oak, bar-length runway, trailing and twirling a long, red-feathered boa as she opens her routine. Ten minutes later, she wears a small gold pendant. And a smile.

"I've been successful here because I've been able to be vulnerable here. When I dance on stage, I can look somebody in the eye and be intimate with them. It doesn't threaten me. I feel totally comfortable without my clothes on," she said. "I'm here to entertain people and give them some sort of enjoyment, regardless of what it is."

"Pretty good," said Mel. "The United Press International. We're everywhere. All over the world."

"It's so weird how I don't even remember this interview," I said. "And how I put some things in the past tense like I was already gone."

"Things change," said Mel. "It's one of life's few guarantees. Then they change again, and not always for the better."

The March issue of *Playboy* came out, and I hosted an autograph signing at Pat Lyons' nightclub, where more than 1,500 men showed up. I sat behind a table, dwarfed by stacks of magazines that marked my second *Playboy* appearance. The publication's perfume-soaked PR person was behind me, making sure I capped the Sharpie in between autographs.

The line disappeared into the dark recesses of a nightclub the size of two city blocks, and I had no idea when it might end. One adoring face, dreamy smile, and kind thought followed another for six straight hours. I loved it.

Playboy
March 1986

Then there's the star of our show, Lucy Johnson, Boston's noted stripper/sex advisor. As Princess Cheyenne, she does visuals during the week at the Naked i Cabaret. Sunday nights, she hosts a sex/talk show called Ask Princess Cheyenne, which by all accounts is far juicier than Dr. Ruth's.

"Perfect," said Lucy when we called to ask a few questions. "I just got out of the shower, and I'm nude."

You've seen Lucy/P.C. on Donahue; read about her in People. She's the Social Register *stripper born to wealth, she traded in her silver spoon for stripping, Seventies' rock star Cat Stevens and sex radio.*

"I get mostly male callers," she says. "A lot of them have already seen me at the Naked i or make a point of coming in. They can't see me on radio."

Poor fellows. But what's this about Cat Stevens?

"We met when I was 16 and again when I was 20," says Lucy. "He was a Muslim by then. I was obsessed with him. We became engaged and I moved to London. I stopped dancing and put on a veil, went to the mosque every day. This went on for about four months until I realized the fantasy was over. I left. It was ironic that I ended up hurting him after years of being obsessed with him. He called me his hardheaded woman. I guess I was too hardheaded."

And that's only one Lucy Johnson story. Want more? You'll have to ask Princess Cheyenne, Sunday nights, on the Hub's WBCN."

The *Playboy* article packed in customers beyond capacity night after night but outside the club, Boston Mayor Ray Flynn was making good on his promise to purify the Zone. Chinatown residents and business owners were tired of their raunchy neighbors, and developers wanted the prime real estate.

Once a stubborn adversary to regulations, the Zone was caving under the weight of license hearings, property values, police crackdowns, and business closings. Many saw the adult entertainment district as a failed experiment, a moral contaminant, or an island of misfit toys. I didn't need the mayor of Boston to read the tea leaves for me. The Combat Zone was fading, and my need to be part of it was fading, too. Until Halloween night.

Dancers were having fun wearing plastic vampire teeth and pumpkin earrings while passing out candy corn. Songs like "Monster Mash" and Thriller" replayed every other set, and someone decided dancers on the floor had to wear witch's hats. My skin felt itchy and dry, and I wanted an argument.

I hoisted the light-up butterfly wings over my shoulders, and the sequin edges on the straps dug into the meat on my shoulders. The wings felt heavier every time I wore them.

"What's your first song?" Janice, the DJ, asked, chomping air bubbles out of her gum from underneath a witch's hat.

How did she forget the song between last fucking night and tonight?

Her gum popping and hat annoyed me.

"Same as the last two thousand times. 'Fantasia.' Please."

"Ugly Head of Greed?" she asked rhetorically, recounting the full name of the song.

Even my hair felt irritated. She started a percussive beat with her two-inch long, red acrylic nails, and I felt like my forehead was about to erupt.

"That's the one," I mumbled before zinging it back. "Geez, Janice, I don't know how you deal with those crazy-looking nails. . . . not only torturous, but semi-ridiculous looking."

"I can still finger my girlfriend, and she doesn't complain."

"Gross."

"Did someone say finger? Of course, you can, darling," said Brittany, yanking at the same white mini dress she'd had forever.

"I hate this costume. I'm choking to death," I growled. "Janice, please do the smoke machine heavily with the strobe."

"Hoping to go up in smoke, darling?" Brittany asked. "I dare say The Princess is rather testy. She must have happened upon a pea between her bedsheets."

Brittany always made me laugh.

I hauled the glorious wings onstage, toggled the light switches and lifted the poles to make lazy turns, careful not to knock out any bartenders. The audience was excited. I felt as vacant as a clam.

Then I saw them.

Four glow-in-the-dark Xs at varying heights caught my interest. I made my way to the runway's end again and realized they were traffic belts strapped to Boston Police motorcycle cops. They liked to step inside to "warm up," even in summer. They kept their gloved hands folded and their heads down, forming a sexy but untouchable line of authority.

I rarely saw their faces, only outside from a distance, when they parked their imposing motorcycles diagonally in front of the club. If they were there when I left, I paused to watch them laugh and mount their bikes as though they were miniature thoroughbreds. I was mesmerized by their regalia, glossy turquoise helmets, tall leather boots, jodhpurs, gloves with gauntlets, leather jackets, and gun belts. The cops never stayed long enough to satisfy my curiosity.

This Halloween night, they lifted their heads and watched me for the first time. I noticed one in particular as I twirled naked on the balls of my feet.

Then Karen, another dancer, weaved toward them, parallel to the bar and holding a champagne glass like it was attached to a flying video stabilizer. She tossed a few stray ribbons of hair behind one shoulder and lurched wildly ahead, right toward the cops. She regained her posture, but three steps later, her five-inch heels crisscrossed and locked. The contents of the champagne glass propelled forward as Karen went down like a loose hand on a clock. All four cops opened their arms and righted her like a Weeble. She yanked off her shoes and turned them upside down, as if the shoes were at fault and not the alcohol.

"That sure was super swe-eet," she said with elongated pronunciation.

After my set, I hurried downstairs. Three of the cops had left, and the one I noticed leaned against the cigarette machine. He wrote his number on the back of my hand and started coming in more often. One night, he suggested I stop by to see him at a detail on nearby Tremont Street and we sat in his cruiser and talked. And other stuff.

Several rounds of sex in a Boston Police Department cruiser with a Boston Police officer inspired me to put together a motorcycle cop act. Donny took me to police supply stores to collect gear and donated a nightstick, handcuffs, leather gloves with gauntlets, an old leather police jacket, Boston Police patches ("They're real," I'd boast.), a turquoise helmet, and clip-on tie.

To add whimsy, I bought six free-standing, blue police lights for the runway and a radio-controlled police motorcycle. Soon, any cop within a half-mile radius came in to see the show, scheduled for 9 p.m. every night.

Jill Duncan, from *The Tab* newspaper, wrote an article called "The Socialite Stripper" and described it:

> *"All the attention of the predominantly male crowd is focused on a slim muscular blonde woman who is parading up and down the elevated runway in a leather police officer's uniform. The costume is made up of an astonishing number of parts, such as three-piece elbow-length black leather gloves and a form-fitting uniform that comes apart and turns into a leather teddy. Throughout it all, the girl remains in motion pirouetting, crouching, and twirling a billy club like a baton. By the end of the half-hour show, the girl wears nothing but a silver cape, and, as the strobe light alternately flashes and goes dark, one can see a flash of silver and a flash of skin—silver, skin, silver, skin—until the image is all but obscured by a haze of smoke. The crowd—separated from the stage by a row of nonchalant bartenders—is pleased but nonplussed by the performance. The girl is smiling."*

I was at the top of my game but felt anesthetized by routine. Even applause didn't shatter the monotony. I wanted every night to be over the moment I arrived so I could be with Donny.

Public enthusiasm for adult entertainment waned, and the Combat Zone was sanitized. Increased law enforcement drove out prostitution and VHS players and desktop computers brought pornography into people's homes. Quirky characters became rare as people moved on in a variety of ways.

Billy, the day manager, died; Ray left for medical school; and Mel had cancer, leaving his son in charge. Hedy Jo and Buzzy moved to Las Vegas and the joke shop was closing. Dancers became opera singers, veterinarians, hairdressers, university deans, aestheticians, professors, cops, marines, wives, and mothers. Guddler stopped coming in with his lobster-filled cooler.

Without the promise of adventure, stripping became drudgery and lost its vocational charm. I just wanted to be with Donny and vigorously attached myself to his interests. I sat cross-legged on the sidelines of Boston Celtics games, enrolled in a scuba-diving course and dove inside the New England Aquarium tank. Every week I went to Sunday dinner with Donny's large family in Hyde Park. After a dozen or so well-done roasts and Carvel Ice Cream cakes, Donny insisted I tell his mother, Virginia, or "Gin," what I did for work.

"So, um, you should probably know something about me," I said, bracing for the worst.

"Oh God, are you going to tell me you're a Kennedy?" she asked.

"No, nothing like that. I'm a stripper. At the Naked i."

"You are? What does your mother think?"

"She hasn't talked to me since I was on *Phil Donahue*. Not that she ever approved of anything I did anyway. Talking to her is like walking the plank."

"What about your Dad?"

"I can't say he's accepted it, but at least we still talk. When he visits, we always go into the club when I'm not working."

"That's good that he keeps an eye on you." Gin's face relaxed and her eyes fixed on me. "Wait a minute, you're Princess Cheyenne."

"Yeah. That's me."

Later, while sitting in the passenger seat of a police cruiser, Donny gave me an offer I couldn't refuse: "Quit dancing and we'll buy a house together and get married."

I left the Naked i in 1988 and my absence barely registered. Strippers didn't have retirement parties, after all.

After racing full tilt into a wild world, I'd navigated it with more than just a smile. I was ready for my second act.

Philip's Letter

Dear Lucy,

Thanks for taking pictures of me and my wife last night outside the Paradise. I wanted to share with you a story. Although words as tools don't always convey the meaning of feelings, I will do my best to explain.

For the past week or so, the lines from Cat Stevens's song were playing in my head; "Oh, very young what will you leave us this time, you're only dancing on this earth for a short while, although your dreams may toss and turn you now . . ." I know that when my mind begins playing music it means the music is hiding a deeper meaning that will ultimately present itself, make its appearance.

I thought it may have been the result of my two older children moving on in their lives and out of town. One is in LA and the other is looking for an apartment in Boston.

Perhaps the music was a harbinger also. I saw you dance once or twice in the late '70s or early '80s. My record keeping is framed by girlfriend relationships. The period of time was the end of a deeply intense and caring relationship I had shared with someone, when I saw you dance. You were a force of nature, a whirlwind, unbridled, on stage. And your demonstration of the willingness to give, touched me deeply then and stayed with me. The beauty of your naked body and the emitted belief in the beauty of yourself and in your performance came through and stuck with me as a place card in memory of what I had and had lost. The confidence you displayed, that image, was not perceived as a show, but rather it was communicated as a condition of your being, of how you chose to live this life that I needed to see; as remembrance

My girl at the time had moved on. The residual guilt was from not having lived my life to its fullest extent resulting in a deeply hurtful loss. The chance sighting of you dancing drew for me a picture of what was lost in me. What you were, the image, helped me visualize what I was no longer, and what I no longer had. Your image, which helped me carry the load, has resided in me deeply as an icon of how to try to live life, an icon of remembrance; remembrance of who I wanted to be, who I lost, and what I thought I was but wasn't.

I hugged you to share that with you and to validate to me that you are real, and that I can touch the image. Make it real.

A few years ago I ran into her again. She was divorced, I was married. John Updike wrote that "... adultery and alcohol ..." are sure ways to destroy a family. Our adulterous relationship nearly destroyed my family and my role in it. It had served two purposes though; 1) it helped me resolve and salve the wound and 2) it showed me and her who we were. I ultimately fought for my family's preservation and my role in it and we remain a family at work helping each other to persevere.

After hearing of your tragedy last night I wanted to share my story with you and to let you know this morning that I felt last night that I had received some of the weight of your tragedy and in receiving I hope that our short conversation and embrace, the touch of a caring stranger, can help you alleviate a bit of the pain that I know you carry.

That which you showed to me and that which remains with me served to depict you as a good person and I hope that this acknowledgement and validation of your personal goodness will offer you and provide you some comfort in sharing the weight of your tragedy with a stranger.

That's what you, as very young, left in your time, as you were dancing on this earth.

Like I said, words as tools can fail. I hope that I have provided you with some spiritual blessing and support.

All the best,
Philip

ACKNOWLEDGMENTS

"Tenk you veddy much."

Agents who requested full manuscripts and almost represented me brightened my day, but the people I'm thanking are far more essential. Like my stepsister, **Kim Walin**, and stepfather, **Bob Walin**, who kept me afloat financially and preserved my sanity while my mother died. They continue to include me as family.

Susan "No Nonsense" Ovans, and her husband, **Roger "Grumpy" Jackson** adopted me. Every week Susan made dinner with vegetables from her garden while I beat Roger at Scrabble. Susan often groused about my writing a book. In the end, she gave it wings and feet like nobody else could.

While I was still self-absorbed and in my mid-twenties, **John Taylor Williams**, or "Ike," encouraged me to put a manuscript together and became my literary agent. Some publishers showed interest and Warner Brothers bought the rights to the story. Thankfully, neither progressed. I was too young to have any perspective.

Author, professor, and one-time ecdysiast colleague **Lauri "L" Umansky** weathered decades of book brainstorming and became my oldest friend, and **CJ Young**'s infectious enthusiasm, deep friendship, and confidence infused me with the energy I needed.

I left Princess Cheyenne in the Combat Zone in 1988, thirty-seven years ago. I moved to the suburbs with Donny Wightman, married, and became a realtor. In 1990, we had a daughter, Torri, who died on a rain-drenched road in a hydroplaning car when she was sixteen.

On the day of her funeral, Torri's face filled the front page of the Boston Herald thanks to journalist **Margery Eagan**. Margery met Torri when we were guests on her radio show co-hosted by one of my favorite people, **Jim "As In" Braude**. Jim helped hold up the scaffolding while it imploded.

When Aerosmith dedicated one of their albums to Torri, avid rock fan **Tracy Rotkiewicz** immersed herself in fundraisers for **Dan Strollo's** crash prevention training for teen drivers.

Despite being baptized Episcopalian, Torri had a Catholic funeral facilitated by **Virginia "Gin" Wightman**, a force of nature and my perpetual mother-in-law. She gave me the community at **St. Mary's Church** in Hanover, Massachusetts who opened their minds and hearts to me. **Father Chris Hickey** clarified much of my confusion while also making me laugh. **Becky Smock, Deacon John Murray, John and Nancy Atturio, Jim Rabbit** and **Trish Bowen** gave me what I needed to stay alive at that time.

As did **Barbara and George Thomas** who befriended, fed, and employed me. George reminded me how important it is to complete things. They kept me laughing and became the strength I didn't always have. I scoffed when George gave me an old set of golf clubs, but a weekly foursome gave me friendships with **Maureen Dewitt** and **Lizzie Kimball**.

One-time testing supervisor, Rorschach authority and playful soulmate **John Miner** gave me the book *Dark Night of the Soul* and wrote, "Yes, let's get out of the pit. It's time to move forward. We're pulling you up and out. Got that? Find that place inside of you to put it away, never forget, and then inch forward."

After finding a St. Benedict medal in my office parking lot, I discovered **Glastonbury Abbey**, a Benedictine community in Hingham, Massachusetts. The monks temporarily housed me and gave me purpose as their photographer. I grieved, laughed, and rediscovered faith in the unknown after spending time with **Father Nicholas, Abbot Thomas, Father Timothy, Father Albrecht, Brother Daniel, Brother David, Brother James,** and **Andrew**. Along with the magnificent monks, **Hayes "The Erg" Shea** and **Chris Nagle** will never cease to amaze me.

Others took me into their nests along the way, like Hayes's friends, **Sandy** and **Isabelle Allen**. **Barbara Blauer** incorporated me selflessly into her life for months and gave me precise manuscript feedback, and I lived with friend **Bessie Wolfington** and daughters **Gwen and Nora** for four amazing years. We often joked about being related. Turns out, we are.

Their neighbors **Pete Fournier** and **Meredith Durant** became family and I stayed with **Tory Minnehan Curtis** while looking for a place to live. **Jill and Matt Murmes** made sure I had a place to go for Thanksgiving, and a place to work out.

No mother can endure child death alone.

Donna Fitzgerald witnessed many joyful beginnings and tragic endings and **Nicole "Batard" Gouvia**, along with husband **Mike** and daughters **Mackayla** and **Emski**, have loved me tenaciously without conditions. Nicole is the only person who calls on Torri's birthday and date of death every year, without fail. **Christine** and **Eric Henrikson** hired me to paint the interior of their home while keeping me close and **Al DeLuca** fed me words of wisdom and gifted me a VW Jetta when I had no car. **Pam Foley** surprised me one day by filling my home with flowers, food, and gifts and **Von**, **Margaret**, and **Zoe Duran** watched over me in multiple ways. As did **Ken Freedman, Victoria Wolfson, Jax Greatorex, Marcie Baskin, Leah Godfrey**, and **Haven "Tickets" Baima**.

Tobin Eckian reminded me to take heart in the things we can't see.

There are others that are gone besides **Torri**. **Mr. Perry Winkle Wightman**, my red toy poodle and the most successful relationship I've ever had. Child psychiatrist **Jeanne "Gigi" Dolan** who sat at Torri's grave with me day after day. **Debi Chute**, neighbor, and treasured friend brought me a rainbow clown wig allowing me to flummox the Fox News surveillance team when leaving my home. **Carole "Green Ticket" Hollander** and I met while in line for Cat Stevens tickets. We remained friends until she left. **Chazy Dowaliby**, Executive Editor of The *Patriot Ledger* in Quincy and *The Enterprise* of Brockton, ran an article about my daughter's death and the headline highlighted my past as a stripper. We became good friends after she published an apology. Renaissance man and attorney **Kevin Gaughen** whose curious appreciation for the unusual made us fast friends. **Deneb Sandack** taught me how to trap and band raptors in Cape May, New Jersey. What emerged was a mutual understanding and love beyond any I've ever experienced. And **Jordan Yazbeck**, who marked the first child death close to my heart after Torri's. **Elie Yazbeck** was kind enough to employ me at his gas station where I came to know Jordan, and Elie's other sons **Mike** and **George**.

As an only child, I came to appreciate the significance of cousins. **Leslie "Lel" Heffernan**, husband **Mike**, and sons **George** and **Will** have supported me through hopelessness, happiness, and everything in between.

Lel has known me longer than anyone. I am also grateful to relatives **Ned** and **Lily Johnson** for including me in their project, "There Will Be Dancing: The History of a Johnson Family," and the unparalleled family reunions that followed.

Birds. The most unexpected piece of my moving forward was bird immersion, and stories about the people I've met could fill a book. My first bird-banding mentor and treasure, **Trevor Lloyd-Evans**, the ornithologist in charge of Manomet Banding Lab, taught academically and practically. He was never short on stimulating questions or stories. Trevor introduced me to another master bander, **Sue Finnegan**, with whom I took a certification course at Wing Island in Brewster, Massachusetts.

Today, I am a proud member of "Sue's Crew" and consider Sue a friend for life. I band birds alongside a group of stellar individuals and new friends like **Michele "Sombrero" Burnat** and her wife, culinary expert **Lesa Milas, Mike "Catbird" Babcock, Reenie "Tights" Dwyer** and husband **Bob Dwyer,** president, and executive director of the Cape Cod Museum of Natural History. The birding skills of fellow Mensan, **Keelin Miller,** conservationist and playful person **Paula Pariseau,** Purple Martin advocate **Mary Keleher** and **Brandi "Rare Bird" Sikorski** are awe-inspiring. I've enjoyed walking and talking with weekend warrior **Gretchen Putonen,** high-school-bird-wiz **Ethan Seufert** and **Gabbie DiNardi** and had many laughs at the banding table with **Lauren "Eggplant" Grimes.**

Yearly trips to fall migration hotspot, Cape May, New Jersey, filled my bird world with experts I've learned, birded, and formed friendships with like **Amy Donovan, Tom O'Toole** and **Ruby, Sue Fortuna** and sister **Anita Holland, Stick LePan, Eileen Mathers, Christine and Gerry DeWaghe, Bobbye Samdahl, Meg Walker-Hedeen** and husband **Dave, Cheryl Riley** and husband **Pete, Liza Gray, Glen and Kashi Davis, Eric Brunke, Mike Lanzone, Trish Miller** and **David LePuma.**

Life today is made more meaningful by **John, Molly, and Gus Dobrowski,** who have pulled me into their enormous, adventurous family and with whom I will grow old. **Jeff Bieling** and I are both strong cups of coffee, likely separated at birth, and his partner, **Lisa Novakoff,** brings some sanity to the mix. **Rachel Cohen** and I support each other through Long COVID, and, most recently, **Wendy Davis** and **Kellie Graham** have entrusted me with their rental home, giving me the ideal green environment to complete the book's odds and ends.

Finally, but with no less gravity, **Ari "Casting" Buchler** and **Howard Zaharoff** gave me legal guidance and **Charles Farrell** intuited that **Kyle "The File" Sarofeen** and I would become trusting friends, even if he didn't publish my book. Charles was spot on. Ours will be an enduring friendship.

Nanly and Torri.

UNACKNOWLEDGMENTS

Massachusetts School of Professional Psychology, Nancy DiZio, Mike Beaudet, Robert Fox, Karen Patrick, Bessel van der Kolk, David Carrasco, Robert Prentky, and former Plympton Fire Chief, David Rich.

About the Author

Lucy Wightman lives on Cape Cod.

Princess Cheyenne is set in 10-point Sabon, which was designed by the German-born typographer and designer Jan Tschichold (1902–1974) in the period 1964–1967. It was released jointly by the Linotype, Monotype, and Stempel type foundries in 1967. Copyeditor for this project was Boutros Salah. The book was designed by Brad Norr Design, Minneapolis, Minnesota, and typeset by Westchester Publishing Services. Printed and manufactured by Lightning Source on acid-free paper.

www.ingramcontent.com/pod-product-compliance
Lightning Source LLC
Chambersburg PA
CBHW030231170426
43201CB00006B/177